Basic
Debate

Third Edition

Maridell Fryar
Independent School District
Midland, Texas

David A. Thomas
University of Richmond
Richmond, Virginia

Lynn Goodnight
National High School Institute
Northwestern University
Evanston, Illinois

Consulting Editor
Carmendale Fernandes
English, Speech, and Drama Department
Fremont High School
Sunnyvale, California

 National Textbook Company
NTC a division of *NTC Publishing Group* • Lincolnwood, Illinois USA

Photo Credits

AP/Wide World Photos: pages 2, 4, 59, 84, 144, 176, 244

Historical Pictures Service, Chicago: page 186

Harold Keller, Davenport West High School, Davenport, Iowa: pages 108, 192, 228, 235, 254, 259, 264, 272, 278, 284

National High School Institute at Northwestern: pages 10, 26, 74, 118, 128, 138, 204, 209

Odis Richardson, Du Sable High School, Chicago, Illinois: pages 32, 52, 90, 172

Art Shay, Photographer: pages 37, 242

UPI/Bettmann Newsphotos: page 220

1993 Printing

Copyright © 1989, 1986, 1979 by National Textbook Company, a division of NTC Publishing Group,
4255 West Touhy Avenue, Lincolnwood (Chicago), Illinois 60646-1975 U.S.A.
All rights reserved. No part of this book may be reproduced, stored in a retrieval
system, or transmitted in any form or by any means, electronic, mechanical,
photocopying, recording or otherwise, without the prior permission of NTC
Publishing Group.
Manufactured in the United States of America.
Library of Congress Catalog Number: 87-63584

3 4 5 6 7 8 9 TS 9 8 7 6 5 4

Acknowledgments

The assistance and support of many people helped complete this book. The families, colleagues, students, and former students of the authors generously provided counsel, suggestions, and examples for the pages that follow. Special appreciation should probably be expressed to the members of the Robert E. Lee High School Forensics Squad and the Auburn University Forensics Squad who tolerated their coaches' preoccupation with this manuscript. A special word of thanks goes to Doni Reiter, Scott Maeberry, and the many Northwestern debaters for their help in gathering new materials and examples for this edition. A special thanks goes to Tom Goodnight for his patience, late night advice, and willingness to listen to countless rewrites as Lynn Goodnight revised and updated the previous edition of *Basic Debate*. A special word of appreciation goes to the National Forensic League for the generosity of Mr. James Copeland, Executive Secretary, in allowing us to use materials published by that organization.

To John Giertz, San Francisco State University, for his help in revising the chapter on Lincoln-Douglas debate, many thanks.

Finally, but not least, special thanks are due to David Mezzera, St. Ignatius College Prep, San Francisco, for revising the chapters on student congress.

Preface

Basic Debate is exactly what its title implies, a basic textbook for beginning-level debate students. In addition, it presents a unique section on Student Congress, a forensics activity growing in popularity.

The organization and scope of this book are also unique among the many available texts in argumentation and debate. It begins with the recognition that certain skills are common to any kind of forensics activity, including the ones on which this text concentrates. The skills of analysis, research, and reasoning are carefully examined in such a thorough manner that teachers in fields outside debate will find this section useful.

Another section deals specifically with academic debate. Unlike many texts written for secondary students, this section offers in-depth discussions of both traditional and innovative case approaches. It treats theory as well as practice, addresses itself to presentation as well as issues, and clarifies the special features of cross-examination, which is now widely practiced at both college and high school levels. In this revision of Basic Debate, a number of changes have been made. This version contains chapters on Lincoln-Douglas debate and the tournament experience. Each chapter ends with Questions for Discussion and Activities. These should help the student put into action the material that is being presented.

Originally written by two outstanding coaches of debate, Basic Debate is based on the latest theory as practiced in actual debate competition. David A. Thomas's previous work, Advanced Debate, is considered a standard in the field. Maridell Fryar has been the recipient of many honors and awards, including Texas Speech Teacher of the Year Award and Diamond Key Coach. Both authors have been active on the debate circuit.

The present text has been updated and revised by Lynn Goodnight, author of Getting Started in Debate and co-author of Strategic Debate. Goodnight is Coordinator of the National High School Institute at Northwestern University. She is also a member of the writing staff for National Textbook Company's yearly debate series.

Contents

Introduction

This book provides you with the knowledge you need to participate successfully in two forensic activities—debate and student congress. Although these are only two of the many forensic activities, they offer you the opportunity to acquire analytical skills, reasoning and persuasion, and critical listening and thinking skills. All these skills transfer directly from the academic world into everyday life.

Part One of this book covers the basic forensic skills needed for success in debate and student congress. Parts Two and Three are devoted to each of these activities in detail. In recent years participation in Lincoln-Douglas debate has grown significantly, offering students a real opportunity to access the values and principles upon which a democratic society is based. For these reasons, a chapter on Lincoln-Douglas debate has been included in Part Two of this text. But before you begin to study the text, you will find it helpful to understand the authors' underlying attitude toward forensics.

Forensics as a Laboratory

Many academic subjects use laboratories to simulate a real world setting, whether in the study of physics or of foreign languages. The same is true of forensic activities. Although student congress, for example, is not the same thing as the U.S. Congress, participating in the former does teach basic principles and information. In forensic activities, you perform under the direction of teachers. You use common formats and follow rules that teach you certain principles and skills. As you speak, you are evaluated so that your skills may improve. Later in life, when you participate in community affairs, your ability to present, defend, and criticize opinions will serve you well.

Forensics as Problem Solving

When agreement is not reached in an initial discussion, polarization may occur. Out of this situation come attempts by an individual or a faction to persuade others to accept a position. This process characterizes argument in the lawmaking bodies of society, in the media, and in the courtroom. Regardless of where it occurs, the basic goal is to win a decision from others in favor of the desired course of action. Confrontation is a part of that process. The aim is not to convince the opposition but to convince a third party, a judge.

In this stage of decision making, an advocate must be familiar with deliberation and confrontation. Fundamental to success is the acquisition of the skills of forensics. Competitive speech events offer you the opportunity to exercise those skills.

Forensics in this Text

This book is designed for beginning forensic students. It focuses on an explanation of some of the theory and background of the rules and practices of academic debate. But unlike most texts designed for beginners, the book also provides substantive new material useful to the experienced competitor.

Currently, there are few materials available on Lincoln-Douglas debate. The chapter in this book provides a background and lays out the fundamentals of this activity. Again, aside from the Congress Manual published by the National Forensic League, there is no comprehensive guide to student congress. The authors hope that Part Three of this text proves a practical guide to the preparation and practice of this rapidly developing competitive activity.

The materials in this book reflect the forensic philosophy of the authors. Like any other academic discipline, there are many different theories and practices that make up the body of literature of forensics. We have attempted to indicate those areas in which we depart somewhat from other authorities. We submit this text as a further contribution to the subject of forensics and hope that it will be useful to you.

Part One

Basic Forensic Skills

Beginning Problem Solving

Before exploring either debate or student congress, you need to become acquainted with some of the basic skills of argument, with forensics. The first part of this text introduces the skills of analysis, research, and reasoning. These form the basis for any work you will do in competitive forensic activities. As you study the chapters in this section, pay very close attention to the explanations and guidelines offered. The skills you acquire will equip you to move with ease through many academic pursuits.

Chapter 1

Debate in a Democratic Society

Objectives and Key Terms

After studying Chapter 1, you should be able to

1. Explain (in a nutshell) what debate is,

2. Identify situations in which debate experience would be of value,

3. Identify skills that are either learned or enhanced through debate, and

4. Identify the principles on which debate is based.

After reading this chapter, you should understand the following terms:

arguments

criticism

debate in a democracy

Y ou live in a society that gives you the right and the responsibility to make choices about how to conduct your life. You are called on to make decisions and value judgments. Every day, you have to decide whether to spend your time at work or at play, by yourself or with others, or planning for the future or thinking about the past. If you use your time wisely, you can create opportunities and make decisions that will lead to success. If you squander your time, you will limit your options and make unproductive decisions.

The Nature of Debate

Learning how to debate can help you develop decision-making ability. Debate is the process of generating argumentative clash. There are many different debate formats. Different forums have distinct formats and procedures. Common to all debating, however, is the intellectual exchange of ideas. Debate involves reasoned argument put forward in the service of statements of belief or propositions of policy.

To debate well, you must be able both to compose precise, stimulating, and well-supported arguments and to critique arguments offered by an opponent. Some people are able to do this easily. Others, either because they are shy or inexperienced, have trouble composing and critiquing. However, all people have a right to express their own opinion and to ask others to provide support for the opinions that they state. To the extent that people can talk to one another intelligently, they can come to productive agreements.

What You Will Learn

In this book, you will learn some new skills. For example, you will learn how to make arguments. This is an important skill for several reasons. First, learning to make arguments requires you to take statements and studies, facts and options, and shape them into a cogent case. In one sense, these formal requirements for finding reasons to support an idea help sharpen your own thinking. Rather than making judgments solely based on likes and dislikes, you will be able to reduce your own biases and reach a more objective judgment about what is really good for you. Second, learning how to make cases increases your ability to influence others. People usually want to do the right thing. To show them what to do, you must provide the right reasons. Argumentation teaches you how to put together strong, clear, forceful positions that lead to good decisions. Without such a skill, you might have good ideas but no way to communicate them.

In this book, you will also learn how to criticize arguments. Sometimes an argument sounds good, but it is really misleading or incorrect. Argumentation teaches you how to examine arguments systematically and see if the proof is sound and if the methods of reasoning are valid. Criticism is not to be confused with mere negative thinking. It is not enough just to reject arguments because you believe they are wrong. Criticism is a powerful corrective. It permits you to isolate what is wrong with an argument, to say why, and to provide a better alternative. In this way, argumentation expands your ability to influence people or at least to clear out bad ideas and make room for better ones.

The Value of Debate

If argument did no more than sharpen your judgment and aid you in influencing your friends, it would be a worthwhile pursuit. But there is much more to the study of forensics than personal improvement. Thus far in life, you have been working and playing in a limited domain. You know your family, your friends, and people you encounter at school. As you approach your eighteenth birthday, your life will take on another dimension: that of an active citizen in a democracy.

The language of democracy is the language of debate. In a democracy, people are given the power to decide for themselves the values of government. A great many issues must be decided, and values often conflict. Should money be spent for more schools or should taxes be lowered? Should one support the Democratic or the Republican party? Should the United States build a strategic defense against nuclear weapons or direct scientific efforts elsewhere? No one has final answers to these questions. There are risks to any choice. Only argument can serve to determine which is the least risky alternative.

You have a responsibility to be a good citizen, and debate can provide you with the communication skills necessary to fulfill that responsibility. Those who are untrained in debate and critical argument may not understand the need for public discussion or even how to evaluate cases that political leaders make for and against changes in public policy. Easily swayed, uncritical listeners may support bad policies and demagogues.

Good argumentation, on the other hand, can provide you with an improved ability to make critical choices. This book is designed to enable you to become familiar with policy debate and argumentative analysis.

Conflicts often arise between rights and freedoms. One way to resolve these conflicts is to develop a consensus through argument.

The Functions of Debate

Debate in a democratic society has many functions.

1. Debate helps people decide the meaning of the past. Arguments in history class, as well as those in the public forum, are sometimes directed to the implications of historical event or document. The Constitution and its intended protections and constraints, for example, have been the subject of controversy for some time. By examining the Constitution, students can come to understand how this historical document shapes present institutions and orders society. By finding the meaning of the past, students can better determine the values that are shared in common.

2. Debate helps people decide the values of the present. In a democracy, there are many competing groups, each with a different history and a different view of the present. Debate brings into focus public obligations and duties. Difficult questions arise concerning conflicts between human rights and freedoms. The best way to resolve these is to develop a consensus through argument, to focus on what *ought* to be done to preserve and advance a just and moral society.

3. Debate permits people to evaluate alternative futures. The status quo never stands still. Problems continue to arise. How should resources be allocated? How should technology be developed? What programs are necessary to secure defense? All these questions can be answered by arguments that in some cases defend existing policies and in other cases provide alternatives. Especially in academic debate, sponsored by the National Forensic League (NFL), questions of public policy are the primary subject.

Academic debate provides training for good citizenship. While the term "argument" might be equated with squabbling or mean-spirited disagreement, this is not what is meant here. Debate trains people in such a way as to maximize the chance that any critical discussion they participate in will be an honest exchange of views leading to an intellectually respectable decision. Toward that end, students should realize that this book is based on an ethic of communication.

In debate, you should always work within a sound intellectual framework. Debate is based on the following principles:

1. The debater should respect the intellectual integrity of argument. Debate requires the search for the best arguments based on the most informed opinion in fields related to the resolution.

2. Debate is based on the fair exchange of opinion. Debate is not an intellectual game that aims at getting in the last word. It can only work when students are committed to advancing and defending ideas.

3. Debate should be conducted with respect for others. Debate that aims only at a display of intellectual dominance is a pointless activity. Rather, debate upholds the dignity of individuals insofar as it affirms their right to be listened to and critiqued.

4. Debate should be the product of honest research and valid evidence. There is no room for distortion or fabrication in forensics.

5. Debate should be treated as a learning experience. The process of debate should be directed not only toward training strong advocates and good speakers but also toward developing open minds and good listening habits. By helping students learn the significance of good and timely arguments, debate should enhance, not impede, communication.

Summary

Debate is more than an academic exercise. The skills and values you will acquire in debate can be applied in nearly every occupation as well as in your relationships with other people. Look on your course in debate as an opportunity.

Questions for Discussion

1. Debate can be of benefit in everyday life. What elements of debate make this true?

2. What is the value of learning to make arguments?

3. If you learn how to criticize arguments, how will you be able to better defend your own position?

4. Describe the functions of debate in a democratic society.

5. How will debate help you to develop an analytical mind?

6. In debate, it is important to have an open mind when you prepare arguments. How does this help you in preparing your positions or in attacking an opposing position?

Activities

1. Keeping in mind your career plans for the future, explain how debate will help you to succeed.

2. Attend the next city council, school board, or PTA meeting. As issues are discussed, identify instances in which speakers are not able to analyze critically the arguments of previous speakers. Also identify instances in which positions were bogged down because the participants did not listen critically to their peers.

3. Using the issues outlined in Activity 2, analyze the position and outline a counterposition (or rewrite a support of the position).

4. Choose an issue currently before the legislature (state or national). Outline the pros and cons on the issue. Try to equalize the number of pros and cons. How has each of these issues been handled in the legislative process?

Chapter 2

The Skills of Analysis

Objectives and Key Terms

After studying Chapter 2, you should be able to

1. Present an in-depth analysis of a debate problem area,

2. Formulate a properly worded proposition that will meet the characteristics of a proposition, and

3. Explain the differences among propositions of fact, value, and policy.

After reading this chapter, you should understand the following terms:

analysis

problem area

problem statement

proposition

proposition of fact

proposition of value

proposition of policy

F orensic events, such as debate and student congress, are modeled after decision-making situations in the "real world," such as the legislature or a court of law. The problems considered in forensic events are similar to those confronted by "real world" advocates. However, the overriding principle remains true. Even in these serious, complex problem areas, the best possible solutions can be found if the best methods of decision making are applied. Before you can effectively take sides on an issue or even develop a personal opinion, you must be able to analyze a problem and its solutions.

Defining Analysis

Analysis is the process of separating a whole into its essential parts. It is the opposite of *synthesis*, which means to combine separate elements into a complete whole. Analysis is an active thought process. Generally speaking, you already analyze many different objects or concepts, using many different methods to break them down into essential elements. In chemistry, you analyze compounds to identify their separate chemical elements. In bookkeeping, you analyze the records of a business to determine debits and credits. In an English class, you analyze a piece of literature, observing its essential features of plot, character, and style.

Analysis can be complicated when you look at the many possible ways to divide concepts into parts. But the purpose of this chapter is to point out the essential elements of analysis used in forensics. Consider three distinct levels that require analytical thinking: the problem area, the problem statement, and the audience.

Analyzing the Problem Area

A *problem area* is a general area of concern to a community. Problem areas are usually broad umbrellas that cover many particular problems. A clean environment may be a problem area. Clean air and water and good land use are specific problems to be discussed within the area. How can a problem area be analyzed? At a minimum, all the pertinent facts about the problem area must be discovered. Use the following questions to discover those facts:

1. What is the goal or ideal thwarted by the problem?

2. How far off is that goal?

3. What are the identifiable reasons for being short of the goal?

4. What possible solutions can overcome these reasons?

5. Which of the possible solutions appears best in comparison with others?

The answers to these questions will show you two important things. First, they will indicate where your knowledge of the problem area is strong and where it is weak. This will then guide your research and further investigation. Second, the answers will pinpoint some of the issues that you must consider in your own presentation of opinion.

Analyzing the Problem Statement

A *problem statement* narrows a general discussion area. Instead of examining all aspects of pollution, you might wish to know why one specific aspect persists or what the merits of a single solution are. The statement of the problem must be analyzed. It has been said, and rightly so, that it is useless to seek agreement on any course of action until agreement has first been reached on the meaning of the terms used. In other words, the beginning point for analysis is a definition of the terms by which the problem is stated. Each forensic event places the problem in a different form, but each states a problem for consideration. Debate asks students to advocate a resolution, such as "Resolved: That the federal government should exclusively control the development and distribution of energy resources in the United States." Student congress presents a bill or resolution to be debated by the group. The place for you to begin your analysis in each of these situations is with the meaning of the terms of the statement.

The logical first step is to consult dictionaries, textbooks, and encyclopedias. You should be particularly aware of specialized dictionaries that include technical terms. Such publications as *Black's Law Dictionary* and *The American Dictionary of Psychology*, for example, should be consulted if the topic, bill, or resolution falls into the specialized areas that such books cover. You should also explore the prevailing connotations for terms and try to use definitions within the social, political, economic, and historical contexts of the statement. Further, you should determine how the key terms are interpreted by the experts in the field.

When you are involved in the analysis of definitions, you should also be aware of the presence of value terms. Words such as *fair, free, new, sig-*

nificant, best, comprehensive, and *control* are vague because the realities to which they refer are not absolute. They are relative to a standard of measurement that is not uniform to everyone everywhere. Before agreement can be reached on a question of policy, there must be an agreement on the terms by which the policy is to be justified. If your task, for example, is to justify a "comprehensive program to significantly increase the energy independence of the United States," you must fully understand what constitutes *comprehensive* and what is a *significant increase.* Thus, your analytical task is to arrive at the best possible understanding of what these terms mean within the frame of reference represented by the total statement of the problem area.

Analyzing the Audience

Once the problem area is analyzed, you must adapt your ideas to the intended audience. It is not enough merely to accumulate and organize a stockpile of information. To achieve your purpose, you must know which pieces of information to select and present to your intended audience. In this stage of analysis, you attempt to determine which issues will best speak to the particular audience you will address. In student congress, you use features of both discussion and debate in a legislative framework. Ultimately, the group will vote on proposed bills and resolutions. Audience analysis should lead you to the selection of information that wins group support for your position. In debate, you may use special forms of issue presentation to influence an expert judge. Specific methods of analysis apply to each of these events.

There is no single method of analysis in forensics. Some methods are used for investigating a problem area, and other methods are used for planning a strategy for presenting a case to a legislative assembly or a debate judge. Regardless of the setting for decision making, whether student congress or debate, the common denominator is the use of the English language. In all these events, you think, speak, reason, persuade, and argue with words and sentences. The beginning point is the *forensic analysis*—the breaking down of the proposition under consideration. Thus, some understanding of the statement of that proposition is valuable.

Stating the Problem

What is a proposition? The root of the word is *propose*, to offer for consideration. A *proposition* is a statement offered for consideration, specifically a statement made to others for the purpose of gaining acceptance after due consideration. A proposition may require explanation, discussion, or proof. Some propositions are uncontroversial; these are rarely debated. Others may be too vague to spark disagreement. When a proposition presents a clear and important choice, it is often the subject of debate.

The function of the proposition is to provide focus for discussion and debate. Specifically, it is the means by which the problem under consideration is explicitly verbalized. It will present or assert a claim for eventual acceptance.

Problem Selection

Where do the problem areas for forensic events originate? Each year, a national debate topic is selected. The topic is then debated for an entire year. The National Federation of State High School Associations conducts the selection. The process is careful, time-consuming, and thorough. An annual meeting of representatives from each of the states is preceded by research and questionnaires. At this annual meeting (usually in August), suggested topic areas are discussed and debated. Following the National Federation selection of three possible problem areas, a national mail ballot is sent to all forensic teachers and even some students to register their preference of problem areas. The first ballot gives the forensic community a chance to voice a preference for a specific problem area. The problem areas are then announced on January 15. A second national ballot is mailed, except this time it concerns one problem area, with forensic teachers and students ranking three specific propositions relating to the chosen problem area. The results of this balloting are announced on April 15. The ballot count and the results are announced by the National Federation of State High School Associations. High school topics for the past several years clearly show the variety and scope of problems the selection process results in:

Resolved: That governmental financial support for all public elementary and secondary education in the United States should be provided exclusively by the federal government.

Resolved: That the method of selecting presidential and vice-presidential candidates should be significantly changed.

Resolved: That a comprehensive program of penal reform should be adopted throughout the United States.

Resolved: That the federal government should guarantee comprehensive medical care for all citizens in the United States.

Resolved: That the federal government should establish a comprehensive program to significantly increase the energy independence of the United States.

Resolved: That the United States should significantly curtail its arms sales to other countries.

Resolved: That the federal government should provide employment for all employable United States citizens living in poverty.

Resolved: That the federal government should establish a comprehensive national policy to protect the quality of water in the United States.

Resolved: That the federal government should implement a comprehensive long-term agricultural policy in the United States.

Resolved: That the United States government should adopt a policy to increase political stability in Latin America.

Once the resolution has been selected, the process of analysis focuses on that resolution. In order to make a meaningful analysis, you should understand the characteristics of the proposition.

Problem Characteristics

Propositions must meet five criteria. First, the problem area should be *significant* in scope, affecting people throughout the country or even around the world. For example, the problem of how to provide for national defense is significant because it affects all Americans. Other examples are poverty in America, world hunger, organized crime, welfare, inflation, access to medical care, civil rights, and energy shortages. All these are significant in scope. By contrast, purely local or state level problems are not chosen nationally for forensic events because they lack sufficient scope to involve students in forensics all over the nation.

Second, a problem must be within the realm of government *jurisdiction*. It is not enough merely to describe a problem, even though it might be significant. It must be possible for a proposed solution to be enacted into law by the government. This characteristic of problems for forensic consideration does not mean that other types of problems are unimportant, only that governmental action must be feasible. For example, we might agree that the lack of religious faith is a serious problem throughout the nation. But it would not be fitting to suggest some new law requiring increased devotion to our religious heritage. Forensic events generally deal with problems for which a concrete solution is possible. This implies problem areas, such as international relations or domestic health and welfare, where there is public interest in government policies and their alternatives.

Timeliness is the third standard that a proposition should meet. Since the success of forensic events hinges on generating student interest and involvement, a problem area must be current. A by-product of timeliness is widespread coverage by the media, government publications, and scholarly journals. A premium is placed on using up-to-date evidence in any forensic event.

Although the problem area must be timely, it cannot be transitory. *Durability* is essential. Caution is exercised in the selection of forensic problems so that the problem will not pass quickly from the national interest or be suddenly resolved by an unanticipated governmental action. A few notable cliff-hangers have occurred in recent years. Probably none have had as much impact as the creation of the Environmental Protection Agency in the middle of the year during which high school debaters considered the resolution "Resolved: That the federal government should establish a program to significantly reduce air and/or water pollution." For the most part, though, national debate questions are selected so as to ensure that they will continue to be problems for the duration of the debate year.

Related to the standard of durability is *debatability*. The problem area must be arguable on both sides. On the whole, the problem should favor neither the affirmative nor the negative. The problem area should be carefully considered before the choice is made to be certain that arguments and issues of merit are inherently contained in either position. If the topic is not debatable, one side has a built-in advantage over the other.

Forensics directs your attention to a significant public problem. The forensic experience permits you to study the problem in depth and debate proposed solutions. Thus, the educational nature of forensic events is established because, through forensics, you become informed about significant and timely problems you might otherwise ignore.

The continuing process of analysis leads from consideration of the meaning of the terms in the proposition to consideration of the characteristics of a good proposition. Now you need to develop an awareness of the types of propositions that can be argued.

Understanding the Types of Propositions

There are three types of propositions in forensics, each calling for its own unique levels of support, explanation, development, and proof. Propositions may be classified into three categories—propositions of *fact*, propositions of *value*, and propositions of *policy*.

The simplest of propositions is the proposition of fact. It involves definition and classification in order to establish the truth or falseness of a claim. Increasing in complexity is the proposition of value, which asks that criteria be applied in order to determine the worth or value of a particular thing. At the highest level of complexity is the proposition of policy, which demands that after establishing certain facts and values, a consideration of such things as expediency and practicality leads people to propose a certain defensible plan of action.

To illustrate the progressive nature of propositions, consider the following case taken from the criminal courts. The charge is that A was wounded by a bullet fired from the gun of B (fact). Additionally, however, it is claimed that B's attack was totally unprovoked, unjustified, and premeditated (value). Consequently, capital punishment is advocated (policy). At each level of complexity, new types of issues emerge, and each successive proposition builds on the preceding one. As a consequence, if you would analyze accurately, you must understand the unique characteristics and the interdependency of each type of proposition.

Propositions of Fact

A factual proposition is an objective statement that something exists. Moreover, the statement can be verified by someone other than the person making the statement. A factual proposition may be about an object or event that can be experienced directly by the senses of sight, hearing, touch, smell, and taste. An abstract statement may also be considered a factual proposition as long as it can be objectively and accurately justified. "Spinach is a green, leafy vegetable" is a factual statement about a tangible object. It can be verified through the senses by someone other than the person making the statement. Even so, it is also classified as a factual proposition because probable truth can be measured scientifically.

Compared with value judgments or policy propositions, propositions of fact are considered the least controversial. Notice, we do not say they are uncontroversial. Disagreements can and do arise over factual propositions. Every trial in a court of law involves at least one factual proposition. That the defendant committed (or did not commit) the criminal act with which he or she is charged is a factual proposition. However, factual propositions are less controversial than other types of propositions because they may be verified objectively by reference to other facts—to what is or what has occurred. They are not obviously in the realm of attitudes and opinions, as are value judgments.

Forensic events require you to be familiar with several different types of factual propositions. An *observation*, or statement of what you observe, and a *description*, or statement of the characteristics of what you observe, are factual propositions. For instance, "That is a car in the driveway (observation). It is my father's red '85 Chevy Malibu Classic station wagon (description)." These are objective, verifiable statements that a thing exists. It is a car. It exhibits specific characteristics.

Statements of fact may be about the past as well as the present. A newspaper report and a story from history thus qualify as factual propositions. The person asserting the fact need not be the same person who witnessed it. The statement must be objective and subject to independent verification. Establishing whether a fact exists (or existed) does not always hinge on the person who makes the assertion, as long as the statement can be verified.

Factual propositions are sometimes more complex. Conclusions drawn from reasoning about a set of facts are also considered factual propositions. However, the process of verifying such conclusions is also more complex, more hypothetical, and more obviously debatable. Such propositions are called *inferences* (conclusions based on possible relationships between known facts). For instance, it is a fact that cigarette smokers have a much higher incidence of lung cancer than nonsmokers.

Based on this observation, we may infer that cigarette smoking causes lung cancer. Here is a situation where the facts are not clear. The tobacco industry maintains that the evidence linking smoking with cancer is not strong enough to prove that one causes the other. Instead, other factors, such as environmental pollution, may be the responsible causative agent. Perhaps, for some unknown reason, persons who are predisposed to cancer are also more likely to be motivated to smoke. We can still treat the proposition "Cigarette smoking causes lung cancer" as a factual proposition, even though it is an inference based on reasoning from the known facts. Naturally, inferences of this sort are more debatable than direct observations, such as "55 million adults smoke cigarettes."

Propositions of fact that might be called "future" in type are predictive in nature. Like the inference, the *prediction* is a statement of how one thinks present facts are related so that one can expect certain results in the future. The concern here is not unscientific predictions like Jeane Dixon's astrological forecasts or the school yearbook's comments on the future career possibilities of Jimmy and Maria. Rather, what is meant are the predictable forecasts and trends based on present observable facts, such as "At the present divorce rate, by 1990 more than half of America's children will grow up in broken homes" and "The United States will rely on foreign sources of petroleum for over 50 percent of its needs within the next three years." As with inferences, the accuracy of predictions hinges on the quality of factual data and the quality of reasoning used in drawing relationships between known facts.

You have seen that a factual proposition is an objective statement about the existence of something, capable of independent verification by others. Among the important types of factual statements are observations, descriptions, history, reports, inferences, and predictive generalizations.

Although national organizations avoid selecting propositions of fact for debate, obviously it is essential for you to be able to prove the facts or refute the claims of your opponents using these factual propositions. In addition, factual statements are useful in the academic application of forensics in other fields. Social studies and English classes as well as psychology, philosophy, and science classes frequently make use of propositions of fact. Clubs and organizations may also consider them more frequently than they do other types of propositions. Thus, the basic issues involved in propositions of fact need to be specified.

The issues inherent in propositions of fact are relatively few. One needs to determine (1) what occurred, (2) what data are required to establish the alleged fact, and (3) what data are available for use. Consideration of these issues will result in the accurate analysis of propositions of fact.

Examples of propositions of fact are the following:

Federal intervention in state policies is unconstitutional.

Shakespeare was not the real author of the literature that bears his name.

America was first discovered by the Norse.

Television viewing contributes to the mounting crime rate.

At current rates of use, the free world will run out of oil within 35 years.

Propositions of Value

Propositions of value express judgments about the qualities of a person, place, thing, idea, or event. Therefore, when you make a statement about values, you move from the realm of senses and inferences into the realm of opinions and attitudes. When you say, "Spinach is a green, leafy vegetable," you make a factual statement. But when you say, "Spinach is *yucky*," you give your opinion of its qualities; you have made a value judgment.

In forensics, understanding value judgments is very important. Although knowing the facts about a problem area is vital to discussing it or debating about it, only our value judgments can serve as a guide to what should be done about the facts.

There are several different types of values. Before turning to those types, a crucial distinction between facts and values as propositions should be made. Facts are either true or false, and their truth can be verified. Values can never be considered as literally true or literally false. You can verify that someone holds a value, but not whether the value is the one he or she ought to hold. To say that "spinach is yucky" is to say something about your attitude toward spinach, not about spinach itself. To someone else, spinach may be "yummy." Whereas values are not literally true or false, they are nevertheless important because people believe them, and people allow them to color their thinking about everything else.

Artistic values, also called *aesthetic values*, express pleasure with a person or an object. Among artistic values, you attach great importance to beauty, symmetry, good taste—and their opposites. You hold the value judgment that civilized people create various works of art, literature, and music and that such creations are good. The standards applied to works of art express taste, whether the objects please or displease. This is true even when you are not conscious of your standards. You may say, "I like that song" or "That picture is pretty." To make such statements indicates that you have critical standards of some sort. It is also important to note here that value judgments say as much about the person holding the opinion as the thing being judged. Value judgments vary from one person to another and from community to community. Someone else may find your favorite poem dull, sentimental, or otherwise displeasing.

Artistic values are often brought into play in forensic events, if only indirectly. In a debate on energy shortages, for instance, the facts may prove it more economical to build all automobiles with one mold for body style and one shade of black for paint. Yet most Americans share the value of having artistic choices even at higher cost. The value proposition "We should build cars in the most economical way" would probably not win many votes if it resulted in denying all possible choices to consumers except a black Toyota.

Moral and *ethical values* form the basis for judgments of right and wrong, just and unjust, good and bad. Of course, our religious heritage teaches us such values, and we live our daily lives more or less according to a learned set of beliefs and convictions. Yet, it is a mistake to pigeonhole all moral and ethical value judgments into sectarian religious doctrines. Many values underlying laws and policies reflect civil values. For instance, laws related to family life and child protection, crimes against persons, and the human welfare triangle of jobs–housing–education derive largely, if not entirely, from moral and ethical value judgments cutting across the boundaries between specific religious groups.

Harvard psychologist Lawrence Kohlberg once provided clear insight into the depth and nature of moral values. Through original research conducted in many cultures other than the United States, Kohlberg found that all cultures share enough moral and ethical values to say that these values are simply human moral values. According to Kohlberg, people relate to one another according to the level of moral growth they have achieved. The lowest level is to feel free to do anything whatsoever as long as the consequences to oneself are not painful. This is an infantile level that nearly all people outgrow. Progressing up the levels of moral development, other moral values include obedience to authority; doing whatever you are told, *plus* considering its impact on others; following the main body of laws governing all people in your community; and undertaking only what is consistent with an abstract, profound, universal ethical code.

The importance of Kohlberg's theory can be seen in terms of policy analysis. For instance, the criminal code places a heavy emphasis on punishment. Criminals are assumed to have few moral values and to cease committing crimes only when threatened by punishment. However, in some jurisdictions, the criminal justice system displays faith in rehabilitation measures and educational programs on the assumption that criminals are capable of acquiring a higher level of moral development.

Related to general moral and ethical values are *political values*, which express judgments as to what is *expedient*, that is, what should or should not be done for the common good. Political values include democracy, rights, justice, and many others. The U.S. system attempts to maintain a historical balance between the values of individual liberty and equal protection under the law. The core value of liberty requires that we believe that the best government is the least government, that government interference and regulation must be checked. The core value of equality dictates that we believe that government should protect the basic rights of citizens to the vote, to police protection, to an education, to decent housing and nutrition, to medical care, and to a job. Often, if one of these core values is advanced, there is a corresponding encroachment on the other. We can expect lively debate over any proposed government action along these lines of political values. In some areas, government involvement is seen to be essential by everyone. Government regulation of the power utilities, provision of fire departments, public schools, and national defense are examples. In other areas, the relationship between government and the people is subject to much debate.

So far, what have you learned about value propositions? They are statements about judgments. They concern a thing's qualities, rather than the thing itself. Judgments are important because they express opinions and attitudes about the underlying meanings of facts and events, whether we like or dislike them, whether they are good or bad, whether or not they should lead to action, and what type of action they lead to. Value judgments may be of an artistic, moral, ethical, or political nature.

Examples of propositions of value are the following:

Communism is a form of government that undermines human dignity.

The use of tax money to support athletics is wasteful.

The United Nations is not worth the money it costs the United States.

By now, it should be clear that value judgments are highly relevant to your participation in forensic events. When you decide that a problem is significant or harmful, you are making a value judgment. To say that a plan has results that could be called advantageous or disadvantageous is to make a value judgment. Ultimately, to decide to take action on a policy change and to specify the types of government actions that should or should not be adopted is to make value judgments. Every persuasive appeal in forensics—student congress or debate—inevitably calls forth the values held by those listening to you. Your success in forensics will be enhanced by a clear understanding of the nature of value propositions, how they function as guides to creating arguments, and how your listeners will arrange your value appeals along their own sets of judgmental priorities.

Group discussions can help you understand how value propositions affect debate.

This final point is crucial to understanding the role of value judgments. While there are many important values, there is no set priority or rank ordering of values. When relevant values conflict, priority must be determined. A good example of competing values was shown recently in the public controversy over mandatory air bags for automobiles. Though few people questioned the fact that air bags installed in all cars could save thousands of lives, the government decided not to require auto manufacturers to install them because it seemed that the public would rather have the choice to buy air bags as a voluntary option. In this instance, the value of free choice was held to be more important than the value of personal safety.

Propositions of Policy

The origin of the term *policy* is the Greek word *polis*, or city, the same root word leading to related modern English words, such as *metropolis, police,* and *politics.* Broadly speaking, a policy is a course of action or a set of rules, regulations, or laws designed to guide present and future government and private sector decisions. In a corporation, for example, company policies govern employer–employee relations. A school district may set up policies governing how the school buildings may be used by outside groups. The body of local, state, and federal legislators passes policies that administrative branches of government enforce.

A *proposition of policy* is a statement of a course of action to be considered for adoption. The spheres of policy formulation include all those problem areas deemed appropriate for government action. In the classic statement of Aristotle,

> Of the subjects upon which all men deliberate, and upon which deliberative orators speak, the chief ones, we may say, are five in number, to wit: (1) ways and means; and (2) war and peace; next, (3) national defense; and (4) imports and exports; finally, (5) legislation.

Theoretically, every question requiring government deliberation falls within one or another of these general categories. Indeed, it is difficult to think of many items being considered today that are not pertinent to at least one category or another. All issues related to spending and taxing (fiscal, budget, or revenue bills) are matters of ways and means. The nation's foreign policy, regarding diplomacy, economic relations, and military matters, seems to be included in Aristotle's reference to war and peace, defense, and trade policy. Finally, all issues of domestic problems, such as welfare, law and order, commerce, and the rest, come within the province of legislation.

The status quo is comprised, in part, of government policies, accumulated over time. Rules, regulations, and laws begin with the basic documents established within a given jurisdiction (the United States Constitution, the constitutions of the various state governments, city charters, and others.) They continue through the body of laws and statutes passed under the authority of those basic documents to govern citizens. There is some overlap between jurisdictions, such as between federal laws and state laws; but generally the existing policies are allocated to different levels of government corresponding to the authority of each level. Usually, the level of government and the nature of a problem fit each other. For instance, local government has primary responsibilities for the public schools, local law enforcement, fire protection, and other matters because it is close to the people served. Conversely, the federal government assumes responsibility for matters of national concern, such as defense and military policies, interstate commerce, and regulation of broadcasting frequencies. It is easy to see why this division of responsibilities occurs. It would be inappropriate, even impossible, for the city of Midland, Texas, to make a treaty with Great Britain. Likewise, the federal government does not concern itself with parking violators in Midland's City Hall parking lot. Nevertheless, in all matters of public concern, policies are established and maintained by some appropriate authority possessing jurisdiction.

Where do policies come from? At this point in history, rules, regulations, and laws stand on the books, ready for easy reference. If you were to ask, "What is the policy of the U.S. Army toward deserters?", you could find the answer by turning to the relevant section of the *Uniform Code of Military Justice*. If you were to ask, "May girls wear short shorts to the senior English class?", you would probably learn the answer from the school's dress code. And you would also discover that these policies, like all rules, regulations, and laws, are binding on your decisions and actions as long as you remain under the jurisdiction of the authority in charge of the policy.

Yet to recognize this characteristic of policies—that they exist and are binding—does not truly explain the answer to the question of where policies come from. Even though policies now exist, they did not *always* exist. At some point in the past, policies had to be created in response to problems as they arose. At some point in the past, there was no answer to the question "What is the policy to guide decisions about such-and-such a problem?" Moreover, there will be situations arising in the future for which no policy now exists, and new policies will be needed to guide decisions. In fact, existing policies are in continuous need of review and change to adapt to changing conditions.

With this explanation of the nature of policy and policy formation, you are now ready to learn some important characteristics of propositions of policy. Keep in mind that a proposition is a statement requiring consideration. First, a proposition of policy reflects a rule to guide action or decision. As such, it differs from both factual propositions and value judgments. A policy is not subject to verification by observation of events or objects, like a factual statement; rather, it is validated by agreement among all the people subject to the policy and enforced by law. Neither is a policy a matter of subjective assessment of artistic, moral, or abstract political qualities; rather, a policy is an objective rule to guide decision or action regardless of any subjective evaluation of it.

Second, because policies are created and maintained ultimately by the agreement of the people they affect, they are considered to be subject to change through orderly processes. Policies are negotiable. On the other hand, a factual statement is either true or false. A fact cannot be amended by majority vote. Likewise, value judgments are not negotiable, although they may change as our attitudes and opinions change. We do not ordinarily think of a value judgment as a policy guiding decision and action among all people within a community. In this sense, you say that you cannot legislate morality. On the other hand, you can legislate a policy.

Broadly speaking, any statement of a policy is a proposition of policy. However, in forensics the attention usually focuses on propositions of policy requiring consideration, that is, propositions for which you seek acceptance. There are three general categories of propositions of policy.

First, you may propose a new policy to guide decisions and actions where no policy exists. This is the starting point for all policies. To illustrate this type of policy proposition, imagine this hypothetical situation. Suppose great strides were made in the area of space travel by the wealthy industrial nations. What policies should guide decisions as to the allocation of space routes, ownership of resources discovered on previously unexplored planets, safety and security regulations in space? The nations involved would naturally be required to work out a set of rules, regulations, and laws binding on all and to formulate a set of policies applicable to these problems. In the past, the development of nuclear weapons and of nuclear energy for peaceful uses generated a need for a whole new set of policies where none previously existed.

Second, you may propose amendments to alter policies that exist but for some reason are no longer satisfactory. The conditions that existed originally may have changed in significant ways, out-moding once-established policies. A good example of an amended policy is the reduction of the speed limit on interstate highways from 70 to 55 miles per hour, in order to reduce the nation's fuel consumption during the 1973 oil crisis. Another example is the return to a higher speed limit on the rural highways of some states in 1987.

Third, you may propose to abolish an existing policy altogether. Once, all high school students were required to study Latin. Now, only a few college graduate programs maintain this policy. At some point, the authorities in charge of educational institutions decided to abandon the policy of requiring the study of a language other than English.

The proposition of policy is highly relevant to forensics. In student congress, contestants are expected to make policy proposals for consideration by the entire legislative body. Whenever such a proposal is made, it is called a *motion*, which is a precise statement of the proposed policy to be considered for possible approval. Once moved, a proposition may be debated, amended, and disposed of by acceptance, rejection, or other means according to the rules of parliamentary procedure.

In debate, the opposing teams are concerned with a proposition of policy. As in student congress, the statement is precisely worded. However, in debate the proposition is called a *resolution*, rather than a motion or question. Unlike student congress, debate does not permit the resolution to be amended. Also, at the conclusion of the debate, the debaters are not expected to agree among themselves as to the disposition of the resolution. Instead, they put their arguments for and against the resolution to an impartial judge who is responsible for making a final decision to accept or reject the resolution based on the merits of the case as presented in the debate.

Examples of propositions of policy are the resolutions for debate in 1987–1988:

Resolved: That the United States government should significantly decrease its military involvement in Latin America.

Resolved: That the United States government should significantly increase its nonmilitary assistance to Latin America.

Resolved: That the United States government should adopt a policy to increase political stability in Latin America.

These statements of proposed policies for debate meet the criteria established for propositions of policy. They propose a rule, regulation, or law to govern decisions within a designated problem area. Although the statements are general, permitting debaters some flexibility in interpreting the specific meaning of the resolutions, they state an agency of jurisdiction ("the United States government") and an action in a specific direction ("should significantly decrease its military involvement...").

Summary

Analysis, understanding the different aspects of the problem under consideration, is the beginning point for any forensic event. In the specific parts of this book that deal with debate and student congress, you will examine how these analytical skills can be applied. For now, keep in mind that the characteristics of the problem area and the nature of the proposition give you specific directions in which to discover the basic issues in problem-solving.

Questions for Discussion

1. Debate begins with the *analysis* of a problem area and its solutions. Define the process of analysis.

2. What is the difference between a *problem area* and a *problem statement?*

3. When wording a proposition for debate, what characteristics should you consider?

4. Propositions may be classified into three categories—propositions of fact, value, and policy. How are they different from each other?

5. There are three general categories for propositions of policy. What are these and how are they different from each other?

Activities

1. Using the resolution "Resolved: That the federal government should exclusively control the development and distribution of energy resources in the United States," outline the meaning of the terms of the statement. Are there any value terms in the resolution?

2. Propositions ought to meet five criteria. Examine the following propositions. Does each meet those criteria? Rewrite in correct form those that do not.

   Resolved: That the federal government should increase social welfare programs in the current budget.

   Resolved: That enrollment in secondary schools is declining.

   Resolved: That the federal government should redesign the tax structure to tax citizens equally and use a significant portion of the tax dollars to improve the educational system.

   Resolved: That municipalities should establish comprehensive security guidelines for airports to make them safe.

   Resolved: That city governments should establish a comprehensive program to improve educational standards in the schools.

   Resolved: That the federal government should establish a comprehensive program to provide medical care for all Americans.

   Resolved: That all United States citizens have a right to clean drinking water.

3. The following are examples of poorly worded propositions. Rewrite these propositions, wording them correctly.

   Propositions of Fact

   Resolved: That action should be taken to balance the budget of the federal government.

   Resolved: That the housing market is no longer attractive to young married couples.

   Propositions of Value

   Resolved: That every citizen should be guaranteed an annual income.

Resolved: That English study develops skills in grammar and punctuation.

Propositions of Policy

Resolved: That the jury system in the United States should not be significantly changed.

Resolved: That the federal government should establish a comprehensive national policy to protect the quality of water and guarantee a future supply of energy.

4. Formulate a proposition of fact, one of value, and one of policy on each of the following topics: arms sales, terrorism, star wars, excellence in education, age discrimination, aviation safety, and protectionism.

Chapter 3

The Skills of Research

Objectives and Key Terms

After studying Chapter 3, you should be able to

1. Conduct a successful library survey on a particular debate resolution,

2. Make a list of private resources in your community to be used for a particular resolution,

3. Explore computerized indexes in your research,

4. Explain and operate under the guidelines for ethics in research, and

5. Make a list of key terms to use when you research a debate resolution.

After reading this chapter, you should understand the following terms:

card catalog

indexes (or guides)

computerized indexes

research

secondary sources

evidence

evidence card

T he analysis that is fundamental to successful participation in forensic events is both an outgrowth of knowledge and the foundation for continuing research. Much of that knowledge will be
general, but more of it will be the direct result of extensive reading, listening, and discussion. Once the process of analysis is advanced enough
for you to be ready to accumulate specific information on which to build
debate cases or write student congress briefs, you must be prepared to use
the skills of research.

Nature and Purpose of Research

Although most people have used the word *research* many times, its actual
meaning frequently escapes them. It means what it literally says: to
search again. How often do you pick up a book early in your search for evidence, look through it, and set it aside permanently? As your own
knowledge increases or your grasp of the problem broadens, you may re-
consider sources. Beginning to research a broad area is a hard job because so much information is available. But with energy and persistence,
the topic gradually will become clear.

The purpose of research is to gather information and evidence and to
classify it so that it is easily retrievable for use in competition. There are
three reasons for this data-based approach to forensics. First, there is the
ethical or moral obligation of anyone who attempts to influence others.
To speak without adequate information is to violate the traditional ethics of public speaking. Second, there is a pragmatic consideration. If you
lack thorough knowledge and adequate evidence, you have little chance
to make your view prevail. Finally, there is the psychological advantage
that comes when you are secure in your knowledge that you have the
greatest possible accumulation of information on a problem area. The
debater who is in constant fear of not having done enough research on a
case and the student congressperson who hesitates to speak when the
opportunity occurs because he or she cannot evidence a position are
both at a disadvantage.

Modern competition in debate and student congress places a premium on printed sources of evidence. In student congress, however,
there is room for the introduction of personal knowledge and experience
as well as information garnered from interviews and correspondence.

These sources may furnish a speaker with a background that enables him or her to interpret the printed sources and gather evidence from them. The competitor in forensics must, regardless of the event, be committed to research.

Finding Evidence

Library Survey

The first research step is a library survey. Find out what is available in your local library. The basic tool to consult in any library is the *card catalog*. This lists all the books in the library by author, title, and subject. You should look under any of the possible subject headings suggested by the problem statement with which you are working. For example, if you are researching the 1987–88 debate topic, "Resolved: That the United States government should adopt a policy to increase political stability in Latin America," the first subject you would refer to in the card catalog would be *Latin America*. Following that, you would refer to specific countries, such as Honduras, Nicaragua, Guatemala, Costa Rica, Chile, and Argentina. Then you might move to subjects such as terrorism, illegal drugs, Contra support, and humanitarian aid. In addition, the card catalog might have other areas cross-referenced. Exhaust the most obvious ones first, but remember that there is a time lag in most libraries between acquisition date and final filing in the card catalog for a book. Develop good relations with your librarians, let them know ahead of time what your debate topic is, and ask to be told of newly acquired books on the topic. Most librarians will respond enthusiastically.

Following a careful look at the card catalog, examine other general reference sources. Most libraries today have *vertical files*. These are collections of periodical and newspaper clippings that relate to topics of current interest. You may have to ask the librarian about this collection. In addition, consult such *guides* and *indexes* as the *Reader's Guide to Periodical Literature* and *The International Index*. These works contain alphabetical listings (by author, title, and general subject) of magazine articles that have appeared in a particular group of periodicals. The *Public Affairs Information Service Index* includes magazine articles, but it also lists selected government documents by title and subject. There are also regular indexes to the *Congressional Record* and *United States Government Publications: Monthly Catalog.* Special indexes, such as *The Education Index*, can be useful if the topic fits the special subject. Most libraries carry the indexes listed above, even though they do not have all the publications indexed in them. Keep a record of the promising articles listed, even if they are not available in the particular library you are using. You may have opportunities to work in other libraries. There is no need to use valuable research time by recopying indexes at each stop. Remember that any index will be organized under many different broad subject headings. Use your imagination. Explore all the possible ways the information you seek might be listed.

Using Computers in Research

An important change taking place in libraries across the country is a shift to computerized indexes. More and more libraries are installing computerized data systems as replacements for the traditional card catalogs for books and bound indexes for periodicals. For the library user who understands such a system, the advantages in facilitating research are great.

To be sure, some library users will view this prospect with hesitation. Some people see the advent of computerized library indexes as another encroachment in everyday life by computer technology. Such people assume that a computerized index is useful only to the expert programmer who can speak computerese. But this is not the case. Computerized indexes are designed to be "user-friendly" so that *anyone* can use them, and it usually takes only a few minutes to master a particular system.

Although there is a wide variety of library computer systems presently in operation, most can be placed in one of two categories. The first includes systems that index items you would find in a card catalog (primarily books). Most of these systems, like card catalogs, are indexed by author, title, and subject. To find listings under a particular heading, you merely enter that heading into the system (usually by way of a terminal, which has a keyboard similar to that of standard typewriters). For example, say that you want to find out which of Mark Twain's books are available in your local library. You first indicate that this is an author search (perhaps by typing the letter "a" and entering it; this varies from system to system). Then, depending on the individual system, you might type in "Twain, Mark" and enter it. The computer then gives you a variety of information about each listing. It provides all the information you would find in the card catalog, such as the call number of the book, its publication information, and perhaps a short summary of its contents. In addition, though, the computer might also list the present status of the book—whether it has been checked out and other libraries where the book might be found. This latter information can be very helpful in facilitating research. You don't have to waste a trip to the shelf to discover that a book has been checked out. In addition, you can determine immediately whether the book can be found at other libraries.

Computerized library indexes simplify research and are designed for easy use.

The computerized catalog can also help facilitate subject searches. Using a standard card catalog to find information on broad topics can be quite inefficient. You can find listings only under very narrow, precise headings, and looking under broad headings can be time-consuming. If you were researching West Germany, for example, a card catalog would only allow you to examine subheadings (such as economy, history, geography, and demographics) one at a time. With a computerized system, you could enter the broad topic of West Germany into the terminal, and it would display all the subheadings at once. You would then know immediately how all the material on West Germany has been subdivided, and you would be able to get all the listings under a particular subheading quickly. This technique of entering broad topics to examine subheadings can also improve the breadth of your research, since the subheadings themselves can spark ideas for new cross-references to check out.

The second category of computerized indexes carries periodical listings. These systems index periodical articles you might find in bound indexes like the *Reader's Guide to Periodical Literature* and the *Social Sciences Index*. The operation of these systems is similar to that of the computerized catalog. You enter a particular heading, and the listings for it are then displayed on the screen. Most of these systems, like the bound indexes, are limited to subject searches.

There are two advantages to computerized periodical indexes. The first is that a computerized system permits the search of many years at one time. With bound indexes, if you want to find all articles written on the MX missile in the past five years, you must go through five or more bound editions of a particular index. A computerized system allows you to search five years at once. This can be particularly useful when you are doing newspaper searches. One computerized index has compiled listings from the five biggest newspapers in the United States (*New York Times, Washington Post, Christian Science Monitor, Wall Street Journal,* and *Los Angeles Times*) over a number of years. Using this index saves you the trouble of looking through five different indexes. The second advantage, peculiar only to a few systems, is that the system may be attached to a printer. This means that after you call up the headings you are looking for, the listings can be printed out as hard copy. Needless to say, you can save a great deal of time by not having to hand copy all the listings you find. Of course, you may also find a system of the first category (listing card catalog items) connected to a printer.

The trend to computerized data systems should not be feared. Such systems are relatively easy to use, even for someone with no computer experience. The advantages of such systems are great, however, in facilitating both the efficiency and breadth of research.

Current Sources

The alert and aware forensic researcher will also survey, on a regular basis, current issues of such noteworthy publications as *Christian Science Monitor, New York Times, Wall Street Journal, Congressional Digest, Congressional Record, Current History, Foreign Policy Bulletin, Nation's Business, New Republic, U.S. Department of State Bulletin,* and *Vital Speeches.* This is not an exhaustive list, but a representative one. The thing to remember is that you can and should attempt to locate the latest evidence, even before it has time to be indexed.

Special Sources

There are some special resources of which forensic competitors should be aware. Many of these provide a way for the student living in a remote area to have the experience of direct research in primary sources. As such, they have particular value. Available in the school year 1987–88 were the following privately published materials:

Social Issues Resources Series—A series of volumes contained in loose-leaf notebooks, each addressed to a different social issue. Each volume contains articles selected from newspapers, magazines, journals, and government publications representing different points of view on the problem. About 60 articles are contained in each volume, and supplements are available each year to keep each volume up to date. (Available from Social Issues Resources Series, Inc., Gaithersburg, Maryland 20760.)

Current History—The May/June and July/August issues of this magazine each year are devoted to the high school debate topic. The issues contain a variety of articles exploring many of the aspects of the problem area.

The Forensic Quarterly—There are three issues a year of this publication from the National Federation of State High School Associations. Much of the material published is written especially for publication in this quarterly and is not available anywhere else. All of it is primary material. (Available from National Federation, 11724 Plaza Circle, P.O. Box 20626, Kansas City, MO 64195.)

Congressional Research Service—Each year, this research volume is published with excerpts of statements, speeches, and debates on the current high school debate topic. The extensive bibliography in this work can shorten some of the time spent in the library. (Available from your Congressional representative.)

Article Reprints—The University Microfilms International in Ann Arbor, Michigan, published an impressive set of volumes on the high school debate topic of health care. Each volume contained direct reprints of articles from a wide variety of current publications.

Congressional Quarterly—This source includes weekly reports on federal legislation and a sampling of expert opinion.

National Journal—This source follows national legislation. It has good summary articles on major policy disputes.

Library Reference Service—A set of three portfolios were assembled by this company in Barnesville, Minnesota, on the high school debate topic. Each of the three contained a different aspect of the question, but all the articles (approximately 300) were direct reprints and constituted primary research.

The materials listed here are not exhaustive. They are listed to illustrate that a forensic competitor, no matter where he or she lives, can get primary resource materials and can experience the joy of seeking and finding answers to the questions formulated in the analytical process.

Private Interest Groups

A small investment of money and a relatively large block of time can garner excellent results from another type of primary resource. The money required is for stationery and stamps; the time is for writing letters to private interest groups for material. The best way to discover the identity of such groups is to pose three questions to yourself: (1) Who might be interested in the problem area? (2) Who would gain from the adoption of the resolution? (3) Who would lose from the adoption of the resolution?

When you have answered these questions, you will have identified a number of groups of people who represent special interest groups, which are usually more than happy to supply material. You will, of course, begin with the understanding that the conclusions and interpretations in the material you receive will not necessarily be objective. This does not mean, however, that the facts and statistics such material might contain are not valid.

At times, discovering the existence of such groups is a matter of creative deduction. Some of them are obvious. When health care is the problem area, your first letter should go to the American Medical Association. However, less obviously, the Social Security Administration, the Congressional Research Service, the Pharmaceutical Manufacturers Association, the World Health Organization, and the Department of Transportation were each discovered to have valuable information, which was freely provided to debaters who inquired. These and several other unlikely sources were found by reading and noticing references to studies or projects. A careful look for citations in handbooks and bibliographies can reveal groups to which you can write for additional information. One debate squad was placed on several additional mailing lists as a result of one inquiry and received a great amount of unsolicited material. Some of it, admittedly, was properly classified as junk mail, but some of it answered questions that were vital to their research.

One team, when debating the question of penal reform, discovered that no comprehensive statistics had ever been compiled about jails on a nationwide basis because of the strictly local jurisdiction over jails. They found, however, that there were statewide studies. They then wrote to the proper state agency in each of the fifty states, asking for selected studies and any additional materials related to the debate topic. They received an overwhelming response, about 85 percent, and materials that enabled them to become experts on the subject.

If the identities of these groups are not obvious, you can consult the *World Almanac*, which lists in excess of 25,000 organizations, or the *Encyclopedia of Associations*. The information available from such organizations may hold the key to specific areas of the topic that can lead to a case construction that might have eluded you otherwise. You must also be aware that such publications naturally reflect the biases of the group they represent.

Private Resources

Often, even in small towns, there are private organizations or individuals who possess materials that can be valuable to you. One high school debate squad discovered, for example, that the local hospital administrator had a wealth of books and periodicals not available anywhere else during the year in which the high school debate question dealt with "comprehensive regulation of the health care system." This group also discovered that the local bar association had an extensive law library at the County Courthouse, which the students used to research comprehensive penal reform. And in a completely unexpected windfall, several debaters discovered that local executives of the major oil companies were willing to share access to many statistical records concerning energy costs, consumption, and importation.

But not only do local individuals and organizations frequently have printed sources, they also may provide unexpected access to experts. For example, local doctors, although far more familiar to you than someone in a distant medical center, may have even better credentials in hospital management, preventive medicine, or drug treatment. The district manager of the utility company in your area may have a high level of expertise on some aspect of energy development and would certainly be up to date on existing government regulations on energy consumption and development. Do you look around your community for possible research sources? Invite such individuals to speak to your forensic class. Tape record the speech or interview, with proper citation of time, place, and date. After you have made an accurate transcription of the material, take it to the individual for verification of its accuracy. Once that is established, you have a copy of expert testimony of the first order. In addition, local organizations may have programs to which they invite guest speakers in some special field of interest. Be sure to watch club notices in the media. Almost any organization would welcome a high school group to be a part of the audience. Tape recorders are again preferable to notetaking. Be sure that you ask permission of all involved and that you explain what use will be made of the material.

Frequently the Public Broadcasting System, educational radio or television, has programs that address themselves either directly or indirectly to current problems. Be alert to television programming. If your school has a videotape recording facility, be sure to get a tape for group viewing later. If it does not, then audio tape recording will suffice. Be sure to get an absolutely exact citation on such a broadcast, along with the particular qualifications of any person you might want to quote. Often you can write to the network for a printed script of the program.

If you have difficulty determining whether a person is qualified to speak to a topic, you should do some research on him or her. This is particularly true if the testimony you wish to quote is basically a judgment or a conclusion. Several biographical works are standard in most libraries. *American Men of Science, Biography Index, Current Biography, Directory of American Scholars, Who's Who, Who's Who in America, Who's Who in the East*, etc., offer information that might make it possible for you to qualify the source of a piece of evidence.

Secondary Sources

Thus far, the discussion has focused on discovering primary resources. However, some secondary sources are also important. The forensic community has many different points of view concerning these secondary sources, usually classified as debate handbooks or evidence books. No one denies the value of original research, seeking out relevant books and articles, and the evaluating positions and opinions in their original context. However, the information explosion had made the debater's task a difficult one and has led many debaters to employ secondary resources. Several observations can be made concerning this practice.

First, there is nothing inherently wrong with handbooks. However, heavy reliance on such evidence sources is not wise for two reasons: First, part of the value of debate is the acquisition of research skills. You forfeit that value if you depend on handbook evidence. The second problem is far more pragmatic. The National Forensic League and most of the State Activity Leagues as well as the American Forensic Association have very strict rules with regard to the accuracy of evidence cited in a debate. These rules uniformly place the responsibility for accuracy on the individual who *reads* the evidence in a round. Even when using a reputable handbook, you should check sources. If a flaw is found in a piece of evidence you read in a round, the claim that it came from such and such handbook will not excuse the error in the evidence. You, as the debater, will be held responsible. Checking evidence you find in handbooks will also give you the opportunity to look for additional resources. Consequently, if you rely on evidence that you did not copy from the primary source, you must have every confidence in the integrity of the individual or group who did copy it. Buy handbooks, then, that are reputable and consistent. Beware of evidence that is "too good to be true!"

A debate handbook works best as an introduction to a topic. It can be a valuable source of background information. A handbook can also provide bibliographical sources to be researched. Many debaters will get a feel for what cases might be developed by other schools, and the evidence and initial analysis provided may spark some ideas that would otherwise have taken weeks of research to find. However, since the evidence is gathered before the season, research must be updated. The argument may remain valid, but as the season progresses new evidence will be needed. Most sources cited should be checked for additional evidence. A handbook will not contain every good card found in a source. Most researchers strive for diversity in their sources. This means that good evidence was left behind. Also, a handbook contains the research of a select group of people. Although their ideas might be good, they are not the only good ideas available. Handbooks are traditionally put together in a very short time period (less than six weeks, in many cases). Moreover, as cases change new evidence must be found. Finally, the topic may go into areas not predicted by even the most expert preseason researchers.

Recording Evidence

Evidence accumulated for debate and student congress must be in a form that is retrievable. In the chapters on student congress, specific suggestions for filing evidence to fit the unique nature of that event is given. For debate, the system of placing evidence on note cards is the best system discovered thus far.

Your analysis of the problem area will identify the broad issues of a resolution, enabling you to sort evidence on that basis very quickly. The divisions and subdivisions of these issues will change and grow as the season progresses. The usual plan for evidence organization is to designate different files for affirmative and negative cards, to classify subdivisions within those areas, and to file note cards under those subdivisions.

In recording evidence, you should exercise great care to insure that all relevant information is recorded on the card. This does not necessarily mean that you will introduce everything into a debate round. But it does mean that if challenged you would be able to produce essential information. Every evidence card in your file should contain

1. A main topic heading.

2. A subtopic heading.

3. The citation: author's name, title of article and magazine or book, place and date published, page number.

4. The author's qualifications. Place under the citation or, if space is unavailable, place on the back of the card.

5. The evidence quotation itself. This must be accurate and verbatim. If you intend to omit part of the quotation in order to save time, copy the entire quotation and then underline or highlight the part to be read. In this way, you can always prove that your ellipsis did not violate the intention of the author.

A typical note card might look like one of these:

AFF/Climate   **Climate Change Harmful**

Hon. James Schiever, CARBON DIOXIDE AND THE GREENHOUSE EFFECT, House Hearings, Committee on Science and Technology, February 28, 1984, p. 4.

"In contrast to the cataclysmic effects of a major exchange of nuclear weapons on the environment, the build up of carbon dioxide and other trace gases is expected to result in slow but inexorable change in climate. The results of both, however, may be equally disastrous."

NEG/Climate   **Climate Change Inevitable**

Rafe Pomerance, CARBON DIOXIDE AND THE GREENHOUSE EFFECT, House Hearings, Committee on Science and Technology, February 28, 1984, pp. 112-113.

"The Environmental Protection Agency says it is too late to stop global warming and that the best policy is to adapt. The National Academy of Sciences concludes that we do not yet know what to do. It recommends waiting while further studies are conducted. The truth is neither. We must prepare for some climate change while also acting NOW to prevent drastic climate modification which will result if current energy, industrial and agricultural policies continue."

It is important to identify directly quoted material with quotation marks, omitted material with ellipses, and interpolated material with brackets rather than parentheses, so that the language of the original quotation can be distinguished clearly from the debater's paraphrasing. After putting an entire quotation on a card, the debater can highlight what he or she will read so that unnecessary phrases like "as in chart 1" will not take up time in a speech. The National Forensic League specifically stipulates that ellipses are not to be used in evidence unless the debater carries a copy of the original source. Should a piece of evidence contain ellipses in the original, this should be indicated in brackets on the evidence card.

Only one item of evidence should be recorded on each note card. The temptation is usually strong, especially for beginning debaters, to record two short pieces of evidence on one card. This hurts the flexibility of the note-card system. Try to avoid writing on both sides of the card or carrying part of the information over onto another card.

Ethics In Research

Finally, it is appropriate here to talk about the ethics of research. The requirement that you provide evidence for all your claims and arguments in a debate is one reason why debate is so educational. Debaters do more research and accumulate more files of evidence cards than just about anyone, especially on a voluntary, extracurricular basis. It is not uncommon for a high school debater to compile 2,000 or more evidence cards during the debate season.

On the other hand, the rule that you must provide evidence as proof in a debate has ironically set up an almost counterproductive situation. What if you need a piece of evidence to say something, and you don't have it? Chances are, you will lose the argument, especially if it is refuted by your opponent. Yet, if you just had that piece of evidence, perhaps you would be able to win the argument instead of losing it. The temptation is to lead the judge into believing that you indeed have the evidence by "doctoring" a card or by simply making up a card to say what you need it to say.

For instance, the affirmative sample debate evidence card shown on page 40 of this chapter says that a change in the climate will be "slow but inexorable." If you are trying to win your case, you could be tempted to make this evidence stronger by reading, "The build up of carbon dioxide and other trace gases is expected to result in *an inexorable* change in climate" instead of "*slow but inexorable* change in climate." When the desire to win a debate becomes strong enough to lead to such a decision, the underlying purpose of debate is subverted. Debate is aimed at making decisions based on the facts. The whole system of school debating rests on truthfulness, especially in reporting research. To misrepresent a piece of evidence is to lie to the judge about what the sources said. If you were the person who wrote the original research report, would you want someone to twist it into something you neither said nor meant?

The misuse of evidence, therefore, is the most serious breach of debate ethics. To misrepresent a piece of evidence is called *distortion*, and to make up evidence is called *fabrication*. The American Forensic Association recommends that the penalty for evidence distortion and evidence fabrication should begin with an automatic loss of the debate. Also, they advocate that the debater who is guilty receive a score of zero speaker points, which effectively prevents her or him from receiving a speaker award in the tournament because such awards are based on the overall average of scores during the tournament. Beyond that, for evidence fabrication at the college level, in particular, a debater found guilty is barred from participating in the National Debate Tournament, and the American Forensic Association is instructed to write a letter of censure to the debater's home school. The National Forensic League also has strict rules in this area. As you can see, the forensic community takes this violation of debate seriously. So, as you record the evidence you discover in your research, do so accurately.

Summary

The core of forensic competition is the research you do. Through research, you prepare the proof to validate your arguments. Research is a careful process of determining what is available, using fully a wide variety of resources, and recording the results carefully and accurately. Once you have begun the research process, you need to turn your attention to the use of that information to establish proof.

Questions for Discussion

1. When preparing to research a proposition, why should you begin by developing a list of key terms?

2. Which type of evidence is considered to be the least educationally defensible? Why?

3. If the library near you has computerized indexes, why would it be to your advantage to use them?

4. If you need to determine how qualified a person is to speak to a topic, where can you find information?

5. Research goes beyond what is found in the library. On any given topic, there are numerous groups that print information concerning the topic. How do you tap these resources, and how do you determine their value?

6. What are the essential items of information that an evidence card should contain?

7. The reading and research skills learned for debate can be applied to other areas as well. Describe some of these other applications.

Activities

1. Using one of the following propositions, make a list of key terms. Use your imagination.

   Resolved: That academic achievement criteria should be applied to extracurricular activities for participation.

   Resolved: That the United States should significantly change its foreign trade policies.

   Resolved: That the federal government should establish a program to provide for aging American citizens.

2. Using one of the resolutions in Activity 1, perform the following tasks (be sure to use your list of key terms):

   a. Make a list of books of interest on the proposition.
   b. Using one of the indexes listed in this chapter, make a bibliogra-

phy of magazines or government documents available on the proposition.

3. Using one of the resolutions in Activity 1, identify any private interest groups that might have materials available on the resolution. Draft a sample letter to send to these interest groups.

4. The following pieces of evidence are flawed. In each, identify the flaw.

Anita Johnson (Prof. of Medicine, MIT), *Environment*, March 1987, p. 9.

"Flame retardants are not labeled, nor are the many extraneous ingredients in drugs, such as flavors and dyes."

Edward Kennedy (Senator, Mass.), Hearings, Subcommittee on Health and Scientific Research, May 17, 1983, p. 4.

"Most patients today are hopelessly uninformed about what drugs really do and cannot do. They therefore make excessive and irrational demands for drug treatment when they see their doctor."

"Another Study Refutes Saccharin/Cancer Link," *Chemical and Engineering News*, March 17, 1985, p. 8.

"Wynder and Stellman state emphatically, 'No association was found between use of artificial sweeteners or diet beverages and bladder cancer.' Alan S. Morrison and Julie E. Buring, who conducted the Harvard study, hedge only slightly by concluding that 'users of artificial sweeteners have little or no excess risk of cancer of the lower urinary tract.'"

David Dickson, *Nature*, January 3, 1986, p. 2.

"Such nonpropellant emissions could bring the total CFC emissions back up to previous levels within seven to ten years."

Lewis A. Dunn (Prof., Harvard U.), *Controlling the Bomb*, 1982.

"It also would lessen the chances of unauthorized use of nuclear weapons in local conflict, thereby dampening one flash point of Soviet-American confrontation."

Ted Greenwood (Professor of Political Science, Un. of Vermont), "Supply-Side Non-Proliferation," *Foreign Policy,* Spring 1961, p. 131.

"In the absence of international acceptance of existing U.S. policy, Congress and the new administration should initiate movement toward a revision of the international nuclear regime. Such revision should be pursued through a process of broad negotiations and agreement. A wholesale dismantling of the regime—all too easy to bring about in the current political environment—would not be constructive and should be avoided."

A. M. Weinberg (Commonwealth Edison), "Can We Fix Nuclear Energy?" *Annals of Nuclear Energy,* 1986, p. 473.

"A one million KW pressurized water reactor contains 15 billion Ci radioactivity. This is about equal to the natural radioactivity in all the oceans; radioactivity that accompanies the decay of the 4 billion tons or uranium and its daughters dissolved in the seas."

Roger E. Linneman (MD) "Medical Aspects of Power Generation. Present and Future," *Medical Research Engineering,* July/August 1984, p. 12.

"Starr, in evaluating both types of power plants of equal size situated in similar population densities estimated that there would be 60 death annually from the fossil fuel plants for each cancer death from a nuclear plant. . . . Dr. Stig Bergstrom of the Studsvik Research Station in Sweden estimates that the effects from operating a nuclear plant are 10,000 less than from an oil-fired plant, and that a savings of $6 million per year in property damage could be realized by generating electricity with a nuclear plant instead of a fossil fuel one."

Chemical Week, January 2, 1983, p. 16.

"Industry sources estimate that another 1,000 to 2,000 doctoral-level toxicologists will be needed by 1991, which is sooner than the nation can possibly generate them warns Lange."

Health Benefits: Loss Due to unemployment, Hearings before the Committee on Energy and Commerce and the Subcommittee on

Health and the Environment, House of Representatives, January 24 and April 22, 1983, p. 16.

"Many working mothers and their children who under the harsh rules demanded by the Reagan Administration are no longer eligible for Aid to Families with Dependent Children (AFDC) have simultaneously lost their eligibility for Medicaid. Individuals who are losing social security disability benefits lose their entitlement to Medicare."

Todd May, Jr. (Prof. of Economics, Boston U.) et al., "Employment: Recovery and Change," *Fortune*, August 8, 1986, p. 18.

"Almost every state has adjusted its revenue base in one way or another, by raising income or profits taxes, canceling cuts enacted earlier, increasing sales levies, or hiking user fees. At the local level there's been action too. Property-tax receipts are pouring into municipal coffers at the fastest pace in more than ten years."

David A. Andelman (The Peace Movement), "Space Wars," *Foreign Policy*, Fall 1987, p. 102.

". . . if the United States possessed an ABM system, the Soviets would inevitably acquire one too."

Chapter 4

The Skills of Reasoning

Objectives and Key Terms

After studying Chapter 4, you should be able to

1. Explain "proof,"

2. Explain and demonstrate the relationship among evidence, claim, and reasoning in the establishment of proof, and

3. List the tests for credibility for generalizations, analogy, cause-effect, statistics, and authority as forms of reasoning.

After reading this chapter, you should understand the following terms:

proof

assertion

generalization

analogy

false analogy

cause-effect

sign argument

reasoning from scientific methodology

reasoning from authority

F orensic events provide an educational laboratory in which to learn and practice the principles of analyzing a problem area in the context of debate and student congress. Methods of analysis were explained to you as the way you organize information. To find the information, you have seen that you must do research. The final task in this section is to explain how to integrate your information and analysis to create convincing proof.

Establishing Proof

In any forensic event, you must present your conclusions to others for their consideration. To do so, you make a claim. You ask for belief in your conclusion. Suppose you are asked, "Why should I accept your claim?" What would you answer? It is not enough simply to say, "You should believe what I say because I said it." If, however, you say, "This is the *reason* you should accept it . . .," and then you furnish a reason for accepting your claim, you have given the other person a basis for considering your conclusion. *Reasoning* is the process of providing support for a claim.

When your reason seems acceptable to the other person, and your claim is believed on the basis of your reasoning, it is said that you have proved your claim. *Proof* is information which, when offered in support of a claim, presents sufficient reason to make a claim acceptable. If the other person fails to accept your reason as sufficient for belief, then you have not proved your claim, even though the person may understand your position better than before. You have given a reason, but not a good enough reason to constitute proof in the mind of that person.

What is the difference between good and poor reasons? The answer to this question is complex. To grasp the concept of proof fully, you must understand psychology and *persuasion* (what causes people to believe or to doubt a statement), and you must also understand the rules and standards applied to proof within various contexts. For instance, if you are making your argument in a court of law, you must realize that there are many rules of evidence to govern what proof may be introduced, in what form it can be offered, and at what point in the proceedings it may be presented. Similarly, other settings for argument have special rules of procedures and standards of proof.

You do not have to become an expert to prove your case in forensic events. You may use some widely shared principles of reasoning and proof. The primary rule in the events of forensics is that all arguments must be based on *evidence*. Evidence consists of those items of information discovered through research and offered as proof in support of your claim. The claims you make must be accompanied by a reference to evidence. Without evidence, a claim has no support and is called an *assertion*. This label is used because you assert a claim based on your own belief and nothing else. In debate, an unsupported assertion is not accepted as proof. But a claim founded on evidence is always accepted as proof until it is refuted.

You must also make clear the connection between your evidence and your claim. Go back to the initial question: "Why should I accept your claim?" Suppose your answer is, "Because I have this item of evidence." Now suppose you are asked, "How do you get your conclusion from that evidence?" You are asked to relate the evidence to your claim. If you fail to make the connection, your evidence will not serve as proof for your claim; it will be considered irrelevant, or unrelated, to the issue. So, in the final analysis, proof might be represented as the equation:

PROOF = EVIDENCE + REASONING

Types of Reasoning

The following diagram illustrates the process of providing reasons for your claims on the beliefs of other people. On the right, you have stated a claim on your belief. On the left, you have an item of evidence.

Evidence	*Claim*
Auto manufacturers are making cars about 500-750 pounds lighter each year.	Cars in the future will be more economical to run.

Reasoning

?????????

How do you get from the evidence to the claim? You must have some reason to believe that the evidence supports the conclusion. In the example, you must reason something like this: "Lighter cars require less fuel than heavy cars; if future cars are lighter, then they will burn less gasoline." If your reason (that lighter cars consume less gasoline) is correct, then the evidence supports the claim. Several types of reasoning are generally accepted in forensic events.

Generalization: Reasoning from Facts

One of the most common forms of reasoning assumes that, if individual members of a general class of objects share a characteristic, then the characteristics will apply to all other members of the class. If you draw a general conclusion based on some specific examples, you have made a *generalization*.

Evidence	*Claim*
My 1982 Buick station wagon gets about 8 mpg on the highway.	Big cars are gas guzzlers.

Reasoning

Generalization—I assume all big cars are like mine.

In reasoning through generalization, what are the major types of evidence used? The evidence offered in support of a generalization is the *example*. When you claim that all members of a class or category are alike in certain characteristics, and your audience asks you to furnish proof, your response should be to point to individual members of the class about which you are generalizing and say, "See, this example (or group of examples) has the exact characteristics I am talking about." Ideally, the more examples you can produce, the better your argument.

Beyond the technique of itemizing specific examples leading to a generalization, you may also select one instance from a general group. This is the basis of survey research, such as public opinion polls. Rather than looking at every member of the population, you look at the sample and then make the assumption that it represents the whole group. There are rigorous scientific procedures you must observe in survey research, but the basic form of reasoning involved is simple generalization.

Several tests help to determine whether your generalizations are sound: (1) *Are there enough examples?* If the generalization is well known and widely accepted as true, just a few examples may serve to substantiate the point. If the conclusion is not so well known, then you may wish to provide quite a few examples. For instance, the conclusion "Playing football is dangerous" might seem untrue. But if you look at the large number of people hurt each year in football games and practices, the conclusion can be proven. (2) *Are the examples typical of the group?* A typical example is one that represents the group as a kind of average case. To prove the generalization that most people on welfare are undeserving, you would have to do much more than find one or two examples of people who did not need aid. You would have to show that the average person does not need welfare. (3) *Are there significant counterexamples?* In some instances, you might find enough examples to prove a claim, and these examples might represent the average case that supports a generalization. What might weaken the support of your claim, however, are a few significant counterexamples.

These are instances where the generalization does not hold true. If you were arguing that it is good to intervene in the affairs of another nation, for instance, you might contend that, on the average, intervention saves the lives of Americans. Historical examples might be used to support the conclusion. The Vietnam War, however, serves as an instance that, according to some people, denies the claim that United States military intervention is good. If you know that there are some important counterexamples to your generalization, you should be willing to modify your claim. Instead of saying all interventions are good, you must say that some or most are good.

In statistical survey research, the tests are very similar: (1) *Is the sample size great enough?* (2) *Is the sample representative of the whole population?* The process of survey research is guided by scientific rules of procedure. For instance, to insure representativeness, the sample is drawn on a completely random basis, which allows every individual member of the population an exactly equal chance to be selected. This avoids introducing bias into the selection process, which would possibly yield an unrepresentative sample. Testing this kind of evidence by these standards is referred to as looking at the methodology employed.

Analogy: Reasoning from a Similar Model

You also reason by *analogy*: You draw a conclusion about an unknown based on its similarity to a model that is known. An analogy, then, is a comparison. An analogy is somewhat like a generalization in that it uses a specific, known example as its basis. However, the generalization draws a conclusion about the whole class of objects from which the example is drawn. The analogy draws its conclusion about another specific example. The analogy makes the assumption "This unknown example is like that known example."

Evidence	*Claim*
The U.S. Postal Service is wasteful and inefficient.	The proposed new energy distribution agency would be wasteful and inefficient.

Reasoning

Analogy: I assume the new federal agency, which is unknown, is like the U.S. Postal Service in the known areas of wastefulness and inefficiency.

The test of an analogy is this: Is the unknown example like the known example in the essential areas being compared? As long as the similarities lie in the areas about which the claim is made, argument by analogy constitutes proof. If the analogy draws its comparisons in an area not relevant to the claim, the argument will be faulty. This fallacy is called the *false analogy*.

You must realize, however, that even the literal analogy is regarded as a weak form of proof. Some authors have called it the weakest form of proof. There are many confounding factors that serve to weaken the power of an analogy because there are always elements that are not comparable between the known and the unknown. To say that one thing is like another thing is not to say the two are identical. Differences between them exist. The closeness of fit between your model and the unknown example you are reasoning about is the most important consideration in evaluating the strength of an analogy. Both sugar and salt have comparable qualities of visual appearance and texture; however, many a bowl of oatmeal has been ruined at camp by pranksters who filled the sugar bowl with salt.

Someone might use the example of the U.S. Postal Service to draw the analogy that any government agency developed as part of an affirmative plan is bound to be wasteful or inefficient.

One form of proof is the extended analogy. The extended analogy moves from a detailed discussion of a known person, place, object, or event to a detailed examination of that which is not completely understood or which is perhaps even entirely unknown to the audience. The argument of the extended analogy proceeds by distinguishing points of essential similarity from characteristics that are circumstantial or nonessential. Consider an extended analogy that members of the United States Congress often use when discussing military affairs in Latin America: Intervention in Nicaragua would be similar to intervention in Vietnam. The Congressional representatives who make this analogy do not want U.S. troops sent abroad. They hope to persuade the President to restrain intervention by suggesting that any intervention in a Latin American country would be just like, or analogous to, U.S. intervention in Vietnam. They hope to prevent the U.S. from repeating the mistake. To extend the analogy, the representatives point out that like the war in Vietnam the war in Nicaragua is a revolutionary struggle, that the turmoil requires a political not a military solution, and that the terrain gives our mechanized army little advantage. They also note that differences are really not essential. Though Vietnam and Latin America are in different parts of the world, what is important is the kind of war and the required solutions. To dispute an analogy, you must determine why the differences between the two things compared are significant. In this analogy, it might be maintained that the Vietnam intervention and a Latin American intervention are essentially dissimilar because in Vietnam China could easily supply military weapons to keep the war going, while in Latin America supply of revolutionary troops would be far more difficult. The extended analogy is an important and exciting form of reasoning.

The ability of an analogy to explain, illustrate, or clarify the unknown matter is great. For this reason, figurative analogies are sometimes used. A figurative analogy is a comparison of dissimilar persons, places, objects, events, actions, or ideas. "A tie in football is like kissing your sister." "The government is like a three-legged stool; it has an executive branch, a legislative branch, and a judicial branch, tied together with the system of checks and balances. If one of these branches were to be destroyed, the government could not stand." In figurative analogies such as these, complex ideas are simplified and made vivid in the minds of listeners. To gain increased understanding and to establish your point of view may be as important to winning your argument as providing more factual and logical arguments.

If you rely too heavily on figurative analogy for support of your argument, you run the risk of easy refutation. Such refutation simply shows that your analogy falls down because you have compared the known model with your claim in the wrong dimensions for comparison, you have overlooked crucial differences that exist between the items you are comparing, or stronger forms of argument can be proved that contradict your figurative analogy. Thus, you need to exercise care in the construction and use of this form of argument.

Cause-Effect: Reasoning from Process Relationships

In concept, the cause-effect relationship is easy to grasp, and it is therefore a familiar form of reasoning. Basically, a cause-effect relationship is one in which two phenomena (objects, events) are observed interacting in some process, and it is assumed that one of them causes the other. The form of the argument is "If . . . then. . . ."

Evidence	Claim
This is the coldest winter since '07.	My heating bill will be outrageous.

Reasoning

Cause-Effect: I assume my furnace will burn more fuel than usual because of the cold weather. "If the temperature goes down, then my thermostat will kick on the burners."

In forensic events, this reasoning form is very important. Most of the events deal with cause-effect relationships: What are the causes of the problem? What are the effects of the problem? What would be the result if this or that change were implemented in dealing with the problem? Understanding the nature of this form of argument is difficult, because it is the most complex form of reasoning. You need to examine it in a bit more detail.

As mentioned, the cause-effect relationship assumes that in the process of interacting, there is a connecting link between one phenomenon and another. It further assumes that this connection is so strong that the relationship is predictable. For instance, what will happen when a bowling ball strikes a pin? In this simple process, would you predict that the pin will fall down? You should, because there is a strong link between the two events of a bowling ball striking a pin and of the pin falling down.

The quality of predictability is very strong when one phenomenon acts regularly and directly on another. As long as other factors involved in the process are unchanged, the results of the interaction between the two phenomena will be the same. Water will always boil at 100° C at sea level, unless other factors intervene, such as dropping a box of salt into the water.

There are also situations in which two phenomena interact not by virtue of a causal link, but by sheer coincidence. It is possible that your golf shot could hit the back of a turtle on the fairway and ricochet into the hole for an ace. Would you like to bet that you could do it again? Coincidences have the quality of unpredictability. They are in the realm of the possible, but not in the realm of the predictable. Even though you play on the same golf course every day and even though another turtle could cross the fairway just as you are hitting the ball, there are too many intervening variables to predict that such a freak event could ever happen again.

The notion of intervening variables is what makes the cause-effect relationship problematic. From a purely scientific point of view, it is next to impossible to create a closed system with only two components operating in an unvarying process of interaction totally immune from any outside variables. A *variable* is a condition that may change and alter the relationship. Some scientists are unwilling to predict with certainty that the sun will rise tomorrow morning, based on the principle that there are so many potential intervening variables in the open solar system.

To make matters even more complicated, many phenomena are linked by connections that are weaker than causality but stronger than coincidence. Imagine a spectrum ranging from zero linkage to total linkage. The coincidental occurrence would rest near the zero linkage end of the range; the cause-effect relationship, near the 100 percent linkage end of the spectrum. Between these extremes are other degrees of linkage. Scientists have conveniently labeled two of these positions: association and correlation.

0% Linkage			*100% Linkage*
Coincidence	*Association*	*Correlation*	*Causality*
An expected outcome is highly unlikely.	Plausible or possible at one level.	Probable and within a confident level of predictability.	Certain and totally predictable.

The concepts of association and correlation allow you to reason about the relationships between phenomena and still take into account intervening variables. The association linkage merely establishes that where one phenomenon is found, the other is likely to be found. No attempt is made to prove that the one causes the other. In fact, in this instance the two phenomena may not be directly related anyway. Rather, each may be closely related to a third factor. There are no pawn shops in Auburn, but there are several in Columbus, 30 miles away. Ft. Benning is adjacent to Columbus. Why are there pawn shops and finance companies in a town near a large military installation? It is not reasonable to assert that the military base causes pawn shops to locate nearby, any more than it would be reasonable to claim that the pawn shops cause the military base to locate there. Somehow, the large population of military personnel in a metropolitan area creates a demand for access to ready cash between paydays. Thus, pawn shops are *associated* with military towns.

A correlation linkage is stronger than an association linkage: Not only are two phenomena typically found together, but they vary together. That is, changes in the scope or magnitude of one are accompanied by corresponding changes in the other. (Note: When one phenomenon increases and the other increases, the correlation is called *direct*. When one increases and the other decreases, the correlation is called *inverse*.) Here, the phenomena in question are part of a larger, interlocking system. Although they are strongly connected, the phenomena are affected by other factors that complicate the relationship and prevent you from being able to make predictions with certainty. You can still make predictions, but you are allowing for some randomness, error, or intervening variables. These predictions have the quality of *probability*, or a high degree of confidence that falls short of absolute certainty.

There are some traditional tests of cause-effect reasoning. You should be able to distinguish between necessary and sufficient causes. The difference is easy to illustrate. Suppose you walk into a dark room. You want some light provided by electricity. You know that to obtain this light there must be wires, a lightbulb, a lamp, and electricity, all in good working order. These are the *necessary* components of an electrically lighted room, but they are not sufficient in themselves. The room remains dark unless another element is added. You must turn on the light. The act of turning on the light, in this context, is a necessary *and* sufficient cause of lighting the room. Remember that phenomena necessary to creating an effect may not be *sufficient* to bringing about the effect. Only when causes are both necessary and sufficient the effect can occur.

This test is important in judging the adequacy of value and policy claims. If someone argues that it is necessary to spend more money on a problem to bring about a solution, this claim can be granted, and you can still refute the argument. You can say that although it is necessary to spend more money, say, to relieve poverty, money by itself will not end the problems of poverty because other factors are involved. If you can find important factors that could prevent the cause and effect relationship from taking place, you can disprove the relationship.

Typically, resolutions that emerge from problem areas of significant social concern involve complicated causal analysis.

In debate analysis, the *stock issues* approach, discussed on pages 80–81, begins with the question "Is there a need for a change?" In traditional debate theory, you have to prove that the present system *causes* the problem and that no changes, short of those contained within the debate resolution, would solve the problem. The second stock issue is "Will the plan solve the need?" To prove this point, you are required to prove that the plan will eliminate the cause of the problem—that is, that the plan will *cause* the solution. The third stock issue, "Is the plan desirable?" calls for an examination of other possible results of adopting the plan. All these stock issues require a high degree of causality between policies or policy changes and results.

On the other hand, the *systems analysis* method, discussed on pages 81–84, investigates all the relevant factors within the present system and compares the predictable results of manipulating one or another of these factors. Since systems analysis allows for secondary causal linkages, the connections may be weaker. They may range within the realm of correlation between policy change and outputs of the system. In both the stock issues and the systems analysis methods of determining solutions, you need to have a basic understanding of cause-effect reasoning.

Sign Argument: Reasoning from Related Observation

Another form of reasoning is argument from sign. *Sign argument*, in its most simple form, says that when one thing occurs so does another. The phenomena are not causally linked, but they always (or almost always) occur either simultaneously or in succession. The *sign* is the observed phenomenon or phenomena. The signified is the phenomenon referred to or predicted by the sign. Consider a basic example:

You are out on a walk in late summer and you observe the following: The squirrels are running about gathering nuts. Many have grown thick fur. Further, you notice that all the birds seem to have flown south. You observe that winter must be coming early. You read from the signs of nature an event that is about to take place.

Notice that the relationship here is not causal. Birds flying south and squirrels gathering nuts do not cause winter to come early. They are merely signs, or symptoms, of early winter. And they allow you to predict that winter is coming soon.

Evidence	*Claim*
Leaves are falling. Squirrels have thick fur. Birds have flown south.	Winter must be coming.

Reasoning

These characteristics are associated with the advance of winter.

Sign arguments are reversible. This means that you can reason from sign to signified, or from signified to sign. If someone told you that Jesuit College Preparator was an excellent school, for instance, you would expect a number of characteristics or qualities that would signify a quality high school. If these signs were *not* there, then you would question the assertion. Conversely, if you could agree on the qualities of an excellent school, then you might look for these signs in investigating a school you desire to attend.

Some sign arguments are infallible. Others are not. An infallible sign argument is difficult to refute, but it is hard to find. Most infallible signs, in fact, do not seem to invite much controversy. Darkness is taken for granted as a sign of evening, even though an eclipse occurs once in a great while. This is an almost infallible sign argument.

Fallible sign arguments, while more controversial, allow greater freedom to speculate. It may be the case that a certain combination of symptoms is a sign that disease is setting in. Even if your certainty level about this conclusion is not great, it might be better to act to prevent the disease—even if there is some chance the sign argument is wrong. Note that a fallible sign argument is weak to the extent that you can find similar objects signified by the same sign or group of signs. A good win-loss record for your basketball team might be a sign that your school has an excellent team and will do well in the playoffs. But it may also be a sign that the team has been lucky, that it has an easy schedule, or that it plays in a weak league. To the extent that alternative explanations can be introduced, the relationship between sign and signified is weakened.

Statistics: Reasoning from Scientific Methodology

There are two typical approaches to explaining statistics in a book of this kind. The first approach is to treat statistics as merely a collection of examples, a survey sample. In this approach, the reasoning form is the same as that of the generalization. Instead of citing a specific example or group of examples, you insert a number into your evidence. You would say something like "'Big cars are gas guzzlers because the average EPA gas mileage estimates are lower for the Chevy Sportvan than they are for the Chevette." The same tests apply: Are the figures based on a large enough sample? Is the sample representative (that is, typical of the population of all members of the class)? Is there another sample with contrary findings?

The second approach to statistics is derived from more advanced scientific methodologies. There are more types of experimental methods than the survey sample and the average score. The objective of advanced scientific research methodologies is to study the precise relationships that exist in a process interaction. The control procedures for conducting research in such process interaction relationships make the method more scientific and the results more precise. The purpose here is not to explain any of the statistical methodologies specifically. Rather, it is to point to a few of the qualities required of statistical studies generally.

Evidence	*Claim*
The studies show that solar energy is economical only as a supplement to a regular heating system, only for heating water, only in certain geographical areas.	Solar energy is not the answer to the energy crisis.

Reasoning

Statistical: I assume the methodology of the studies meets scientific standards.

Notice that in this form of reasoning, the connection between the data and the claim is not an assumption about the facts themselves, but rather the method of the study. In this example, the method is not made explicit. Suppose the particular evidence is well known in the field, and you are familiar with how the evidence was obtained. Suppose further that it is derived from a computer simulation of future energy use and based on projections of future energy costs assuming a certain rate of price increases and on current solar technology. A computer simulation can make calculations with great precision, but it is limited to the data programmed into it. Hence, the calculations are subject to possible variations if energy prices do not behave in the field as predicted in the simulation or if solar technology achieves a presently unforeseen breakthrough. In other words, whenever reasoning is based on a method of statistical analysis, the important thing to remember is that what is claimed is not based so much on the results of the calculation as it is on the quality—and the limitations—of the method used.

In testing reasoning derived from statistical methodologies, it is not enough merely to ask, "What's your methodology?" Finding out what methodology was used is only the starting point. It is also important to know the assumptions used in conducting the experiment. Small variations in assumptions can produce large variations in the calculations. Therefore, it makes little sense to test the results of the calculation without first examining the assumptions used in the methodology.

The findings of any scientific study are strictly limited to the population tested, under the conditions that prevailed during the test. It is contrary to the scientific method to make extensive extrapolations of the findings into realms where the same conditions do not exist. For example, if a study was conducted specifically to test the effectiveness of air bags in front-end collisions at speeds less than 50 mph, it would be fallacious to expand the statistical results to apply to all automobile accidents.

Authority: Reasoning from Source Credibility

Up to this point, this treatment of the forms of reasoning has been based on the different kinds of reasoning about facts. Generalization, analogy, cause-effect, sign, and statistical reasoning all begin with concrete data.

Forensic events also use reasoning based on evidence drawn from the opinion and testimony of authorities. The principles of reasoning involved differ considerably from any discussed so far.

Evidence	*Claim*
The President said the nation should develop a defense against nuclear weapons.	The nation should develop a defense against nuclear weapons.

Reasoning

Authority—I assume that the President knows what he is talking about.

In this sample of reasoning, the claim is based entirely on what the authority said. This argument contains no generalization, no statistics, no analogies, no scientific studies. All that is presented to you is the testimony of an authority.

The tests of reasoning from authority are basically the same as the tests of source credibility in rhetoric. First, is the source quoted an expert? Is there reason to believe the person is competent to voice an opinion? Second, is the source quoted trustworthy? Is there reason to trust the sincerity, objectivity, and good faith of the person? Third, does the evidence agree with that of other authorities? This question is important because no data is given in support of the testimony; therefore, there is a need to have an independent check on the claim.

After making these tests of reasoning from authority, you then apply the routine tests of evidence. Is the quotation consistent with the context from which it was taken (or consistent with other known statements of opinion from the same source)? Is it the most recent evidence? Was the statement meant literally or figuratively? This test is especially important when the source uses figures in the statement, such as "Ninety-nine times out of a hundred, we would not have run out of coal in the city during the winter months."

Authoritative evidence is qualitatively different from empirical or factual evidence. Each kind of evidence has its strengths and liabilities. When your argument is over propositions of fact, empirical evidence is superior to testimony and opinion evidence. When proving the significance (that is, the measurable scope or magnitude) of a problem area, it is better to use concrete evidence. However, when the issue is over goals, values, or principles, the opinion of respected authorities is preferable. For example, if you want to prove the extent of unemployment among black youth in the nation's cities, simply cite the statistics given by the Department of Labor's Bureau of Labor Statistics. This form of evidence is better than a quotation from an authority who believes that "very high" unemployment exists. However, if you want to prove that unemployment rates among urban black youth is "the worst social problem confronting America," this is a value judgment and would be more persuasive if quoted from Jesse Jackson or some other person whose views and opinions are respected.

Summary

When research provides data relevant to the problem your are analyzing, your real task is to integrate your data and analysis into proof. This proof is necessary in order for you to support the conclusions you draw about problems and solutions. In all the events that are classified as forensics, the reasoning skills hold the key to eliciting the belief of others.

Questions for Discussion

1. Explain the concept of proof.

2. Why is it important that an argument be based on evidence?

3. In reasoning by generalization, what are the major types of evidence used? Describe three tests that help to insure that your generalizations are sound.

4. How is reasoning by analogy helpful to someone who is listening to your argument? Define a false and extended analogy.

5. Most events in forensics deal with reasoning from cause and effect relationships. Define reasoning based on cause-effect sequences. Provide an example. In your example, are there any intervening causes?

6. The argument that "Our school has a great football team and therefore should do well in city competition because it has lost only two of its last ten games" uses what type of reasoning? How could such an argument be challenged?

7. What is the value of using statistics to support your reasoned conclusions?

8. When examining statistics for use as evidence, why is it important to understand the methodology?

9. Forensic events often use evidence drawn from opinion and testimony or both. To support the claim, "The United States should maintain a balanced budget," find two pieces of evidence which rely upon authority. How do your authorities meet tests of source credibility suggested by rhetorical considerations? Next, apply routine tests of evidence.

Activities

1. Using the claims provided below, demonstrate how you would prove or disprove each. At the end of the activity be sure you have used all the forms of reasoning covered in this chapter.

   Claim: In the future, most Americans will drive small cars.

   Claim: The cost of houses has kept many first-time buyers out of the housing market.

   Claim: A college diploma is a prerequisite for a good job.

   Claim: A two-income family is becoming a necessity in today's society.

   Claim: Funding "Star Wars" research will help the administration when negotiating arms control.

Claim: Pollution is destroying the ozone layer.

Claim: Children testing positive for the AIDS virus should be allowed to attend public schools.

2. Using a current issue, find examples of reasoning through generalization. Use magazines such as *Time, Newsweek,* and *U.S. News & World Report.* Diagram the generalizations.

3. Develop an analogy, an extended analogy, and a false analogy on each of the issues to follow:

Issue: U.S. involvement in the military affairs of other nations.

Issue: The U.S. postal service versus private mail service.

Issue: The increasing federal deficit.

Issue: Student dress codes in secondary schools.

Issue: Funding of elementary and secondary education.

4. Using an issue affecting your personal life (for example, curfew, car privileges, allowance, and phone use), outline your position using cause-effect reasoning. Outline a refutation of your position. Be sure to look for flaws in the cause-effect relationship.

5. Using one of the following issues, develop an argument (for or against) with statistics. Use your local newspaper, the *New York Times,* the *Wall Street Journal,* or *Newsweek.* Demonstrate the validity of the statistics.

Issue: The relationship between U.S. trade policies and unemployment.

Issue: Decreasing inflation is indicative of a healthy economy.

Issue: Decreasing energy prices have increased the use of foreign oil.

Issue: Storage of toxic wastes—effects on the environment.

Issue: Safety of nuclear power plants.

6. Using a current issue, look for evidence drawn from opinion or testimony. Find three credible statements and three statements that do not meet the tests of credibility. Explain the differences between the two sets of statements.

Part Two

Debate

Winning Decisions in Confrontations

Every year, thousands of students in junior and senior high schools, colleges, and universities participate in academic debates. They have different levels of success depending on many factors—motivation, dedication, and talent. The fact that you are studying this book is an indication of your desire to acquire or improve the skills necessary for success.

The preceding section of this text discussed the basic skills of analysis, research, and reasoning, which are applicable to many forensic activities. This section introduces the rules and strategy of academic debate.

Chapter 5

Fundamental Considerations in Debate

Objectives and Key Terms

After studying Chapter 5, you should be able to

1. Explain "burden of proof,"

2. Understand what is required for a *prima facie* case,

3. Explain "stock issues,"

4. Explain systems analysis, and

5. Understand how to design and justify a plan of action in response to the resolution.

After reading this chapter, you should understand the following terms:

burden of proof

prima facie case

stock issues analysis

systems analysis

presumption

affirmative plan

A cademic debate is a forum for developing the skills of advocacy. Within clearly prescribed limits, you are encouraged to analyze complex issues, reason from your evidence to solid conclusions, think quickly in the face of your opponents' arguments and refute them logically, and defend your case all the way through to the end of the final rebuttals. Hence, debate offers an ideal setting in which to develop your ability to advocate public policy, to dispute values, and to learn how to test propositions of fact.

Debate is the most widespread of the forensic events. Over the years, more schools have sponsored debate teams than any other forensic event although student congress is gaining increasing popularity. Of the events, debate offers the greatest opportunity for frequent participation because there are many more debate tournaments during the typical season of competition than there are opportunities to compete in student congress.

Debate is an intensive activity. The breadth of the debate resolution requires you to gain a great deal of knowledge about the facts and issues involved. Moreover, in competition with debaters from other schools, you are required to be well enough informed to be able to refute their arguments as well as to be prepared to prove your own. Since debate is a team contest, you have a partner to help you, and of course the whole squad in your school will work together in preparing for tournaments. Even so, if you want to succeed, debate requires a significant investment of time, thought, and work. It takes both time and experience to master all the elements necessary to be a championship debater. Gaining mastery of the knowledge and skills involved in activities such as band or chorus, athletics, or drama involves high levels of determination and commitment. This is no less true in debate and other forensic events.

You will find that debate pays off in personal achievement and satisfaction. Even one year's participation will provide you with valuable skills for organizing your thoughts, thinking logically, and speaking with confidence and force. The longer you stay involved in debate, the more you will learn—and win. Debate serves another important personal function: Your association with a group of people working together toward the common goal of excellence in debate can be very satisfying. You will enjoy a sense of belonging and acceptance, a sense of worthwhile achievement and growth as a part of an important activity, and a sense of contribution. Even if the tangible results of a season of competition seem modest in terms of trophies and awards won, these intangible satisfactions will ultimately loom large in your feelings. For these reasons, many adults today remember their experiences as debaters with pride and warmth.

Debate as Confrontation

There are two sides in a debate—the affirmative and the negative. The side in favor of the resolution affirms it, and the side opposed to the resolution negates it. These two sides confront one another in the debate and place their arguments about the resolution before the judge. Based on the arguments developed in this confrontation, the judge decides the winner of the debate. The judge is an impartial person with regard to the resolution. The decision is not based on how the judge feels about the resolution personally, but strictly on whether your arguments have adequately supported your position. Thus, the debate is won or lost on the basis of your skills in analyzing the resolution for the judge, proving your arguments with superior reasoning and evidence, and refuting the arguments and case presented by your opponents.

When you participate in a debate, the emphasis in the confrontation is always on the issues and evidence presented. Debate is a confrontation of ideas rather than personalities. For this reason, debate permits you to argue and disagree with your opponents without being personally disagreeable. In fact, sarcasm and insults have no place in debate, and most judges will severely penalize you if you resort to such behavior. By keeping the debate on an intellectual level, you learn to participate in the process of making decisions about the significant problems and proposed policies of your time through reasoning and facts, rather than emotions.

Debate is the most competitive of the forensic events. In student congress, debate is used as a decision-making tool, but the objective of that debate is to win the support of the other members of the congress. To this end, the bills and resolutions may be amended either to remove barriers to agreement or to add elements designed to make them more acceptable to the majority. Cooperation is the key word.

This is not so in debate. The affirmative and negative sides are expected to remain firmly committed to their side of the resolution to the very end of the debate. It is not your task to come to an agreement with your opponents over whether the resolution should be accepted. It is your task to convince the judge of the reasonableness of voting for your side and against your opponents. The rules and procedures of debate are designed to make it possible for you to have a fair, equal opportunity to win the judge's decision. The debate format, which emphasizes confrontation of evidence, ideas, and arguments, allows you to take this competitive stance with dignity, respect for each other, and, ultimately, zest and enjoyment. Although competing debate teams are adversaries during the debate, it is possible for them to remain friends both during the round and afterward. In much the same way, the prosecutor and the defense attorney in a courtroom remain friends despite their opposing roles in the trial. Indeed, friendships frequently grow among debaters as they gain mutual respect for the forensics skills each possesses.

Analysis in Debate

In academic debate, as in other forensic events, analysis is a crucial skill. To understand the methods of analysis in debate, you should first have a clear idea of the aim or objective of the contest. Most important, it should be noted that policy debate involves some special assumptions about how argument emerges and how it should proceed. By understanding these rules, you will be able to begin to construct speeches and take sides in the argument.

A resolution of policy requires an affirmative and a negative. The affirmative is the champion of the resolution. The negative plays devil's advocate, closely questioning the resolution's necessity and desirability. As policy debate is presently set up, all resolutions are designed to call for a change from the present system. To affirm the resolution is to say in effect that the status quo is in some way defective and a better alternative is possible. The reason for creating resolutions that mandate change is that debate itself is thought to be a process of testing policies. A good policy should be able to withstand severe criticism. Although it is possible, and even desirable, to debate the value of existing policies, the educators who created academic policy debate believed that it is better to discuss new alternatives. The affirmative, then, proposes. The negative opposes.

Debates are judged by a neutral third party. The affirmative resolution is submitted to a judge for approval. The negative argues that the judge should not grant approval or even that the judge should render firm disapproval. Note that a judge need not believe the resolution is a bad idea to vote negative. He or she may simply say that there is not enough proof to tell whether it is good or bad and may simply withhold consent.

The Burden of Proof

How does the judge know when an affirmative has presented enough proof to justify assent? Debate theory provides guidelines for making a fair allocation of responsibility between the affirmative and the negative. Because judges disagree about proof standards, however, the guidelines for determining the minimal level of proof required to earn a decision vary. The current state of thinking about this subject is explained briefly at this point; additional explanations will be provided later, as you explore case strategies available to both the affirmative and the negative sides in a debate.

A good starting point is the realization that in order to deserve the decision of an impartial judge for a proposed debate resolution, the affirmative is required to prove that the resolution merits adoption. It is not sufficient merely to suggest a change in the present system of dealing with a problem area. The traditional rule is that change is not a good in and of itself. The responsibility to prove a case for the resolution is known as the affirmative *burden of proof*. The affirmative must prove something before it can hope to win the judge's decision.

The phrase *burden of proof* has a special meaning here. You understand, of course, that each debater in the round, whether affirmative or negative, has the burden to prove any asserted argument with evidence. The mere assertion of a claim is rarely accepted as a valid argument. In this broad sense, all debaters have a burden of proving.

Beyond this general burden, however, the affirmative has a specific requirement to prove its case for the resolution. Unless the case is proven by the affirmative, the negative has every right to expect the judge's decision. To turn the equation around, the negative does not have to prove that the resolution should be rejected. If the judge were asked to render a decision prior to hearing either side speak, the decision would be for the negative because no case has been offered to support the resolution to change the present policy.

What must the affirmative prove? The usual answer to this question is that the affirmative must present a case sufficient to convince a reasonable and prudent person that the proposed resolution merits her or his acceptance. Such a convincing case is called a *prima facie* case, one that is convincing on its face, or at first glance. If the affirmative fails to offer a *prima facie* case for the resolution, then the impartial judge cannot give assent. On the other hand, if you succeed in presenting a *prima facie* case, then the negative has the burden to refute it and convince the judge not to accept the resolution. Just as the affirmative has the burden of proof with regard to the resolution, the negative has the *burden of refutation* with regard to the affirmative case.

What constitutes a *prima facie* case? Analysis in debate means to break the suggested proposal into the essential elements that enable a judge to see the reasons the proposal should be accepted. In debate, analysis is largely limited to case analysis.

Stock Issues Analysis

One form of debate analysis is called stock issues analysis. A series of questions about the resolution under debate makes up the stock issues. This is the most traditional and most widely understood form of analysis because it has been used in academic debate for decades. To understand the logic of the stock issues, you must realize that the debate resolution is a proposed action to change the present system of dealing with the problem. You assume that the debate judge does not know why the change is being proposed, and then a series of questions tells you what information you need to present to convince the judge to accept the proposal.

(1) *Is there a need for a change?* This is the first stock issue. You must show that the present system causes the problem and that, moreover, nothing can be done to solve the problem except for the proposal being advocated. If there is no need for the proposal, then the judge will not accept the proposal. (2) *Does the need for a change inhere in the status quo?* One might find a significant problem, but if it is likely to go away of its own accord, no alteration in the status quo would be necessary. Recently, many politicians called for public works programs due to a rise in unemployment. But the increase was not long-lived. Economic stabilizers alleviated the suffering of the unemployed even while the economy rebounded to provide new jobs. If the status quo is capable of solving its problems through existing mechanisms, then the resolution is not necessary. Without a unique justification for the resolution, there is no reason it ought to be adopted. (3) *Will the proposal solve the problem?* Once you have shown that the problem exists and will continue despite every effort to correct it, you must show how the proposed change would work to re-

move the causes of the problem and thus allow for a solution. If your proposal will not solve the problem, the judge will not accept it. (4) *Is the proposal desirable?* This fourth stock issue asks the judge to consider whether the proposal is a good one, assuming for the sake of argument that a need exists and that the proposal will solve it. At first glance, this stock issue looks paradoxical, since a proposal that would solve the problem would seem to be desirable by definition. However, there may be other considerations involved if the proposed change is accepted. Suppose the change in the present system would create new problems of its own. If the new problems are worse than the problem solved by the proposal, then the judge will not accept the proposal on the grounds that it is not desirable.

These four questions create the stock issues in debate. Notice that the affirmative must prove all of them because if any one of them is answered in the negative, then the judge will not accept the proposal. Who would want to make a change without justification?

The stock issues approach assumes that the judge has an initial presumption—that the present system is dealing adequately with the problem area. This initial presumption is what you must overcome. You do this by using the stock issues to show the following: There is a need to change the present system; your proposed change is the only way to achieve the best solution to the problem; the program would work; and it would be desirable to make the change. If you fail to prove any one of these arguments, then the presumption is that the present system should not be changed, and things should continue exactly as they are.

The stock issues method of analysis is criticized largely because of its basic presumption that the present system for dealing with problems can and will continue unchanged unless a positive decision to change it is made. In reality, the present system itself is undergoing changes all the time due to changing conditions. For instance, as the population grows, the economy alters, and the status quo changes accordingly. New problems arise and old problems change in character, so national policies are constantly being adjusted to accommodate natural changes in the environment.

Systems Analysis

Systems analysis is a method used to determine what changes should be made in laws and policies dealing with problems. Rather than presuming a static, unchanging environment, systems analysis presumes that everything is in a state of constant change. By keeping a careful watch on the situation, it is possible to make predictions and projections about where evolving problems are likely to arise within the system. Thus, the underlying principle of systems analysis is to try to make ongoing decisions about the kinds of changes you want, rather than the simple decision about whether you want to make any change at all. If change is inevitable, it would be better to adjust the policies to control the direction and extent of change, rather than do nothing and allow the situation to undergo changes on its own.

As a method of debate analysis, the systems analysis approach calls for each side to uphold a particular system for controlling the changes the present system is going through. The debate resolution upheld by the affirmative represents only one possible method of controlling and directing change. The negative, which is opposed to the affirmative method of controlling change (reflected in the resolution), must also support a system for controlling and directing inevitable change.

A critical difference may now be observed between the logical requirements for a *prima facie* case using the traditional stock issues method of analysis and the more recent case form using systems analysis. In the former, the affirmative has the burden of proof to overcome an initial presumption in favor of the present system. Unless this presumption is overcome, the judge must vote for maintaining the present system. However, in systems analysis, the prejudgment in favor of maintaining the present system is greatly diminished. This does not mean that the judge has no standard criteria for accepting or rejecting the resolution; presumption still exists in the debate. However, instead of initially presuming that the present system should be maintained, the judge reserves presumption for the proposed system that affords the greatest probability of benefit against the least measure of risk. The competing systems supported by the affirmative and the negative are compared. The one with the most favorable cost-benefit ratio becomes the one that the judge presumes is deserving of the decision in the debate.

In systems analysis, then, the negative is required to offer a proposed system for controlling and directing change. It is not adequate for the negative simply to launch attacks against the affirmative case in hopes of defeating one of the stock issues. Even a system with perceived problems is presumably better than no system at all. It is presumably better to live under conditions of known risks than to take a chance on the unknown risks of an uncontrolled, undirected system. Having said this much, it should be emphasized that the negative is not obligated to propose a counterplan in every debate. If you wish to continue using the present system for dealing with the problem area rather than the affirmative proposal for changing the present system, you may do so. The systems analysis approach only requires that you explain how the present system reflects a better choice of methods for controlling change than does the affirmative proposal.

An important distinction between the stock issues form of analysis and systems analysis in debate is that the concept of *presumption* varies considerably between them. As you have seen, in the stock issues method, the status quo, or present system, is presumed to be adequate and will continue to function adequately in the event that no *prima facie* is proved to overturn this presumption. Seen in this way, presumption is a rule allowing the judge to entertain a prejudgment in favor of the negative because he or she may base the decision entirely on the presumption of the present system without requiring the negative to prove its merits.

On the other hand, in the systems analysis approach, the judge's decision may not be based on a prejudgment in favor of an unexplained system. Here, the task of the judge is to compare alternative methods proposed by opposing debate teams for the purpose of controlling and guiding inevitable future change. In such a method of decision making, the presumption or prejudgment is in favor of the system offering the greatest level of benefits based on the least cost, or risk.

The choice of argument model to use in creating a case for change may depend on your own political values and the nature of the resolution. The stock issues approach reflects a conservative bias. Note that a resolution has to be thoroughly tested and proved, while the negative need only poke a single hole in the affirmative's logic to win. This model is the political preference of a conservative who likes to see change come about quite slowly. The conservative is likely to believe that, all things being equal, problems are caused by acting too quickly. The systems analysis approach is often attractive to liberals. The liberal likes to see change. Even if a change may not solve all the problems, it should be tried. Moreover, the negative cannot win simply by saying that there are a few problems with the proposed change. What the negative must do is to prove that the status quo will end up worse for the change. Thus, the negative must establish the value of the status quo.

To select a particular approach to creating a case, you should see if the resolution seems to suggest a more liberal or more conservative approach to public policy. Liberal approaches, in the domestic arena at least, usually increase government intervention to solve problems. Conservative approaches sometimes decrease or eliminate government. Note that the negative, too, may select a position based on the nature of the resolution.

Interpreting the Resolution

So far, you have seen that the objective of debate is to convince the judge that the resolution should be accepted or rejected. The resolution represents a proposed change in the present system for dealing with a problem area. The method of analyzing the resolution is to narrow it to its essential elements or issues.

Limiting the Resolution

The resolution for a change in present policies is always stated broadly. For instance, the three resolutions for 1987–1988 call for changes to be made in the United States foreign policy toward Latin America. Consider the specific wording of the primary resolution, "Resolved: That the United States government should adopt a policy to increase political stability in Latin America."

The affirmative team might suggest that changing U.S. immigration laws would promote political stability in Latin America.

This is a broad resolution. Who should be able to interpret what changes are required? There are quite a few possibilities, and not all of them can be part of a consistent policy. One affirmative might prohibit U.S. military intervention in Latin America for the express purpose of maintaining political stability in a particular country or in the region as a whole. Another affirmative might mandate the disbursement of humanitarian aid for similar purposes. Still other affirmatives might legalize drugs, strengthen the U.S. economy, change certain banking regulations, change policies affecting immigration, all of which could have the effect of increasing political stability in Latin America. Moreover, the scope of the required action is not clear. Must the affirmative be concerned with every country in Latin America, or is affecting the major countries enough? Or, then again, can the affirmative legitimately focus on, say, the 400,000 citizens of Suriname? Certainly, there is ambiguity in this policy resolution.

The affirmative has the choice to define the resolution and establish the grounds for debate. The affirmative need not defend all interpretations of the resolution. There is not time to do so, and interpretations can be contradictory. So long as the affirmative definition of terms is reasonable, the debate should proceed without objection. Even if the judge does not agree completely with how the affirmative has defined the resolution, unless challenged by the negative, definitions should not be at issue. Once the negative claims that an affirmative interpretation of the topic is unreasonably narrow or even completely incorrect, however, the question of the meaning of the topic (or what is called topicality by debaters) is as debatable as any other issue.

Designing the Plan

Next, in interpreting the resolution, the affirmative team also has an obligation to present a specific plan for consideration. It is not enough for the affirmative team to focus on the problems that exist in a reasonably limited area; it must also provide a plan for a solution that could be implemented. This plan is usually presented in the form of a proposed law for Congress to pass. As such, the plan must include certain minimal components, or planks. These include the following:

1. The *principle,* or the legislative intent that the plan is designed to implement.

2. The *mechanism,* or specific action that must be taken in order to implement the stated principle or legislative intent. The mechanism in turn consists of certain essential planks:

   A. An agency designated to administer and operate the plan. This may be an existing agency granted new legal powers and duties or a newly created agency designed for the affirmative plan.

   B. The powers and duties granted to the agency by the affirmative plan, that is, what the agency is supposed to do.

   C. Administrative details, including provisions for manpower and funding, limits on the agency, and enforcement measures (including penalties for violations of the plan).

Justifying the Plan

In addition to proposing specific legislation that would implement the resolution, the affirmative must also offer a convincing rationale or reason to accept the resolution as expressed by a plan. No matter how complete a plan appears to be, the rule in debate is that "A change is not a good in itself." The affirmative team must prove that there is good reason to adopt its plan.

The rationale for a plan consists of four basic elements. First, the plan must respond to some problem area in the status quo. The problem can be a general one, like diminishing water resources, or it can be simply the absence of a benefit—the lack of a less costly, more efficient alternative to present programs. Second, the plan must provide potential benefits that are unique to its adoption. If the status quo could obtain the benefits offered by the plan, there would be no reason to adopt the resolution. Third, the plan must be able to work. A fine plan that might offer substantial benefits should not be adopted if it is too complex or too difficult to enact. Finally, the benefits should not cause significant side-effects. It does no good to cure the disease if the patient dies from the treatment. Although the affirmative does not have to show that the plan does not have bad side-effects, it should be prepared to refute claims that significant disadvantages apply to the plan. These requirements will be discussed in greater detail elsewhere. Suffice it to say that together they constitute the *prima facie* burden of an affirmative team: If any one of the first three categories is not established at the outset of the debate, there is no reason to adopt the resolution.

Consider, then, the relationship between resolution, plan, and rationale, as the affirmative position is brought together to justify the resolution.

Resolution

expressed by . . .
Specific Plan for Proposed Legislation

supported by . . .
Rationale for Adopting Proposed Plan

When the affirmative interprets a broad resolution to mean a specific proposal for legislation that, if adopted, would mean the resolution is adopted, and if the affirmative also presents a good reason for adopting the plan, it has fulfilled its basic analytical obligations. A case presented to the judge containing these elements would be adequate for a favorable decision, and it would be up to the negative team to refute it in order to turn the decision around.

Summary

Regardless of how much or how little experience you have with debate, you will quickly recognize that debate deals with argumentation and that it involves confrontation. The formats and time elements that control debate have a definite purpose. The side that each team assumes in a debate has clearly defined obligations. Your skills in debate are built on your understanding of basic concepts, such as the burden of proof, types of analysis, and the function of the resolution. As you move into building cases, these are the fundamental considerations that will guide you.

Questions for Discussion

1. What is the difference between a resolution and a plan? If a resolution is a call for action, why is a plan necessary?

2. In debate, the affirmative and negative present their arguments about a resolution before a judge. How does the judge make a decision about the resolution? What is the advantage of being evaluated on the confrontation of ideas rather than personalities? What role should personal prejudice play in the evaluation of a debate?

3. In a debate, what is the fundamental difference between the affirmative and the negative?

4. In debate the affirmative is said to have the "burden of proof." What does this mean? What is it that the affirmative must prove?

5. What does *prima facie* mean? What happens if the affirmative does not present a *prima facie* case?

6. In the stock issues form of debate analysis, a series of basic questions are raised about the resolution? What are these four questions?

7. What is systems analysis? In systems analysis, how is the negative's responsibility changed? How are the requirements for a *prima facie* case different under systems analysis from under a stock issues model?

8. The rationale for a plan consists of four basic elements. What are they?

Activities

1. Listen to a debate and be sure to take notes on the arguments. What type of debate analysis (systems analysis or stock issues) was used by the affirmative? Did it work well for the affirmative? Why?

2. Watch a segment of "60 Minutes" or a program similar in format. By debate standards, did the reporter meet the burden of proof when presenting the news story? Why or why not?

3. Using stock issues analysis, look at the following examples of problem areas and proposed solutions. Do the examples meet the four stock issues? Why or why not?

Problem area: Unemployment is increasing because of increased imports.
Solution: Tighten restrictions on imported products that compete in industries in the U.S. experiencing increased unemployment.

Problem area: Population in third world countries is increasing faster than these countries can provide for their new people.
Solution: Family size would be restricted to two children per family in third world countries in order to stabilize population growth.

Problem area: Dependence on foreign countries for oil is increasing and endangers the stability of an energy source.
Solution: Implement a program of energy conservation while investing money in research for new and improved energy resources.

4. Using the resolutions found on page 48, formulate an affirmative plan of action. These are not expected to be final products. Be sure to check your plans against the four basic elements of an affirmative plan.

Chapter 6

Presentation of the Debate

Objectives and Key Terms

After studying Chapter 6, you should be able to

1. Describe the different debate formats,

2. Describe the concept of preparation time,

3. Explain the obligations of each speaker in a debate round,

4. Organize a speech for presentation,

5. Explain the concept of and formulate an affirmative or negative brief,

6. Understand the concept of flow-sheeting, and

7. Start a system of abbreviations for flow-sheeting.

After reading this chapter, you should understand the following terms:

    constructive speech

    preparation time

    rebuttal speech

    speaker responsibilities

    briefs

    flow-sheeting

    delivery

I n traditional academic debate, a team is composed of two speakers. In a round of debate, there are two teams, one designated on the affirmative side and the other on the negative. During the debate, there are four constructive speeches and four rebuttals. Each speaker, then, is obliged to give a constructive and a rebuttal speech. Cross-examination debate builds on traditional academic debate, providing each debater the opportunity to question his or her opponent between the constructive speeches. The duties of the affirmative and negative during constructives and rebuttals are the same for traditional and cross-examination debate. The added duties for cross-examination debate are discussed in Chapter 9.

The *constructive* speech is the longer of the two designated speeches each team member gives. Its name indicates the fact that all case-building (construction through the introduction of arguments) must be done during that speech. In the affirmative constructive speeches, the justification for change and the method of change must be presented. The negative, on the other hand, must set up the negative philosophy, any defense of the present system, and objections to the affirmative plan during the constructive speeches.

Rebuttal speeches are delivered after the constructive speeches have been completed and are only half as long as constructive speeches. Their purpose is to attack and defend contentions introduced into the debate during the constructive speeches. The traditional rule of debate is that no new arguments may be introduced in rebuttal speeches. This is sometimes misunderstood by beginning debaters to mean that nothing can be said during rebuttals that has not been said before. This is not true. Additional *evidence* not only may but should be heard. Extensions of arguments already introduced should be made. However, a whole new line of argumentation cannot be introduced in the rebuttal speech. For example, if the negative has not debated the topicality of the affirmative case in one of the two constructive speeches, it may *not* be discussed in rebuttal. If, however, topicality has been introduced as an issue in a constructive speech, it can be developed and extended in rebuttal.

Purpose of Positions

Affirmative

The affirmative position in any debate should affirm the resolution. The speeches given by the affirmative are designed to explain what the resolution means and to show that its adoption will be advantageous to society. The affirmative supports the resolution calling for change by showing how the status quo is lacking. The role of the affirmative is comparable to that of the prosecuting attorney in a court trial. The affirmative charges that the present system is failing to accomplish a desired outcome. Because of its attack role, the affirmative must speak first, for the negative cannot defend the present system until it knows the charges against the system. By the same token, since the affirmative attempts to prove guilt, it is allowed to make the final summation to the judge. Thus, the affirmative speakers begin and end the debate.

Negative

The negative role in the debate is to deny that the affirmative rationale is true. Once the charges against the innocence of the status quo have been introduced, the negative must immediately employ a number of alternative strategies to defend the present system and to impeach the advisability of the proposed change. This basic position in the debate also determines the order and sequence of the negative speeches.

Formats of Debate

In academic debate, three formats seem to be popular. The first is the traditional time and arrangement that is sometimes referred to as Oxford or standard debate. Many state activities leagues and a large number of invitational debate tournaments still use this format. Many tournaments offer standard debate for novice teams. This enables beginners to work on the fundamentals of debate before adding in the cross-examination periods. Usually after one semester (or at the most one year), the debater will begin participating in cross-examination debate. In standard debate, the speeches occur in the following order and times:

First Affirmative Constructive	10 minutes
First Negative Constructive	10 minutes
Second Affirmative Constructive	10 minutes
Second Negative Constructive	10 minutes
First Negative Rebuttal	5 minutes
First Affirmative Rebuttal	5 minutes
Second Negative Rebuttal	5 minutes
Second Affirmative Rebuttal	5 minutes

In standard debate for novices, some tournaments use an eight-minute constructive/four-minute rebuttal format so the debater will be accustomed to these time limits when cross-examination periods are added.

The second format used in academic debate is called cross-examination. At the high school level, the cross-examination format has been used for a number of years by the National Forensic League. It was adopted as the official format for intercollegiate debate at the National Debate Tournament sponsored by the American Forensic Association.

In cross-examination debate, the speeches occur as follows:

First Affirmative Constructive	8 minutes
Negative Cross-examination of First Affirmative Speaker	3 minutes
First Negative Constructive	8 minutes
Affirmative Cross-examination of First Negative Speaker	3 minutes
Second Affirmative Constructive	8 minutes
Negative Cross-examination of Second Affirmative Speaker	3 minutes
Second Negative Constructive	8 minutes
Affirmative Cross-examination of Second Negative Speaker	3 minutes

Rebuttal speeches are in the same order as they are in standard debate, but they are only four minutes in length. Specific information on cross-examination debate can be found in Chapter 9.

The third format used in academic debate is Lincoln-Douglas debate. It differs significantly from the other two formats in that each team has but one participant instead of two. This form of debate was adopted as an official event at the NFL National Tournament in 1980. A further explanation of the fundamentals of Lincoln-Douglas debate and its format can be found in Chapter 10.

Preparation Time

There are various rules and practices with regard to the elapsed time between each of the speeches, which is usually referred to as *preparation time*. Two of the most common preparation-time rules will be discussed here. However, you should make it a practice to determine which rules prevail in each tournament you enter. Some invitational tournaments and many of the state leagues, especially those using the standard debate format, use the *one-minute rule* (or the two-minute rule). In this rule, each speaker is allowed one minute from the time the preceding speaker sits down in which to gather materials and approach the podium to speak. If a speaker exceeds this time, the additional time is subtracted from her or his speaking time.

The second, and probably more common, practice is the *eight-minutes rule*. This is the practice of allotting to each team a cumulative total of eight minutes between speeches during the course of the debate that can be used for preparing to speak. Time is tallied by the time-keeper, who informs each team of the passage of their preparation time. There is no specification as to how the debaters may allocate their time. Thus, the negative may choose to use two, four, six, or eight of their eight minutes before the first negative speech, giving that speaker whatever preparation time he or she needs. The affirmative may choose to use most of its preparation time before the first affirmative rebuttal so that this important speech can be carefully planned and organized. This practice has also been used with five or ten minutes of prep time instead of eight minutes. Always check the tournament rules to determine which practice is to be followed.

In Lincoln-Douglas debate, each debater is allowed a total of three minutes preparation time during the debate. The rules for using this prep time are the same as for the eight-minutes rule.

Overview of Speaker Responsibilities

Details concerning the duties and opportunities of each side and each speaker position in a debate will be presented later; what follows is an overview of the speakers' responsibilities to help you understand the rules of the game. After all, as complex a game as chess may be, it must be learned by understanding the initial movement of the pieces.

During constructive speeches, the affirmative and the negative speakers have a chance to develop and critique contending positions. Rebuttal speeches follow the constructives and are much shorter. Rebuttals are used to extend criticisms already begun in constructives and to sum up the affirmative and negative positions.

Note the sequence of speeches in a debate. The affirmative always goes first. The debate is commenced by asserting that a resolution is true. The first negative constructive follows by refuting the affirmative contentions. The second affirmative constructive speech then attempts to rebuild the affirmative case. The second negative constructive usually adds new objections by attacking the affirmative plan.

Rebuttal speeches are begun by the first negative, with speakers alternating so that the affirmative has the last chance at persuasion. The first negative rebuttal argues against the responses developed by the second affirmative constructive. The first affirmative rebuttal must respond to all the negative argumentation. Note that by the time of the first affirmative rebuttal, the negative will have had 15 minutes (12 minutes in cross-examination debate) to develop the opposing position. Obviously, the first affirmative rebuttal must respond to new arguments in a succinct fashion and also respond to important arguments made in rebuttal.

The last two speeches in the debate sum up final positions. The second negative rebuttal selects, from all the objections to the affirmative case made in the round, the few that are most important. The second affirmative rebuttal answers the remaining negative objections and returns to the affirmative case to remind the judge of its merits.

The following chart will help you remember the order of speeches and duties in a debate:

First Affirmative Constructive

1. State the resolution.
2. Define terms.
3. State the affirmative case.
4. Present the affirmative plan.

First Negative Constructive

1. Object to affirmative definition of terms (attack topicality).
2. State the negative position.
3. Attack specific affirmative contentions.

Second Affirmative Constructive

1. Respond to any objections to definition of terms.
2. Attack the negative philosophy.
3. Respond to the objections to the affirmative contentions.

Second Negative Constructive

1. Attack the affirmative solvency.
2. Present disadvantages to the affirmative case.
3. Develop any new argumentation on topicality.

First Negative Rebuttal

1. Renew the attack on topicality.
2. Renew the attack on the affirmative case.

First Affirmative Rebuttal

1. Refute the new material presented by the second negative constructive.
2. Select the most important issue in the first negative rebuttal.
3. Refute the key issues against topicality and case.

Second Negative Rebuttal

1. Select the negative's strongest issues.
2. Explain why these issues are sufficient to merit a negative ballot.
3. Explain why other issues do not merit an affirmative ballot.

Second Affirmative Rebuttal

1. Respond to remaining negative objections against plan.
2. Respond to remaining negative objections against case.
3. Explain why the issues which you are winning merit an affirmative ballot.

(The responsibilities of speakers during cross-examination periods are discussed in Chapter 9.)

Apart from the first affirmative duties and the injunction to develop no new arguments in rebuttals, the speaker duties represented here do not always occur in this precise sequence. For example, sometimes the first negative constructive might have an objection to the affirmative plan. To some extent, the order of speaker responsibilities will vary by region of the country, depending on what the judges prefer. The chart describes a typical order of responsibilities.

The debater should note that duties in the negative speeches are flexible. Sometimes the first negative might wish to attack the plan, while the second negative argues against the case. Also, the first negative might wish to state a disadvantage and let the second negative expand the argument. As long as the strategy is clearly defined and the judge does not object, such positioning is acceptable.

Basic Affirmative Duties

First Affirmative Constructive

The practice in academic debate is to make the first affirmative constructive speech *all-inclusive*. That is to say that all the affirmative contentions, both case and plan, are included in that speech. A *contention* is a claim, most often stated in a single declarative sentence. Examples of affirmative contentions are (1) Water pollution is a significant problem; and (2) The affirmative plan can solve water pollution. In constructing the first affirmative speech in this manner, the entire affirmative mandate for change is in contention from the beginning. Many people feel that this results in better debates, more clearly defined and developed issues, and greater opportunity for both teams to analyze and extend arguments. It has also led to a highly defined division of labor on the part of negative speakers, which will be discussed later in this chapter.

Even if the first affirmative speech is not all-inclusive, certain elements of the affirmative case must be presented in the first affirmative: the first affirmative speaker must state the resolution, define terms, and present the justification for change. Consider two different rationales for change. A comparative advantage case would have to be presented in its entirety because the plan is necessary in order to present the advantages that justify the change. In the need-plan case approach, the option available to the affirmative is to reserve the presentation of the plan for the second affirmative. These affirmative case approaches and others will be discussed in greater detail in Chapter 7.

An outline of a traditional first affirmative constructive speech is presented below.

1. Statement of proposition.

2. Definition of terms (these may be operationally defined through the plan).

3. Need/harm contentions that establish reasons for change.

4. Presentation of affirmative plan.

5. Advantages of plan (optional, but often included).

The first affirmative constructive speech for a comparative advantage case, criteria-goals case, or net benefits case would follow the pattern above but would incorporate the special materials that will be outlined later.

Second Affirmative Constructive

The second affirmative constructive speech has three primary purposes: (1) to reestablish the affirmative position and analysis in the debate, (2) to refute the major contentions presented by the first negative speaker, and (3) to extend affirmative arguments and present any remaining constructive materials for the affirmative side. In the format of debate currently popular, the first negative speaker usually deals exclusively with need issues or advantages, leaving attacks on the plan for the second negative. As a consequence, the second affirmative constructive speaker will extend first affirmative arguments dealing with justification for the change, read additional evidence to support first affirmative arguments, and answer negative attacks on that justification.

The second affirmative constructive speaker should be ready to extend and answer typical case side arguments. The second affirmative speaker should be prepared to prove that its case is one that justifies the topic, doing neither more nor less than the topic requires (*topicality*). The speaker should be prepared to prove that the harm exists, is significant, and is likely to grow worse (*significance*). He or she should be able to demonstrate that the harm inheres in the status quo or that the advantage is unique to the affirmative plan (*inherency*). These three issues are known as *case side arguments*. Depending on the nature of the affirmative case, however, the variety of case side arguments may change. For example, it is possible for a negative to question the ability of the plan to meet the need or gain an advantage (*solvency*). These instances will be discussed in greater detail in later chapters. Suffice it to say at this point, the second affirmative should be ready to refute anything the first negative brings up. In this way, the validity of the affirmative case is reinstated after the first negative attack.

The second affirmative constructive speech might be outlined as follows:

1. Overview of debate thus far by showing the relationship between the affirmative case and the negative philosophy.

2. Reestablishment of the affirmative contentions and answering of negative refutation. The primary goal of this part of the speech is to return the debate to affirmative ground.

3. Attack any negative constructive materials. As much as possible, the speaker should use already established affirmative contentions to answer such things as the negative philosophy or status quo defense arguments.

4. Summary with emphasis on negative's failure to answer arguments dropped and emphasis on affirmative's responses to major negative contentions.

First Affirmative Rebuttal

The first affirmative rebuttal speech demands systematic organization and concise use of language. This four- or five-minute speech (depending on which debate format is being used) must respond to 12 or 15 minutes of uninterrupted negative argumentation. The primary duty of the first affirmative rebuttal speaker is to answer new material brought up by the second negative. Typically, these arguments will focus on the plan. If the negative has followed the usual division of labor, this will be the first opportunity for the affirmative to respond to those arguments. However, the first rebuttal speaker must reserve some time for a response to the most pressing of the case side attacks, too. In other words, much ground must be covered, and covered quickly enough to stay within time limits but thoroughly enough for the responses to have impact on the debate. You will have to decide for yourself within any given round what the best allocation of your time will be. Remember to watch the time carefully, allocate it wisely, and make every word count as you speak.

Second Affirmative Rebuttal

The second affirmative rebuttal follows the last negative speech in the debate. The second affirmative rebuttal is the conclusion of the arguments in the round. Like any other rebuttal, the second affirmative rebuttal should not contain new arguments. What is a new argument? It is one that introduces a completely new line of reasoning or emphasis to a debate. This character of argument is sometimes clear and sometimes not.

The last affirmative speaker has several duties. First, the round must be put in perspective for the judge. Over the course of the arguments, a judge may become confused. There can be many issues in a debate round. The rebuttalist should not only continue to try to win issues but he or she should put them together. It is the duty of the arguer to explain what the arguments mean in terms of the context of the debate round. For example, to say that some advantage will come about because of the affirmative case is not necessarily to make a telling argument. The advantage may have a small impact. However, if the debater puts the advantage into some perspective, then it might become an important issue. If there is not much of a proven disadvantage, then even a small advantage merits attention. Second, the last rebuttal speaker should try to win particular issues. This might be accomplished by reading more evidence, by establishing the importance of extensions to which the opponents have failed to respond, or by refuting claimed opposing positions. Third, if a position cannot be won, then at least the final speaker should try to explain why the judge should not vote on that particular issue. Naturally, the last affirmative speaker ought not misstate the negative's position in the round. That would be unethical.

Summary of Affirmative Duties

In summary, the affirmative in any debate has the burden of proof and must present a case in the constructive speaking period that meets the burden. In addition, the affirmative team must defend the case against all negative attacks and must be prepared with adequate second line evidence and argument extensions that will accomplish the defense. Each of the affirmative speeches in the round has its own unique place in that scheme, with specific expected tasks associated with it.

Basic Negative Duties

It is difficult to outline the specific responsibilities of each of the different negative speakers because the negative position in any academic debate is a relative one (within certain predescribed duties). However, some regularly practiced conventions in academic debate have proven effective. These have developed as a result of two fundamental characteristics of the negative speeches. First, the negative constructive speakers are in the position of needing to fulfill the negative burden of clash and at the same time to construct a negative position as a framework for the debate. Second, the negative constructive and rebuttal speeches are so arranged as to construct what is referred to as the negative block, a period of extensive and uninterrupted negative speaking in the middle of the debate. The negative strategy for each speaker is somewhat predetermined by these characteristics.

First Negative Constructive

The first constructive speech of the negative team is in direct response to the first affirmative constructive speech. In terms of staking out a negative position, four arguments must be raised in that speech if they are going to be raised in the debate at all. These arguments cannot be delayed until later in the debate:

1. If the negative is going to object to or take issue with any of the affirmative definitions of terms, it must do so in the first negative constructive. This should be presented as a full argument with explanation and evidence and with a designation of impact on the affirmative case.

2. If the negative intends to develop a topicality argument in which the affirmative case is demonstrated to fall outside the parameters of the topic, this argument must be introduced in the first negative. It can, of course, be extended in the second negative's plan attacks, but if the negative position is going to be that the affirmative analysis is nontopical, that argument must come in the first constructive.

3. If the negative intends to establish constructive arguments of its own, specifically a negative philosophy that forms a framework for the entire debate, it should do so in first constructive.

4. If the negative plans to offer a counterplan, it must be given in the first constructive speech.

Each of these four arguments is optional. It is essential to realize that no negative team is obligated to raise any of them. But it is equally necessary to remember that if any one of them is going to be made, it must be done at this point in the debate.

Aside from these four unique obligations, the first negative constructive speaker responds to the affirmative case, leaving the plan objections to the second negative. This is the usual division of labor for negative teams and has the advantage of keeping the issues organized and cleanly structured. If the negative team does not follow this division, it should clearly organize the issues in some other manner so that the debate is not muddled.

Regardless of what case construction the affirmative has used, then, the first negative speaker will probably be concerned with attacking the justification for change. The following is one possible outline of the first negative constructive:

1. Clear statement of the negative position or philosophy. It should give the negative position with regard to this particular affirmative case and should constitute a negative constructive argument that can be an issue in the debate.

2. Definition of terms. If the negative is going to disagree with the affirmative's definitions, this is the time and place for that argument to be placed. The disagreement should be developed as an argument. There should be counter evidence or authorities to support the negative position. You should show how the definition affects the affirmative case.

3. Preview the major issues of your speech. Show the judge your external structure.

4. Structure each of your refutations. The following format will serve for each point:

   a. State the affirmative point in contention. Use the affirmative's headline.
   b. State your position relative to the affirmative contention.
   c. Explain and evidence the negative point.
   d. Relate the impact to the affirmative case. What damage does your point do if it carries?
   e. Restate your position succinctly.

   Remember, your structure should be apparent. Utilize numerical and alphabetical designations to keep the substructure clear.

5. A restatement of the negative philosophy or a summary of the impact you have had on the affirmative case overall can make a strong appeal for the negative position.

Organization is the hallmark of a skillful first negative speaker. You might adopt the following maxim that one successful college coach imprints in the minds of his first negative speakers.

> If an observer walked into the round at the beginning of your first negative speech, you should organize and headline in such a fashion that at the conclusion of your speech he would have in front of him the totality of both the affirmative and negative issues.

Second Negative Constructive

This speech is usually reserved for plan attacks. There might be time to deal with a particularly troublesome contention on case side, but you must not forget that you are the first speaker of the negative block. Thus, the arguments on case side can be dealt with by your partner in the first negative rebuttal. An outline of possible construction for this speech would be as follows:

1. Preview the approach with reference to the negative philosophy established by the first negative constructive.

2. Attack the affirmative plan by an attack organized under the following major headings:

   a. Inherency. Challenge the extent or nature of the change. Demonstrate that it is not a structural change.
   b. Solvency. Develop here any and all attacks by which you demonstrate that the affirmative's plan is incapable of meeting the need or achieving the advantages by which they have offered justification for its adoption.
   c. Disadvantages. Develop here any and all attacks by which you demonstrate that even if the affirmative plan could solve the need or achieve the advantage, it would create disadvantages that would offset its desirability. Such elements as cost, social or economic dislocation, the extent of their significance, and other negative results of the plan should be developed. It is important in developing disadvantages to demonstrate that they are unique to the affirmative plan.

Here is a word of caution to second negative constructive speakers: Guard against falling into a contradiction between inherency arguments on case side (in which you postulate that the present system is already accomplishing the goals of the affirmative) and then going on to present all the massive disadvantages that would come about from the affirmative's proposed change. Careful wording of the disadvantages can avoid this.

First Negative Rebuttal

This speech follows immediately after the second negative constructive and therefore should be an absolute continuation of negative impact. Cover, refute, extend, and develop the case side arguments that were introduced by the second affirmative. Structure these arguments and relate them to your existing negative philosophy. At the conclusion of this speech, reserve a little time to relate case side position to the plan objections that your partner has just introduced. A good structure here is an "even-if" development establishing that the need doesn't exist but that, even if it did, the plan is significantly unable to meet it or creates disadvantages that merit rejection of the plan. Such a summation at the conclusion of the first negative rebuttal makes a complete unit of the negative position and establishes a sound team effort by the negative. It also establishes a preemption of the affirmative's attempt to handle arguments in isolation and forces the first affirmative rebuttal to attempt both case and plan refutation.

Second Negative Rebuttal

This is the negative's last opportunity in the debate. It is imperative, therefore, that you select your arguments for this speech wisely. You must attempt to discover the voting issues and to be sure that, when you conclude this speech, these issues will stand firmly on the negative side of the flow. Look especially at the inherency, significance, and disadvantages as they have evolved in the debate. Be selective and impactful.

Summary of Negative Duties

The negative side of a debate is one of constant challenge. Although it is traditionally said that the negative has presumption on its side and that the present system is judged to be satisfactory until proven otherwise, the negative comes into the round without precise knowledge about the issues. However, if the research you have done is adequate and if you really understand the negative position relative to the change advocated by the affirmative, you will discover that negative debating is not only challenging, it is fun!

General Considerations of Presentation

Planning

Affirmative and Negative Briefs

Debate is a unique and exciting combination of speaking from both a

prepared and an extemporaneous stance. Of the eight speeches in a debate, only the first affirmative constructive speech should be totally prepared in advance. Every other speech, although it may contain elements
that have been prepared in advance, must be responsive to what has gone
before it in the debate. If this is not the case, the debate will lack the essential element of clash. It will not only be dull; it will be almost impossible for the negative to win.

At the same time, however, teams can prepare a great deal in advance
for use in the debate. The affirmative should have attempted to anticipate every possible line of argumentation against its case. The team
should have thought through its own analysis in response to these arguments, located evidence to prove that analysis, and organized that material in advance. Affirmatives frequently develop affirmative briefs. Advance preparation can also be done by the negative in the form of
negative briefs, analysis, and evidence organized in advance for cases
that the team has already met on that year's topic. Such advance preparation is a good way to guarantee the ability to respond to the opposition
in an organized and thoughtful fashion.

When making preparations for a debate, remember that no two
teams will argue in exactly the same way on a given issue. Therefore, be
sure that you relate your prepared materials to the specific case you are
debating during a given round. If your responses sound canned, most
judges will rank you very low on analysis, and you will probably miss vital
points and argue off-center to the voting issues in the debate.

A brief is a method of organizing issues and evidence. On some topics, there will be arguments recurrent enough to predict that they will appear in many—if not every—round of debate. The negative should always be able to question affirmative arguments in a spontaneous manner,
but it also helps to prepare thoughtfully. This is the function of a brief.
To prepare a brief, three things must be done. First, the debater should
find evidence pertaining to the general topic. If the resolution calls for a
universal system of employment guarantees, for example, the negative
will almost certainly have to prove that unemployment is not harmful.
Evidence stating that unemployment does not cause harm is thus useful.
This evidence should be categorized by specific type of harms: unemployment does not cause (1) stress, (2) alcoholism, (3) mental illness, or
(4) spouse abuse—to name just a few evils. Second, the categorized evidence should be placed with its appropriate label on a sheet of paper.
Only one or two of the best pieces of evidence should be written under
each point because time is limited. Third, the brief should contain a

short explanation as to why the negative evidence is conclusive. The more concise the brief, the better. Remember, time in debate rounds is quite limited.

Many debaters find it useful to develop briefs with first, second, and third lines of evidence and responses. Some go as far as rebuttal responses. As the brief grows in length and becomes more complicated, a system must be devised for easy use. Not all the evidence or responses on a brief will be read in every round. In order to stay organized and not waste precious speaking time, the debater can do one of two things. The first is to enclose all briefs in plastic sheets (sometimes called slick sheets). Once this is done, the debater can then mark the evidence and responses to be read with a grease pen or with paper clips. At the end of the round, the marks can be wiped clean or the clips can be removed, and the brief will be ready for use in the next round.

Flowing is one of the most important strategies for success in debate. You cannot deliver an organized response to the opposition if you have not recorded their arguments accurately.

Flowing the Debate

Vital to successful debating is your ability to listen carefully, flow arguments accurately, analyze your own responses, and organize needed materials. These tasks must all be accomplished during the time in which the opposition is speaking and during any additional preparation time that the rules of the particular tournament allow you. Nothing can substitute for accurate flowing of a debate—that is, taking notes. You simply cannot argue points if you are unaware of them. You cannot maintain an organized response to the opposition if you do not have their arguments accurately recorded.

There are as many methods and arrangements for flowing a debate as there are debaters. Your own coach and members of your squad can show you how to place your notes on a flow sheet. There are only two important rules to remember. First, you must flow for yourself. Do not attempt to use your partner's flow, for each person develops special abbreviations and personal codes. Even if you feel inadequate, you must do your own flowing, in order to develop the skill. The second rule is that you not only need to form the habit of flowing the headline for the opposition's arguments, but you should listen carefully to evidence. Listen particularly to vital elements, such as the date, the qualifications of the source, and any limiting words, such as *may, could be,* and *projected.* Flow these evidence characteristics; they often become crucial in the debate. To get as much information as possible you will need to develop a system of shorthand (or abbreviations). Using symbols such as = for equals will enable you to get down more information.

Most experienced debaters find that a larger-sized note pad, such as a legal pad or an art pad, is best for flowing debates. It has become common in recent years to arrange separate sheets on the flow pad corresponding to each of the case contentions and to record the plan on another sheet. In this fashion, the debaters will instruct that they are "going to case side" or "going to plan side." This is all a matter of personal preference. The cardinal rule is that you must flow the debate. If you can interpret the flow accurately, it is a good one.

Organizing

No single debate skill is more important than organization. No matter how brilliant your argument or how cogent your evidence is, if neither the judge, the opposition, nor your partner can decipher which of the

CASE ARGUMENTS

Tournament: FALL CLASSIC

Round: 3

First Affirmative Constructive	First Negative Constructive	Second Affirmative Constructive	First Negative Rebuttal
OBSER-FARM SURPLUS SUCC. FRMG. JE '87 COMM. SURPLUS SCI. MG O'85 STARCH PRDS. BIO-DEGR. J OF COMM. MR '81			
I. INHER.—SQ FAILS → TO SO GOVT. HOLDS NO OPEN MKT BW JL '86 2. 5 BB SURPLUS CHR. SCI M '86 LEG. NEEDED TO SOLVE NYT M '85	→ I. INHER. ── A. MUST SHOW CORE MOT. MUST SHOW BARRIER PROVE STRUCT INHER	→ GOVT. OWNER NOT WISE → GOVT. ANTI-ENVIR. X 1986	→ I. NO CORE MOTIVE 2. NOT ASSUME OTHER ACTORS
ADVANTAGE I. BETTER USE OF SURPLUS A. IMPROVE FRM. ENVIR. —FRMS USE PLASTIC MULCHING CHR. SCI. M '86 — NOT BIO-DEGRD USNWR '86 — CAN START NOW X I. REVERSE LVG IN COMP. W NATURE	B. VIOLATION ── NO CORE MOT C. ROLE 1. NOT NEED RESOL 2. VOTING ISSUE 3. APPLICATION 1. NO IMPACT 2. NOT SOLVE -ONLY PLAS. X X 3. ≠ HARMONY W/ NATURE X	→ EVID. SAYS NEED LEG. STRUCT. INHER. 1986 NEED TO TAKE ACTION NOW → MUST VOTE TO IMPROVE	→ I. NOT DENY BURDEN 2. SQ CAN SOLVE X X 3. NO EVID. ON PERMA. → I. NO LAWS-NOT STRUCT 2. NO EXAMPLES – OTHER ACTORS PROVE SOMEELSE NOT SOLVE TREND IS BURDEN FOR INHER.
2. BENE. FUTURE GENE. → X X	I. NO MORAL IMPERATIVE TIME 2. NO OBLIG. 1980 3. FOCUS ON LT IGNORE ST USNWR	9M. STEPS HELP HARMONY → NYT NOT GIVING UP EVERYTHING FOR FUTURE	→ I. NO EVID. TO IMPR. AGR ENVIR. 2 ALL CARDS ARE GEN. ON ENVIR. 3. 9M. STEPS FOR ECOL. CONSC. 4. LT FOCUS IS DANG. NOT A VALUE
X = EVIDENCE READ			

Affirmative: _14X_

Negative: _6X_

First Affirmative Rebuttal	Second Negative Rebuttal	Second Affirmative Rebuttal
	SURPLUSES ≠ PLASTICS ⟶	
1. THINK HELP FRMRS NOW	1. PERMANENCE STAND IF NO HARM	
2. GVT. WILL NOT DO	2. MUST SHOW TREND	GVT. ANTI-ENVIR.
3. GVT ANTI-ENVIR.	3. STRUCT. INHER-WHAT⟶ MUST HAVE LAW	
4. NYT NO TREND	IS THE BARRIER	
5. NEED LEG. TO SOLVE	1985	
GVT. WILL KEEP SURP.		
	PRICE COMPET. IRRELEV.	
⟶ DROP ────────────	────────────────	⟶
EVID. FROM 1AC NOT DENIED MUST LOOK AT LT	────────────	⟶

©1986 National Textbook Company • Lincolnwood, Illinois 60646 U.S.A.

Symbols and Abbreviations

T	topicality
Inh	inherency
DA	disadvantage
PMA	plan-meets-advantage
PMN	plan-meets need
Circ	circumvention
PS	present system
SQ	status quo
TA	turnaround
CP	counterplan
Sig	significance
OBS	observation
U	unique
NU	non-unique
thr	threshold
$	dollars, money, finance, revenue, funding
MR	minor repair
EXT	extratopicality
x	dropped argument
NE	no evidence used
??	(used before an argument or card to show you're not sure you flowed it correctly)
CX	statement from cross-ex.
>	greater than
<	less than
↑	increase
↓	decrease
⟶	causes
↛	does not cause
=	equals, is
≠	does not equal, is not
w/	with
w/o	without
w/in	within
b/c	because
avg	average

CASE ARGUMENTS

NTC

Tournament:_____

Round:_____

First Affirmative Constructive	First Negative Constructive	Second Affirmative Constructive	First Negative Rebuttal
B. IMPR. LIFE OF FRMR.			
— COST TO DISPOSE → <u>USNWR '86</u>	DOES NOT SAY FIN. → HARM	LOSE $100-200 PER ACRE → <u>X</u>	DOES NOT SHOW CASE SOLVE
— INCOME EXPECTED → TO GO↓ <u>NYT M '87</u>	FRMR. REALISTIC → <u>TIME</u> <u>BW</u>	NOT SAVE ALL FRMRS. → <u>X</u>	GOVT. NOT RESP. WSJ
— MUST MAINTAIN → <u>TIME F '85</u> FAM. FARM GVT. RESP. ETHICAL REASONS <u>X</u>	FRMR CAN FIND → OTHER JOBS <u>BOGART '85</u>	1. MANY CANNOT → <u>X</u> 2. FARM LOSS INCOME <u>1985</u> 3. STILL SHLD. HELP	JOB ARE AVAIL.
C. SOLVENCY →	1. NOT SOLVE ENVIR. →	1. <u>CSM '86</u> — SOLVES ENVIR.	
1. TECH. AVAIL. <u>CHR. SCI. M. O'86</u>	2. MUST PROVE BUS. WILL DO THIS.	2. HAS BEEN TRIED WORKED	
2. HAS BEEN TRIED <u>X</u>		3. FARMERS SAVED	
3. SAVES FARM <u>X</u> <u>X</u>			

*Affirmative:*_____

*Negative:*_____

t Affirmative Rebuttal	Second Negative Rebuttal	Second Affirmative Rebuttal
TO BETTER USE ⌐		1. $100-200 PR. ACRE ADVANT.
IS THE CAUSE ⌐ ⤷DROPPED		2. GOVT. RESPONS.
FORCE TO CHANGE ⌐ GIVES ALTER.		3. TECH. AVAIL. TO SOLVE

———————————→

©1986 National Textbook Company • Lincolnwood, Illinois 60646 U.S.A.

Symbols and Abbreviations

T	topicality
Inh	inherency
DA	disadvantage
PMA	plan-meets-advantage
PMN	plan-meets need
Circ	circumvention
PS	present system
SQ	status quo
TA	turnaround
CP	counterplan
Sig	significance
OBS	observation
U	unique
NU	non-unique
thr	threshold
$	dollars, money, finance, revenue, funding
MR	minor repair
EXT	extratopicality
x	dropped argument
NE	no evidence used
??	(used before an argument or card to show you're not sure you flowed it correctly)
CX	statement from cross-ex.
>	greater than
<	less than
↑	increase
↓	decrease
→	causes
↛	does not cause
=	equals, is
≠	does not equal, is not
w/	with
w/o	without
w/in	within
b/c	because
avg	average

opposition's contentions you are addressing, then you have not advanced a coherent position and have lost most of the impact of the points presented.

Headline Value

The first step in making arguments clear is to word them with headline value. Imagine for a minute what the morning newspaper would look like without the presence of the bold, concise headlines it contains. Nothing would be more important than anything else, and most of the news would be lost in a great mass of black print. By the same token, if you begin speaking and reading evidence in a debate without labeling arguments with brief, specific headlines, then you may not be able to distinguish one argument from another. You should word contentions in a concise form. You should use that form each time you refer to that argument. This headline becomes a point of reference for both teams and for the judge. The argument is less likely to get lost if it is properly headlined.

Internal Structure

In addition to headline value, each argument should have internal structure. You should use numerical and alphabetical designations for the arguments you present so that they are easy to flow and to relate to the case of the opposition. For both the affirmative's constructive presentation and for negative and affirmative refutation, the internal structure of arguments is vital. The affirmative construction of each contention should (1) state the contention headline, (2) explain the contention, (3) evidence the contention, and (4) restate the contention. In refutation, both teams should use internal structure: (1) state the contention to be addressed, (2) structure answers as subpoints and evidence each one, (3) relate answers to the total impact of the opposition's case, and (4) restate the contention briefly.

External Structure

The external structure of your speech is important, too. Not only must each argument presented be well organized, but the total speech must have a structure—and you must make the judge aware of that structure in advance. A statement such as "In this speech, I am going to examine three major issues: topicality, significance, and inherency" gives the judge advance notice of where to look on the flow and identifies for the judge the issues in contention. If your topicality argument, for example, is composed of three basis responses, indicate this, enumerate them with headline value as you present them, and remind the judge at the conclusion that you had three responses to topicality. Too many beginning debaters seem to adopt the motto "If you can't beat them, confuse them." Unfortunately, the person most often confused is the judge, and few ballots are won by unorganized debaters. You are always ahead if everyone in the round—judge, opposition, and, most of all, you—can accurately place your arguments on a flow sheet.

Delivering

Debate is an oral activity. It differs from events like original oratory or dramatic acting insofar as it contains more intellectual content and spontaneous commentary. However, if the debater or the coach forgets that information must be communicated in a limited amount of time through oral means, the event can become quite frustrating. Anyone who has gone to a debate tournament has seen speakers talking at a rapid rate of speed. These are usually experienced debaters who have learned to think fast while talking quickly. You may be tempted to imitate this practice. Don't. What will come out is only a jumble of words. Just as you had to learn to walk before you could run, so you must practice speaking *clearly* before you can speak *quickly*.

There is no substitute for practice in preparation for debate tournaments. Practice includes participation in rounds of debate with your classmates. These rounds offer you the opportunity to give a speech once and then to deliver it again, with improvements. Practice should aim at reducing the number of nonessential arguments. Eliminate the weakest arguments, and you will be able to slow down to a reasonable rate of speed and still say all that is important.

One thing that may be difficult for you is to seek advice on public speaking. No one likes to be criticized, but it is possible that you have annoying habits of speaking simply because you have never been informed of how to speak well. Ask your teacher or your debate coach about your speaking. Make sure that you have the right tone, pitch, and level of articulation for debate. Rather than tarnishing your ability to speak well, debate should enhance it. The best debaters are not necessarily the fastest; they are the ones with the ability and experience to argue essential points and persuade the audience.

Summary

This chapter has examined the basics of academic debate. You should now be able to identify the elements of an academic debate, the duties of each speaker, the obligations and opportunities of the affirmative and the negative, and some of the typical kinds of arguments that are made. You should also be able to identify ways to prepare for a debate, plan arguments, arrange briefs, and structure specific arguments and entire speeches. Finally, you should be aware of the need to practice these arguments in developing skills of oral presentation. The following chapters present some strategic considerations for fulfilling these requirements in rounds of debate in which diverse arguments are made.

Questions for Discussion

1. Even though most of each debate round is an extemporaneous activity, you must spend some time organizing your thoughts. Explain the rules governing preparation time. Why are such rules necessary?

2. Define a constructive speech and a rebuttal speech. What is the difference between the two?

3. What are the parts of a first affirmative constructive speech?

4. The second affirmative constructive speech has three purposes: describe them. What must the second affirmative speaker be prepared to argue in regard to topicality, significance, inherency, and solvency?

5. In terms of the responsibilities of the negative speakers, what is the difference between the first and second negatives? Outline the strategy for each.

6. What is the purpose of preparing affirmative and negative briefs prior to a debate?

7. What is the value of taking a flow in a debate round?

8. What is to be gained by keeping each speech organized?

Activities

1. Using the current issue chosen on page 71, organize and prepare an affirmative or negative brief. The brief should deal with a single issue.

2. Develop a list of abbreviations and symbols that could be used for taking a flow (note taking).

3. For the next week, use the list developed in Activity 2 when you are listening to class lectures, the nightly news, or a news radio station.

4. Collect five articles dealing with the current issue chosen on page 71. Using headlines and internal structure, organize the issues contained in the articles.

Chapter 7

Affirmative Case Construction

Objectives and Key Terms

After studying Chapter 7, you should be able to

1. Explain the essential characteristics of each type of affirmative case construction,

2. Explain how one decides which case type to use,

3. Produce an affirmative case and plan, complete with evidence, and

4. Discuss what makes a harm inherent and significant.

After reading this chapter, you should understand the following terms:

case

need-plan case

harm

inherency

significance

solvency

contention

comparative advantage case

criteria-goals case

net benefits case

T here are numerous methods of constructing an affirmative case. Generally, all the recognized affirmative case forms are derived from sound theories of logic and persuasion. Affirmative cases are built by applying the principles of organizational structure to the information and facts you have discovered in your research. In this book, you will learn some good ways to build affirmative cases. Specifically, this chapter will cover the traditional need-plan case, the comparative advantage case, the criteria-goals case, and the net benefits (systems analysis) case.

The Traditional Need-Plan Case

The traditional need-plan case format is appropriate for debating whether or not a new policy should be initiated in an area where no policy exists. In resolutions dealing with adjustments in the level or direction of an existing federal policy, the traditional need-plan case is less suitable for supporting the resolution.

To understand the traditional need-plan case, you need a bit of historical perspective. School debating has been going on for several decades now. At the time it became popular to use a national policy as the subject of the debate resolution each debate season, the federal government had little responsibility in domestic social areas. Consequently, most school debate resolutions called for the federal government to initiate some new policy in an area where there was no federal policy. Some of the actual resolutions debated in intercollegiate tournaments were these:

1931: Resolved: That the Congress should enact legislation providing for the centralized control of industry.

1936: Resolved: That Congress should be empowered to fix minimum wages and maximum hours for industry.

1940: Resolved: That the nations of the Western Hemisphere should form a permanent union.

1949: Resolved: That the United States should nationalize the basic nonagricultural industries.

As recently as 1965, high school debaters were debating "Resolved: That social security benefits should be expanded to include medical care." A key factor that these and similar resolutions had in common was the call for a federal action in an area where the national government was not already involved. It is difficult for many of us to recall a time when the federal government was not integrally involved in social areas and international organizations. But in a larger view, it really has not been long since there was no Social Security, no Medicare, no United Nations.

In such a perspective, it becomes easier to see how a need for federal action could be a regular subject for policy debate. In that climate, the stock issues form of analysis was the only form acceptable in a debate. There was either a *yes* or a *no* answer to the debate resolution—the federal government either should or should not initiate a policy in a given problem area. This perspective is important because when more recent developments in case forms are discussed, such as the comparative advantage case and the net benefits case (based on systems analysis), the resolution for debate will assume that the federal government is already involved in the area of concern. The issues will be over the degree or kind of involvement that is desirable.

With this historical context understood, you are in a better position to examine the defining characteristics of the need-plan case. The basic format of the need-plan case is the same as the statement of the stock issues: First, the case develops the argument that a need for a change exists. Next, the case develops the plan and shows how the plan meets the need. Finally, the case develops the argument that the plan would be beneficial.

The heart of the case is that there is a need and that the plan will meet the need. In this emphasis, the benefits of the plan assume a role of secondary importance. Judges are not asked to vote for a plan that fails to meet the need, even if it is a beneficial plan.

As a logical theory, the traditional need-plan case is the same as a problem-solution outline. Much of the underlying theory of the case is very similar to the Dewey method of critical thinking: Identify and analyze the problem; select the best solution. However, in debate, there are a few distinctive twists on the theory.

Characteristics of the Need

First, the need or problem has to be *compelling*. This means that you have to select an area in which the present system is woefully inadequate, and people are severely suffering, economically or physically, as a result.

Next, the need has to be *inherent*. In traditional need-plan analysis, inherency typically means a logical relationship between a specific condition existing as an effect of the present system and the specific characteristic of the present system that causes it. To prove that a need is inherent, you must demonstrate that the harmful condition you isolate is caused by that part of the present system that your plan is designed to correct. If the harmful condition or need can be remedied by measures other than your plan, it is not considered an inherent need, according to this analysis.

What could constitute such a characteristic of the present system? The law itself. If the law requires the present system to operate in such a way that the harmful result inevitably occurs, then the need is inherent. The need is created by the structure of the present system, the body of law. Only a plan to change the law can solve such a problem. An example of a structural inherency during the 1950s and 1960s was segregation and the discriminating body of laws regarding public accommodations, jobs, housing, and voting. Only a change in the law could remedy racial segregation; nothing else could solve that need.

Of course, in keeping with the historical analysis of the growth and development of the traditional need-plan case, inherency also is created by the absence of necessary legislation. The problems that exist as a result of the inability of government to act without any legislative authority can only be remedied by the creation of enabling legislation, together with its agencies and adequate resources to fulfill the intent of the law.

Characteristics of the Plan

The plan has to meet the need. The inherent and compelling need has to be completely solved by the affirmative plan. Judges will not accept a proposed federal policy that cannot overcome the causes of the problem and meet the need entirely. Partial solutions will not do.

The plan has to be *practical*, feasible. Even if a plan could theoretically meet the need totally, judges will refuse to accept it if it seems to be an impractical solution.

Originally, as the need-plan case developed in school debates, judges expected the affirmative speeches to be organized in a particular way. The first affirmative speaker presented the need, and the second affirmative speaker presented the plan and made the arguments about its workability, practicality, and extra benefits. Judges seldom voted for a plan because of its benefits, but they expected the affirmative to point out the benefits just the same. Currently, however, affirmative teams have begun to reveal the entire case—need, plan, and benefits—in the first constructive speech.

Need-Plan Case

Resolution
    I. There is a need for a change.
       A. The need is compelling.
       B. The need is inherent.
   II. The plan will meet the need.
       A. The plan is workable.
       B. The plan is practical.
  III. The plan has extra benefits.

It is difficult to adapt the requirements of a need-plan case to a topic that calls for incremental reform. If the United States is increasing or decreasing welfare, arms control, or environmental protection, the direction of policy may create more or fewer benefits, but the policy itself cannot be said to be a solution to a need. At best, it is only an incremental adjustment to the present situation.

The traditional need-plan case is designed to fulfill the affirmative team's burden to prove a case for a new policy. Essentially, it is a problem-solution construct. The distinctive arguments required in proving the need-plan case are that the need or problem is compelling and inherent, the plan will meet the need entirely because it is workable and practical, and the plan promises added benefits. In terms of organization, the need is always presented before the plan because it constitutes the mandate for the plan.

The Comparative Advantage Case

The transition from the traditional need-plan case to the comparative advantage case was a gradual one that took place during the 1960s. Today, the comparative advantage case is the most popular and widely known form of affirmative case analysis. Examining some of the factors involved in the transition from need-plan to comparative advantage cases will help you grasp the reasoning and theory behind the comparative advantage case as it is now used.

Again, remember the historical perspective we have already examined. In the 1930s and 1940s, the federal government could be described as low profile. The Depression of the 1930s and World War II in the 1940s combined to generate a much more active and powerful federal presence in both domestic policy and foreign policy. Consequently, the wording of debate resolutions began to mirror that change. No longer did they call for establishing a new federal policy where none previously existed. Instead the resolutions called for increasing or decreasing federal influence in a problem area where federal policy already existed. Some actual resolutions debated in intercollegiate tournaments during this period were as follows:

1965: Resolved: That law-enforcement agencies in the United States should be given greater freedom in the investigation and prosecution of crime.

1966: Resolved: That the United States should substantially reduce its foreign policy commitments.

1968: Resolved: That executive control of United States foreign policy should be significantly curtailed.

1971: Resolved; That greater controls should be imposed on the gathering and utilization of information about United States citizens by government agencies.

As you can see, the common feature in these resolutions is a call for modifying an existing federal policy, in contrast with the earlier period, when the common feature of debate resolutions was the call for initiating some new policy where none previously existed. The shift in the wording of debate resolutions created a new way of looking at affirmative obligations.

In large part, the movement away from the need-plan case to the comparative advantage case was generated by the difficulty many affirmative teams had in winning debates. During this period, American federal involvement mushroomed in public problem areas. It became very difficult to establish an inherent (or unique) need to solve a problem through a new federal program when there were federal programs in place. The negative could easily show that the existing programs could be effective if sufficient money, manpower, or enforcement were used. Or they could take the position that the federal government could never solve the problems, if existing programs were not able to do so. As a consequence, negative teams simply repaired existing programs or destroyed the credibility of government efficacy.

The comparative advantage case developed as an affirmative strategy to counter this strong negative position. Affirmative teams showed that, although existing programs could possibly be modified in the present system to achieve a solution to the problem area, the affirmative proposal could do the job better. On a comparative basis, then, it would be more advantageous to accept the affirmative resolution than to stay with the present system, even if it were modified a bit. Inherency became a major difficulty because of changes that occurred in the actual political events of the nation.

Inherency was not the only major difficulty for the affirmative teams in this transition period. Solvency, the ability to correct the demonstrated problem, also became difficult under the traditional stock issues analysis. In the need-plan case, it was imperative for the proposed plan to solve the need completely. However, changing social and cultural patterns in our society made such a burden almost impossible. Experts began to characterize social problems as highly complex, with multiple causes. Increased mobility and density of population, intensified family pressures, and the emergence of economic ties and industrial conglomerates all served to complicate solutions to problems. Yet, if today's problems cannot be totally solved, they can at least be ameliorated through the constant review and correction of the policies that govern them. It was not always possible for the affirmative to prove that a plan would eliminate a problem completely, at least not at a feasible cost. Affirmative teams made the argument that this stock issues requirement was too rigid—that, in real world decision making, policy changes are accepted if they seem to be advantageous. Even if adopting a policy does not totally solve a problem, if it produces benefits, it ought to be accepted. This argument focused debate on the comparison between the affirmative plan and the present system. If the plan offers the greatest advantage possible, it should be considered worthy of acceptance.

A homely analogy was argued. Why do people trade cars? If your family already has a car, there is no need to buy another one when you use the need-plan case as your rule for decision. However, if your family can get a better car—newer, nicer, more comfortable, and more economical— then, in all probability, a trade will be made. Likewise, why buy a word processor when you have a typewriter? Not because you have an inherent need for a personal computer, but because of the advantages that come from acquiring a faster, easier way to write papers.

Although such arguments were not completely convincing, they made enough sense to sustain the shift in affirmative case analysis techniques from the need-plan to the comparative advantage. However, some people still objected to the comparative advantage case as a theoretical framework because it dilutes the logical rigor that was the hallmark of stock issues analysis. For this reason, the comparative advantage case incorporated, with modifications, many of the same logical requirements of the stock issues or the traditional need-plan case.

The basic idea of the comparative advantage case is to show that in comparison with the present system the affirmative plan is advantageous—hence the name, comparative advantage. In order to make the comparison, the affirmative team presents its plan first and the advantages later. This is one major difference from the traditional need-plan case. Moreover, since the plan is no longer withheld from the negative until late in the debate, the current practice is for the affirmative to present its entire case in the first affirmative constructive speech, regardless of which case structure is used.

Characteristics of the Advantage

The *advantage* constitutes the rationale presented to support the adoption of the plan. Because the concept of the advantage is the most important difference from the need-plan case, you should understand the arguments necessary to prove the comparative advantage case with regard to the claimed advantages.

First, the structure of the case remains essentially a problem-solution outline, except the solution is presented first and its effects are presented later. The proposed plan is the solution. By increasing or decreasing federal action in a problem area, the plan causes certain changes in the effects of the present system. These changed effects represent the advantages of the plan. Since the comparative advantage case is derived from the stock issues, as modified during the transitional period, the advantage must be shown to be related to the plan along the same lines as the relationship between a need and a plan. For sound organizational structure, there must be a direct comparison between the present system and the proposed change. Specifically, an advantage must be shown to be *sig-*

nificant (corresponding to the requirement that a need be *compelling* in the traditional need-plan case). It must be *unique* to the plan (corresponding to the requirement that a need be *inherent* in the traditional need-plan case).

An advantage is said to be *significant* whenever it is an important outcome of the plan. Significance has a quantitative and a qualitative dimension. Ideally, an advantage should represent a plan outcome highly valued by society that applies to a large number of people for a long time. Here are some ways to discuss significance.

Significance may be demonstrated by four different methods of measuring the amount or degree of change: (1) *Absolute significance,* the total number of units affected by the change wrought by the affirmative plan. How many more people will be employed, how many lives saved, how many units of energy or dollars conserved? (2) *Risk significance,* the fractional proportion of the potential population exposed to jeopardy by the policy system. For example, major medical expenses affect relatively few individuals in any given year. However, the potential risk of major medical expenses affects virtually everyone because serious illnesses and accidents can and do occur. Moreover, when considered over a longer time span than a year, say, over a generation or a lifetime, the percentage of people actually affected by financial catastrophe as a result of major medical expenses escalates. So the risk of financial catastrophe resulting from major medical expenses poses a significant problem area. Where risk to human life is involved, public policy change may also be warranted. The recent experimental findings that common sugar substitutes may be carcinogenic (cancer causing) led to tighter restrictions on the sale and use of saccharine, even though not one person could be found with cancer that could be directly linked to the product. The degree of risk was considered great enough to motivate policy change, especially in light of the absence of any significant negative impact to making such restrictions tighter. (3) *Degree of significance,* or the relative value of the advantage. Public policy deliberation is affected by minor problems only when great numbers of people are involved, but a problem area involving great consequences in terms of values (either beneficial or costly) receives prompt attention even when relatively few individuals are subjected to the harm. The greater the consequences of benefit or harm, the greater the relative value attached to the policy. The degree of significance directly affects the required magnitude of the scope of the problem needed for policy action. A large number of people might be merely irritated as a side reaction to a specific prescription drug. This probably would not constitute a significant justification for a policy change. However, if that same drug had some powerful side effects (such as the drug thalidomide had on pregnant women), immediate withdrawal of the drug from the market would be ordered by the Federal Drug Administration. Hence, the harm of the drug could be said to be significant in degree. (4) *Duration of significance,* or the persistence of a problem. In this sense, the condition of inherency overlaps the issue of significance. Temporary problems (or temporary advantages) constitute much less of a rationale for policy change than permanent ones.

An advantage is shown to be *unique* to the plan whenever the advantage can be achieved best by the affirmative plan and not by any other means. This represents a major change in emphasis from the logical requirements for establishing inherency in the traditional need-plan case. There, the need had to be created by the structure of the present system, and it could not be susceptible to a solution by any measure other than the plan. In the comparative advantage case, the issue is not whether

Many disadvantage and plan-meets-needs arguments against an affirmative case can be anticipated and refuted during team discussions.

other means of achieving the advantage exist, but whether the affirmative proposal is the *most* advantageous means. The advantage is considered unique to the plan when only the plan can achieve the advantage to the same extent of cost efficiency, speed (rate of achieving the goal of the present system), or effective coverage. By being relieved of the burden of identifying a law on the books that causes the problem or the absence of a law to solve the problem, the affirmative was free to describe other hindrances to the best operation of the system. Hence, there arose a new line of argument in affirmative case analysis called *attitudinal inherency,* the tendency of agents charged with creating or carrying out the law to avoid their responsibility. The condition of attitudinal inherency exists in such features of the present system as corrupt officials (as in organized crime), pressure groups and lobbies, conflicting laws and goals, and even general apathy. As long as the affirmative plan contains provisions to change or circumvent such attitudes, and the present system has no such mechanisms to step up its ability to do so, the affirmative can claim the advantage as being unique because only the plan could do it.

A second area of argument relates to the comparisons made between the proposed plan and the present system. Comparisons are made between the plan and the present system in relation to their relative success in achieving the goal in question. When the locus of argument is over increasing or decreasing federal action in an area in which the federal government is already active, the first step is to identify the goal that the present policy seeks to achieve. Once the goal is identified, it is possible to compare the operation of the present system with the projected changes in operation made by the proposed plan in terms of achieving the goal.

The primary areas in which relative comparisons are made in debate analysis include cost, speed, and efficiency. A plan is advantageous if it can achieve the goal more *economically* than the present system, more *quickly* than the present system, or more *efficiently* than the present system.

Comparative Advantage Case
Resolution
    I. Goal of the present system.
    II. Plan.
    III. Statement of advantage: Plan will achieve the goal (cheaper, faster, better) than the present system.

A. The advantage is significant.
    1. Scope and limits of present system.
    2. Increased scope or achievement of proposed plan.
B. The advantage is unique to the plan.
    1. Limitations of present system.
    2. Removal of those limitations by proposed plan.

Two additional points should be made about the comparative advantage case. First, the case may include more than one advantage for adopting the plan. If the affirmative team shows that two, three, or more advantages stem from the adoption of the plan and, moreover, that each of the advantages is independent (capable of achievement without a necessary connection to whether other advantages are achieved), then any one of the advantages can stand as the rationale for adopting the plan. This argument is strategically important, because the affirmative could be defeated by negative refutation on one or more of the advantages and still win the judge's decision, provided there is still at least one advantage to adopting the plan. This strategy is a refinement of the transitional argument that an acceptable proposal is not required to solve the need totally.

Comparative Advantage Case with Multiple Advantages

1. Plan
Advantage 1: Reach goal more economically.
Advantage 2: Reach goal within shorter time period.
Advantage 3: Cover more of the problem area or otherwise claim
             greater efficiency.

According to this strategy, the affirmative team could lose advantages 1 and 2, but still win the debate because advantage 3 is a reasonable, independent rationale for adopting the proposed plan.

The second point is that there is a second level of comparison to be made. Not only is the plan compared with the present system (which is the focus of the affirmative case), but also the advantages of the plan are compared with its disadvantages (which is the focus of the negative attack). This point will be developed more completely in Chapter 8, where negative strategies are discussed. The affirmative should be aware that the comparative advantage case must have advantages that not only outweigh the present system but also outweigh potential disadvantages of the plan.

The comparative advantage case grew out of the need-plan case. Today it is the most popular form of affirmative case analysis. As a form of problem-solution argument, the comparative advantage case presents a proposed plan to change existing policy and bases its rationale on the ways in which the results of the change in policy (the plan) would be improvements over the present system. Comparisons are made between the proposed plan and the present system in achieving a specific goal. To justify the proposal plan, the claimed effect or advantage must be significant and unique to the plan when compared with the present system or any other alternative policy. Comparisons are made between the proposed plan and the present system on the dimensions of cost, speed, and efficiency. More than one advantage may be presented to support the proposed plan, and if the advantages are shown to be independent reasons for adopting the plan, only one of the claimed advantages need be carried by the affirmative in order to win the judge's decision. Another important argument relevant to the comparative advantage case lies in the potential disadvantages that can also be attributed to adopting the plan. This major negative argument will be explained in the next chapter.

The Criteria-Goals Case

The *criteria-goals case* format is basically an elaboration on the comparative advantage case in which greater emphasis is laid upon the policy goals of the present system. The comparative advantage case is based on the requirement that the affirmative must show how its plan is a better way to fulfill the goal toward which the present system is working. In the criteria-goals case, the affirmative incorporates the identification of the goal of the present system as an integral part of its analysis. Then, the affirmative sets up the criteria by which any policy should be judged in the fulfillment of those particular goals.

Once the goal is identified and the standards are set whereby a policy designed to meet the goal should be measured, the affirmative shows that its proposed plan meets the criteria better than the present system does.

However, in current debate theory, meeting a set of abstract, ideal standards of policy formation is not adequate in and of itself to support a proposed resolution. Beyond this argument, the criteria-goals case proceeds along lines similar to the usual comparative advantage case and demonstrates that the plan will accrue significant and unique advantages. The strength of the criteria-goals case is that it offers a separate line of argument against negative refutation. Even though the negative may be able to show how the present system or some other alternative policy could also achieve the advantages, only the affirmative plan can do so while simultaneously fulfilling the criteria of the ideal policy approach to meeting the goal.

Criteria-Goals Case
Resolution
    I. Goal of the present policy.
    II. Criteria for measuring policy designed to meet the goal.
    III. Plan.
    IV. Show how affirmative plan fulfills criteria.
    V. Advantage(s).

The criteria-goals case is an elaboration on the comparative advantage case. However, the criteria-goals case places an initial emphasis on identifying the goal of the present policy and sets forth the criteria by which any policy designed to meet that goal should be measured. Then, the affirmative plan is shown to fulfill the criteria. Beyond this, the criteria-goals case proceeds to justify the plan on the basis of its advantages, as in a comparative advantage case.

The Net Benefits Case

An innovative affirmative case idea is the net benefits case. Unlike the criteria-goals case, the net benefits case was not evolved directly from existing debate theory. The net benefits case differs from the more traditional theory of debate founded in the stock issues. To understand the net benefits case, you need to begin from a different frame of reference.

The net benefits case is based on systems analysis. The differences between stock issues analysis and systems analysis have already been partly explained. Briefly stated, *systems analysis* assumes that legislation of policy takes place in an environment that is constantly changing. The present system is seen as ever-changing due to natural changes, for example, in population growth, economic fluctuations, and demographic trends. Also, it is assumed that policies already exist in all the problem areas considered by the policymakers. Consequently, there is no need to debate over whether a policy should be adopted—policy has already been adopted. What is at issue is how our existing policies can be adjusted to accommodate the continual changes occurring all around us. Therefore, there is no presumption that policies should remain unchanged until a need is demonstrated to change them; rather, what is debatable is the degree and direction of changes that should be implemented by law on an ongoing, continual basis of revision and adjustment.

Basically the net benefits case incorporates four steps: (1) Apply systems analysis to the problem area, (2) determine the components that make up the system and the rules that govern how the components are interrelated, (3) analyze and project what differences could be predicted following a change in policy governing these interrelationships, and (4) determine the most favorable ratio between the costs and the benefits of the proposed change in the system. As translated into an affirmative case outline, the affirmative must not only show the advantages accruing from the plan, but also demonstrate that the plan would result in the greatest net benefits possible considering both the predicted advantages and the predicted disadvantages. When defending the proposal, the affirmative would demand that the negative not only attempt to refute their case, but also present a counter-policy system of its own on which the judge could base a comparison of the methods of controlling and guiding inevitable change.

Proponents of this approach make the point that it is a closer approximation of the way many decisions are made through policy deliberations in government. Congressional committees and administrative agencies do not debate as often over whether the federal government should initiate a new policy (whether based on traditional need-plan or comparative advantage) as they engage in a continuing process of amending, adjusting, and fine tuning the laws already on the books. The basis for real world decision making appears to be based on the relative net benefits of making this proposed change in the overall system as compared with other proposals.

Systems analysis has many implications for debate. First, the affirmative team is able to admit that the proposed resolution has disadvantages as well as advantages. The basis for systematic decision making is the net benefits after taking account of both the pluses and minuses.

Second, for purposes of debate, the basis for decision cannot be simply the significance of the net benefits of the affirmative plan. Instead, there must be a comparison between the net benefits of the affirmative plan and the net benefits of an alternative system proposed by the negative. If the negative team is not prepared to defend an alternative system, the affirmative system must be accepted because the known risk of a system is preferable to the incalculable risk of having no system. This does not mean that the negative is now obligated to present a counterplan. The present system may be defended. The important point is that the negative must be prepared to show that the net benefits of continuing the present system, or any other system, are superior to the net benefits of the affirmative plan.

Net Benefits Case

Resolution
    Plan: policy changes in system
    Rationale:
        I. Net benefits of present system.
           A. Costs.
           B. Benefits.
       II. Net benefits of proposed affirmative system.
           A. Costs.
           B. Benefits.
      III. Relative cost-benefit ratios favor affirmative plan.

The net benefits case is an innovative approach to affirmative case construction. Unlike other cases discussed in this book, the net benefits case is not an evolutionary outgrowth of traditional debate theories and practices. It is a new approach derived from systems analysis as employed in contemporary governmental decision making. A primary distinction of the net benefits case is that it calls for the negative team to uphold a system of its own for purposes of deciding which competing policy system would produce the greatest net benefits, using a comparison of the cost-benefit ratios of the two systems as the basis of choosing one over the other. No automatic presumption or prejudgment exists in favor of any given system. The net benefits case argues that the net benefits of a proposal, after considering both the advantages and the disadvantages, is a better measure of the acceptability of a system than a consideration of the advantages alone.

Summary

Several methods of affirmative case construction have been described: traditional need-plan, comparative advantage, criteria-goals, and net benefits. Each has been examined within a context of historical and theoretical perspectives.

Imagine that instead of examining methods of proving that a debate resolution should be adopted, you have been examining how to sell real estate. The traditional need-plan case is comparable to persuading the judge that a trading post should be built in Indian territory where no white settlements have penetrated. In the absence of any policy, a new policy should be implemented. In order to build the outpost, you must show that a need exists, that the settlement would meet the need, and that it would be desirable.

The comparative advantage case would be comparable to persuading the judge to buy a store on Main Street because it does an impressive gross business. You would wait for the negative team to bring out the overhead costs and other disadvantages.

This analogy applies to the criteria-goals case as well because it is based on the comparative advantage theory. However, you would add that the store you are trying to sell meets certain standards for doing business.

The net benefits case is similar to trying to sell the judge a company on Main Street on the basis of its net profits, compared with the net profits of any store a competitive real estate broker might offer. If no other store is offered for sale, then yours is the only one for the judge to buy. As long as your store shows a profitable net benefit, the judge should buy it even if the negative team tries to reduce the attractiveness of the deal by thinking of ways to reduce your store's profits or increase its costs.

Questions for Discussion

1. Discuss the essential differences among the four types of affirmative case structures. What are the advantages and disadvantages of each?

2. Why is inherency the key term in the need-plan case?

3. What brought about the emergence of the comparative advantage case? In the comparative advantage case, how have the concepts of inherency and solvency changed?

4. How is the net benefits case similar to policy making in the real world? Provide an example.

Activities

1. Using one of the resolutions listed below or the current NFL topic, identify a case area caused by attitudinal inherency. Outline the problem and tell why the present system cannot solve it.

   Resolved: That the Congress should provide financial support for all private elementary and secondary schools.

   Resolved: That the method of selecting presidential and vice-presidential candidates should be significantly changed.

   Resolved: That the federal government should establish a comprehensive program to increase significantly the energy independence of the United States.

   Resolved: That schools should establish criteria for exemption from final examinations.

   Resolved: That the federal government should provide employment for all U.S. citizens desiring work.

   Resolved: That all U.S. citizens are entitled to a home and minimal nutrition.

2. Using one of the resolutions in Activity 1, define the terms of the resolution and decide on a case area for debate. What case format should be used and why?

3. Outline the affirmative case chosen in Activity 2. Research the contentions and gather evidence to support the case claims. Write a two to three minute speech on one of the contentions or advantages.

4. Draft a two to three minute speech covering the remaining contentions or advantages. Do not include a plan in this speech. At the end of this activity, you should have the body of a first affirmative constructive speech, short of the affirmative plan.

5. Using your affirmative case outline, draft an affirmative plan. Be prepared to discuss the plan in class and any potential problems in supporting the plan.

Chapter 8

Negative Analysis and Case Approaches

Objectives and Key Terms

After studying Chapter 8, you should be able to

1. Explain and present the arguments a negative should use against each type of affirmative case,

2. Explain topicality as an issue and demonstrate the ability to argue both for and against the topicality of a particular case approach on a topic,

3. Explain the characteristics of a counterplan and the guidelines for presenting one, and

4. Explain and demonstrate the use of plan attacks.

After reading this chapter, you should understand the following terms:

topicality	workability
extratopicality	disadvantages
straight refutation	counterplan
minor repair	negative strategy
defense of the present system	circumvention

T he negative in any debate has a single burden: to refute the affirmative case. The negative does not construct its own interpretation of the resolution and then show how that interpretation should be rejected. The affirmative's burden is the successful defense of its own case. The affirmative is not obligated to defend any and all conceivable interpretations of the resolution. Consequently, the starting point for negative analysis is to realize that negative responsibilities are fundamentally linked to what the affirmative does in the debate.

Negative Analysis

The negative obligation to come to grips with the affirmative case has traditionally been lightened somewhat by some varying assumptions about debate. One assumption is that a debate is like a courtroom trial. The affirmative is assigned the role of the prosecutor who must prove all charges, and the negative is assigned the role of defense, who pleads the defendant not guilty and then waits for the prosecutor to meet the entire burden of proof. Another possible assumption is that a debate is like a lawsuit over ownership of land or property. Here, the affirmative is assigned the role of claimant, and the negative is assigned the role of defense. In this assumption, possession is nine-tenths of the law: The claimant must prove the case to remove the defendant from physical possession of the land or property in question. The defense does not have the opposite burden of proving that the claimant is *not* entitled to take the property away. A third possible assumption is that a debate resolution is a proposal to change an existing policy. In this instance, the affirmative is assigned the responsibility of proving that the policy should be changed; the negative is given an initial advantage in that it is not required to prove that the resolution for changing the policy should be rejected.

These models of debate differ from one another in some respects, but they are similar in the common assumption that the affirmative has the greater burden of proof. This advantage for the negative is termed *presumption*. The present system is presumed to be adequate until and unless the affirmative fulfills its burden of proof by presenting a *prima facie* case for the adoption of the resolution. *Presumption* is an initial prejudgment that the resolution should not be adopted. Because that is the position upheld by the negative, this prejudgment favors that side of the debate.

Presumption is often left uncontested by debaters. Most of the time, it does not play an important role in a debate. It can be crucial, however, in case of a tie. Suppose that neither team in a debate presents convincing reasons to adopt the resolution or to reject the resolution. Each reason for or against the proposition is refuted by the other side. How can the debate be decided? A judge may vote for the side that has presumption. Traditionally, the negative has presumption because, all things being equal, one should not change the status quo unless there is a good reason. The reason this rule is followed is that chaos would result if laws were made without sufficient reason. Does presumption always reside with the negative (the team that is charged with defending the status quo)? Not always. In some situations, there is no status quo policy, and the presumption resides with doing something, even if the proposed policy is of doubtful value. In addition, if a present policy contradicts a deeply held value, then arguably presumption may reside against the status quo. Since presumption need not necessarily reside with the negative, affirmative teams can argue that presumption should be given to the resolution. In case of a tie, the resolution is more representative of the course of prudent change than the status quo. Obviously, the negative will wish to contend the contrary.

Some other general principles of negative analysis should be explained before specific negative approaches to various affirmative case constructions are explored.

Topicality

It is the affirmative's privilege to define the resolution and to select the case area(s) to be debated. Provided the affirmative interpretation is deemed reasonable, the negative has the obligation to accept the affirmative interpretation for the purpose of the debate. But what is a *reasonable* interpretation?

Although the negative has the burden of refuting any reasonable affirmative case, the negative is not obliged to accept any affirmative interpretation as reasonable. The negative may challenge the affirmative interpretation of the resolution as the basis for the debate. If that challenge is successful, the judge will conclude that, even if the negative fails to refute the specific affirmative case, acceptance of that case would not be the same as accepting the debate resolution.

Such challenges are called *topicality* arguments. The basic idea is that both teams are invited to a tournament to debate a common resolution. The topic for debate is bound up in the statement of the resolution. If the affirmative interpretation strays too far from the stated resolution, the negative argues that the affirmative is off the topic and that the case therefore cannot be used by the judge as the basis for accepting the resolution.

There are several different headlines that these arguments may carry in the negative speech. For example, the negative may charge that the affirmative plan fails to implement the debate resolution in its full, intended meaning. The headline for this argument is that the affirmative is guilty of incomplete analysis. For instance, consider the resolution "Resolved: That the federal government should exclusively control the development and distribution of energy resources in the United States." The negative could object to an affirmative plan aimed simply at building a coal slurry pipeline from the West to the Southeast, because such a plan apparently encompasses only the distribution of coal energy resources and not their development.

Justification

In addition to topicality arguments, there is also the line of argument known as justification arguments. The negative may charge that the affirmative rationale for change fails to justify the proposed policy. Suppose, in the preceding example related to the coal slurry pipeline, the affirmative plan also included itemized planks aimed at fulfilling all the terms of the resolution, but the affirmative case included advantages derived entirely from distributing the Western coal into the Southeastern region. In this instance, even though the affirmative proposes a topical plan, the negative could apply the rule that a change is not good in and of itself. Hence, only the distribution plank of the plan is justified because only that plank provides the claimed affirmative advantage.

A second negative challenge could be launched against affirmative advantages stemming from planks of the plan not necessary to implementing the resolution. The headline for this argument would be that the affirmative advantage stems from an extratopical plan plank. For example, suppose the affirmative plan for a coal slurry pipeline included a finance plank using the progressive income tax to pay for the pipeline construction. The negative could argue that no advantage stemming from using the progressive income tax may be used to justify the resolution because the advantage comes from an "extratopical" plank of the plan. You don't have to use the progressive income tax to implement a federal energy development and distribution proposal. Conversely, the advantage of progressive taxation may be gained equally from non-energy federal projects that rely on this tax.

Just as the affirmative might be unreasonable about claiming advantages from the means through which the resolution is implemented, the negative might be unreasonable in claiming that those means are not strictly part of the topic. If an affirmative instituted a program of water quality through taxing the sources of pollution, a picky negative might say that the resolution calls for guaranteeing water quality and that the affirmative program is a tax system. Clearly, taxing is necessary to produce an advantage, for without raising costs polluters will still pollute. This argument is unreasonable because any resolution is necessarily silent on some points. A resolution that requires the affirmative to guarantee water quality is silent on the means by which the guarantee is established. So long as the means of implementing the plan are not specified by the resolution, the affirmative has a right to select the method of plan implementation.

An advantage is only *extratopical* when the reason for adopting a policy resolution does not stem from the intrinsic policy but from a side benefit. In the example cited above, if the affirmative claimed as a rationale for the resolution that pollution taxes will generate revenue for the federal government, the advantage is extratopical.

Whenever the negative argues against the reasonableness of the affirmative interpretation, the rule "They who assert must prove" applies to them as well as to the affirmative. The negative may not simply assert *that* the affirmative interpretation is unreasonable; it must show *how* the interpretation is unreasonable. Likewise, to argue that a plan does not implement the full intent of the resolution or that the advantages are extratopical also requires the negative to show good reasons for the judge to accept these challenges.

The Plan and Its Rationale

In describing the affirmative approach to analysis, it was stated that an affirmative case must include both a plan for implementing the resolution and a rationale to support the adoption of the proposed plan. These elements naturally suggest possible negative avenues of attack in meeting the obligation to refute the affirmative case. Traditional debate theory outlines the general lines of negative attack to include the defense of the present system, repairs of the present system, the counterplan, straight refutation, and plan objections.

Straight Refutation

How does the negative go about attacking the affirmative case for change? The most direct way is simply to say that the affirmative reasons for change are wrong or lack proof. Thus, for every claim that the affirmative asserts is true, the negative offers a counterclaim asserting that what the affirmative says is false. Alternatively, the negative might say

When debating an issue such as water quality, the affirmative must prove that an example of pollution is typical of the status quo, rather than an exception to it.

there is not enough proof to tell one way or another. The technique is known as *straight refutation*. Straight refutation says to the judge that the resolution should not be accepted because there is insufficient positive evidence to indicate that claims supporting the resolution are true. Straight refutation leads the negative to make the following claims:

There is no problem in the status quo. This is often a difficult claim to prove. If the affirmative has done its homework, it will have isolated some problem. Remember, a resolution emerges from discussion of a topic like poverty, crime, the environment, or foreign policy. Usually, the status quo will be less than perfect in one of these major areas.

Instead of arguing that there is absolutely no problem, the negative may wish to modify its claim and say that *there is no significant problem in the status quo*. Significance is a quantitative and qualitative measurement.

To say that there is no quantitative significance to a problem means that even though a harm has been isolated, one cannot generalize to the conclusion that the entire status quo is jeopardized by the problem. For example, even if an affirmative is able to show an awful harm to the status quo policy, unless the harm is widespread, change cannot be said to be justified. Suppose the affirmative was able to show that the toxic chemicals at Love Canal were very harmful to the people there. Unless they can show that Love Canal is typical of the status quo, rather than the exceptional example, a national water policy might not be justified.

To say that there is no qualitative significance demands that the affirmative prove that the problem violates a significant value. Even if there are many instances of a harm, unless the harm can be shown to be something people care about, it does not constitute a reason for change. An affirmative may be alarmed about soft-drink machines that are broken and cheat people out of their money. However, given that the amount of change each person loses is small, there is no reason to worry about a national policy. Even if the affirmative claims a policy is important because it will resolve a number of individual harms, unless these harms are recognized as dangerous or deleterious to individual well-being, the case for change cannot be said to be significant.

Sometimes, the negative finds cause to question the affirmative's evidence. The affirmative might have evidence that suggests that the magnitude and quality of the harm is bad, but the evidence itself may be suspicious. Sometimes a biased source is used to establish the truth of the argument. For instance, if the American Enterprise Institute, a business-related research institute, claims that strikes are jeopardizing

American productivity, one might request a less biased, more independent source. Sometimes, sources rely on out-of-date statistics. Although it is true that in the early 1970s many experts talked about a fuel shortage, since then fuel prices have risen and energy seems to be plentiful. The negative should check to see if the harm still pertains. The evidence for establishing a harm may depend on theories that are subject to question. There has been a long-standing debate between meteorologists over the issue of climate. Some say the world will soon end in fire because the climate is getting hotter. Some say the world will end in ice because the climate is getting colder. There are signs both ways, and there are theories to support each conclusion. When consensus is not present in the expert community regarding the direction and nature of a harm, the negative has the right to request inaction on the grounds of significant uncertainty.

Another technique of refutation is to *deny that any problem that does exist will exist in the future.* Here, the negative makes the claim that the affirmative's inherency position is untrue. There are essentially two lines of argument against inherency. The first reasons from a new causal factor that has appeared on the scene and will cause the problem of itself to diminish. For example, the recent problem in the stock market is said by some experts to have resulted from computer trading. Very large quantities of stocks are indexed by computers to market conditions and can be sold quickly, without human intervention. When stock prices fall, these programs can accelerate the decline and perhaps cause the whole market to crash. Hence, experts say that federal regulation of computer trading is desirable. A negative position against this kind of case might say that the very decline of the market will lead to self-regulation of computer trading by people involved in the market. Because brokers have an incentive not to see a crash, they will regulate computer use. Thus, the negative argues that a new factor has arisen in the status quo that will diminish the original cause of the problem.

Another inherency tactic is to argue that *the present system could (if it wished to) channel more resources into existing programs and resolve the problem.* This method of refutation is known as defending the efficacy of the present system. The logic behind this argument is the idea that quantitative increases of effort are not the same thing as a bona fide change in the status quo. Sometimes, younger teams become confused by this argument. To challenge the affirmative team to prove that the status quo cannot adopt the affirmative plan is unreasonable. If the plan could never be adopted, then it could never work and the affirmative could not win. Similarly, to say simply that the status quo could change its mind and implement the affirmative plan if it wished is not to refute the fact that there is little likelihood for lawmakers to act differently, given inherent barriers to change. Rather than focusing on why the plan cannot be adopted or whether lawmakers might want to adopt the plan, a structural inherency argument simply says that putting more resources in the status quo programs would be just as good as the resolution, perhaps even better. Such an argument deprives the affirmative of its rationale for change.

Straight refutation also covers plan issues. Most often, the straight refutation on plan centers on the ability of a plan to solve problems or gain an advantage. These plan-meet-need or plan-meet-advantage arguments are frequently argued by the second negative, while inherency and problem arguments are introduced by the first negative. Ideally, the plan arguments would fit well with the inherency arguments, providing a complete rationale explaining why a problem can be solved so much by the status quo and why any plan can go no further.

Defense of the Present System

This line of argument attempts to establish that the present system as it exists is fully capable of dealing with the problem area. One way to defend the status quo is to offer a minor repair. A *minor repair* is an alteration of present policy that gains the affirmative advantage but involves substantially less change than that suggested by the resolutions.

In this line of argument, the negative proposes to compromise by admitting that it is possible for the present system to be deficient in some aspect of meeting its goals, but, if so, the existing mechanisms of the present system can be modified to achieve the same advantages the affirmative claims. In making this argument, the negative shows that the present system has sufficient policy foundations, including laws on the books and agencies in the field of concern, but what is needed is more extensive funding or manpower. It further charges that the affirmative policy change is unnecessarily radical, costly, or unwieldy.

If an affirmative is arguing, for example, that the United States should not intervene in the affairs of Latin America because such intervention is illegal and harmful, the negative might wish to repair the present system by tightening regulations on the Central Intelligence Agency's conduct of covert operations. Thus, the problem of illegal operations could be eliminated without an overall policy that would ban intervention. The point of the minor repair is to eliminate a problem without going as far as the affirmative plan or the resolution intends.

Straight refutation is often used in combination with defense of the status quo. Notice that straight refutation does not require the negative to give a consistent picture of the world. The negative makes a number of claims, not all of which are entirely consistent. The negative, arguing straight refutation, claims that there is no problem; that the problem is not significant; that the status quo is taking care of significant problems; that nothing can be done to alleviate the problem further. Why can the status quo work if the affirmative plan cannot? Why is something being done to alleviate a problem if it is truly insignificant?

Straight refutation always leaves these questions. Consequently, many negatives try to develop a consistent picture of the world. Rather than simply saying no to all affirmative claims, the negative tries to show how the present system is doing the best that can be done in a problem area. Whatever faults the status quo has can be easily repaired, but, beyond the parameters of present programs, no fruitful action can be taken. Thus, defense of the system uses straight refutation to deny claims about the significance of harm or the degree to which it inheres in present policy. It adds to straight refutation explanations about why present policy is working and cannot be improved. Straight refutation does not require the negative to say that the status quo is very good or working at maximum capacity, it simply demands that the affirmative be rejected because its claims are not substantiated.

Straight refutation can and often is used in combination with a defense of the status quo. The essence of this position is to claim that the opponent's claims about the inadequacy of the present system are wrong or that the present system can be made sufficient through minor repairs of existing mechanisms. These arguments tend to minimize or eliminate the significance of a claimed advantage. They also tend to show that the affirmative plan is not essential to cause the claimed effects. These lines of argument, in other words, are used to attack the significance and the inherency of the affirmative case.

Workability

A plan may not meet the need or gain an advantage because it is unworkable. Recall that the general requirement for a plan includes the following planks: (1) *principle,* or legislative intent, and (2) *mechanism,* or specific legislative proposal through which the principle is to be fulfilled. The mechanism should be described in the affirmative plan, including the specific agency to be used, its powers and limits, and its administrative details such as funding, personnel, and enforcement. All of these components must be present in the proposal, or the negative can challenge the workability of the plan. After all, how many times has the legislature passed a bill for purely political reasons, without including sufficient funds or staff to make the bill work or without an adequate enforcement plank to make sure that violators would be discovered and made to comply. Some laws that seem good on the drawing boards are unworkable in practice. Seatbelt laws, for instance, if enforceable, would undoubtedly save a large number of lives, but it is very difficult for a police officer to tell who has a seatbelt on. Moreover, given the shortage of police, no one can expect that a large amount of time will be spent enforcing the law.

Even the presence of these planks may not be adequate to insure a plan's workability if the negative can show that the affirmative provisions have holes in them, that adverse circumstances will occur, or that personnel with the necessary skills do not exist. The key to analysis of the workability arguments is to discover why, if the status quo cannot meet a problem, the affirmative thinks that it can. Perhaps there really is no good solution at present. For instance, the reason toxic poisons leak into the atmosphere is that there is no good way to contain them. If such is the case, despite the best intentions of the affirmative, in the long run toxins will harm as many people as if a program was never adopted.

Next, the plan may not meet the need or accrue the advantages claimed for it. There is a major distinction between this argument and the preceding one. This argument assumes that, although the plan itself may include all the necessary planks, the affirmative analysis has overlooked important factors in the present system that will continue to work against the effectiveness of the plan. The negative argument is that other causes exist for the problems noted in the present system instead of, or in addition to, those causal factors identified in the affirmative case. The plan will be hampered by those factors, just as the present system is, and so the advantages will not accrue. Suppose the affirmative plan is to remove a certain amount from the military budget, arguing that excessive spending causes budgetary imbalance. If the reduction in government spending reduces overall demand, industries might produce less, and this could decrease the number of jobs, which in turn reduces the number of people paying taxes. Reduced taxpaying increases the deficit. The plan would not resolve the problem of deficits because of the chain of cause and effect it starts in motion. In general, the negative should look for the persistence of causal factors not addressed by the affirmative plan but still substantial enough to perpetuate a problem.

Disadvantages

Disadvantages are very important arguments for the negative. Disadvantages are offered in almost all rounds of debate. A disadvantage, in effect, asks the judge not to vote for the resolution on the grounds that it will probably cause substantial harm. To the extent that the harm brought about by the resolution is greater than the good that it does, common sense dictates that the resolution be rejected. Even if the advantages are slightly ahead of the disadvantages caused, the resolution may be rejected if its residual benefit (the total amount of good it does over and above the harm it brings about) is not great.

Disadvantages can be used with straight refutation or with a defense of the present system. A disadvantage used in straight refutation simply says that any effort taken to resolve the problem, including that presently at work in the status quo, is wrong. Harms will result. No solution to a problem is presented by the negative in this context; no policy is defended because there is nothing more that should be done. A disadvantage coupled with defense of the status quo must be argued differently. With this strategy, the negative says that the status quo can provide a solution but that the resolution will bring about unique disadvantages. If a disadvantage applies equally to the affirmative plan and to the status quo, then there is no reason to reject the resolution on grounds of policy comparison. Both will get the disadvantage.

Disadvantages are generally of two types. The first argues that problems related to the topic area will become worse as a result of the affirmative plan. If the negative can demonstrate that the plan leaves the status quo worse off in the very area it is proposed to benefit, then a powerful argument has been made against the resolution. Consider this example: The affirmative argues that present immigration laws are bad because too many illegal aliens are crossing the border. The result is poverty and suffering for those who come to the United States and do not find jobs. The plan closes the southern borders of the United States. The negative might argue that the poverty and suffering will be worse for the same people because Mexico has poor economic conditions and has fewer employment opportunities than the United States.

A second mode of advancing disadvantages is to argue that the plan will bring about effects unanticipated by the affirmative. These effects are usually not directly related to the topic area. For instance, a comprehensive national water policy might clean up water pollution and save a large number of lives but still be undesirable. Why? Controlling water pollution is expensive. The Congress is in no mood to embark on new spending programs. Water pollution spending will detract from other programs that might be more cost-effective in saving lives. Especially at a time when Congress is talking seriously about deficit reduction and automatic cuts have been put into place at the federal level, additional funding may squeeze out important programs, like health research or famine aid. Thus, even though a water pollution program will accomplish goals internal to the policy, its external consequences might make it undesirable.

No matter what kind of disadvantage is argued, the negative should compose disadvantages in the following way: First, the negative must identify how the plan causes the disadvantage. Perhaps the affirmative brings about a new state of affairs that solves one problem but causes another. Perhaps the new state of affairs resolves the topic area problem in some ways but heightens it in others. Second, the negative should identify the impact of the disadvantage. Just as the affirmative must prove the significance of its claims to an advantage, so must the negative prove the significance of the disadvantage. Third, the negative must be prepared to balance the advantages and disadvantages. Where the areas of contention are similar, the comparison is made through discussing the magnitude of the advantage versus that of the disadvantage. Where the area of contention is dissimilar, the comparison must be made through discussing relative merits of the reasons for accepting the consequences of one policy as opposed to another.

Counterplan

Another avenue of negative argument is to present a counterplan. A counterplan is a proposed new policy for dealing with the problem area. It differs in major ways both from the present system and from the affirmative resolution. This strategy is used when the negative chooses not to defend the ability of the present system or minor repairs of the present system to measure up against the affirmative plan. It chooses, instead, to present its own alternative.

The negative should present the counterplan in the first negative constructive speech. It is considered inappropriate for the negative to withhold a major line of argument until after the affirmative constructive time periods have ended. To present a counterplan represents a total commitment to a basic negative position; it is not just another argument among arguments. The negative cannot initially argue that the present system with repairs is as effective as the affirmative plan in meeting the goals of the present system and then present a counterplan for changing the present system. Nor can the negative deny the existence of a need or problem and later present a counterplan in order to meet a need or problem.

The counterplan is a more popular negative strategy in debate practice than it was several years ago. In fact, once negative teams rarely used the counterplan against the traditional need-plan case because it meant that the negative gave up the presumption of the present system, one of its strongest positions. Today, however, influenced by systems analysis, the negative frequently proposes a counterplan as its preferred method for controlling and guiding inevitable change in the policy system of concern.

Whenever a counterplan is presented, it must be competitive with the affirmative plan. That is to say, it must be impossible for the judge to accept both the affirmative plan and the counterplan at the same time. Only when the counterplan is an alternative to the affirmative plan and not merely a supplement to it can the judge vote to reject the affirmative plan. If he or she can accept the affirmative plan and the counterplan at the same time, then the affirmative wins the debate because the counterplan furnishes little reason for rejecting the affirmative plan.

The counterplan should represent a superior choice. It should produce greater benefits, at lower cost or risk, than the affirmative plan. This is the main reason for proposing a counterplan. If the counterplan is an inferior policy choice to the affirmative plan, then it makes little sense to accept it. Conversely, if the counterplan achieves the affirmative advantages, but the affirmative plan accrues disadvantages not related to the counterplan, then the counterplan is superior.

Finally, and most important, the counterplan must be outside the affirmative resolution. Consider the example of the resolution that the federal government should exclusively control the development and distribution of energy resources. The negative counterplan must not fulfill these terms. If the affirmative plan is to build a federal solar power plant in the Arizona desert and the negative counterplan is to build it in Texas instead, then both policy alternatives would seem to fulfill the resolution. The judge must vote for the affirmative no matter which system seems most practical and cost-beneficial. In this example, both the affirmative plan and the negative counterplan implement the resolution. In order to stand as a reason to vote for the negative, the counterplan must implement a policy that is not compatible with accepting the resolution.

In each of the lines of argument described above, the negative takes a position for a particular policy with regard to the problem area. The negative stance is that if the present policy is inadequate, it can be replaced by a counterplan that is competitive, superior to the affirmative plan, and nontopical.

Negative Case Approaches

By now, you should be acquainted with the basic options open to the negative. Debate is like chess, however, in that just describing the moves of the pieces does not give you a very good feel for how the game is played. To understand how negative arguments are used in combinations, you must learn more about each of the case forms identified in the previous chapter. You will recognize many of the concepts already mentioned. The discussion that follows should give you a feel for the special ways negative positions can be constructed from individual arguments to make a powerful case against an affirmative justification for change.

The Traditional Need-Plan Case

Since this case is built on the stock issues, with presumption assigned to the present system, the negative approach to the need-plan case focuses on efforts to defeat the affirmative on any of the stock issues.

First, the negative argues that *there is no need for a change.* This corresponds to the first stock issue. In developing this argument, the negative first analyzes the need as presented by the affirmative to determine whether it is a *compelling* need. In this approach, the position of the negative is that whatever significance is presented by the affirmative, no harm to anyone is indicated. Even though the affirmative indicates that many people are being affected by the present system, the negative response is that these numbers merely describe the present system but do not indict it for a significant problem. In other words, "*So what* if a large number of people are involved in a policy area? What's the harm? There is no harm."

In addition to challenging the judgment of the affirmative that a compelling need exists, the negative also develops the argument that the need is not inherent in the present system. In this argument, the negative interprets the affirmative analysis to mean that only the plan can solve the need. Following this interpretation, the negative shows other mechanisms existing within the present system that could, if employed, solve the problem identified by the affirmative. Or the negative shows that the structure of the present system is not at fault, only surface elements, such as funding or administration.

When the negative shows that the affirmative has failed to prove or cannot prove (due to contrary arguments) that there is a compelling and inherent need, then this stock issue defeats the affirmative. Note that either dimension, harm or inherency, is enough to do the job.

Next, the negative argues that *the plan will not meet the need.* Assuming, for the sake of argument, that there is a compelling and inherent need in the present system, the negative directs its attack toward the solvency of the proposed affirmative plan: If the present system cannot solve the need, neither can the affirmative plan. This argument is developed on two planes. First, the plan is unworkable. In this argument, the plan is analyzed for internal deficiencies to show that, if enacted as a law by Congress, not enough detail has been included for the law to work to solve the need as outlined. There is no possibility for it to work due to an inept agency, vague or incomplete statement of powers given to the agency, insufficient resources allocated, or toothless enforcement provisions. Second, the plan will not overcome the inherent barriers. Assuming that a law could put the affirmative plan into effect, the causes of the problem identified by the affirmative case will not be removed by the plan. There may also be other factors within the present system not considered by the plan. For these reasons, the plan will not meet the need. Even if there is a compelling and inherent need, the failure of the affirmative plan along either dimension of workability or practicality is enough to swing the vote of the judge against the affirmative.

These are the major lines of argument against the need-plan case. Other lines of argument may, of course, be added, such as topicality and plan disadvantages; however, the above listed arguments against the need and the plan strike most directly at the essential structure and heart of the case.

The Comparative Advantage Case

In this affirmative case construct, the emphasis is on comparing the advantages of the affirmative plan with the present system. The negative task is to engage in this process of comparison and to add a second level of comparison, which is the disadvantages of the affirmative plan against its advantages. Just as a compelling need must be present in the need-plan case, so must the advantage in the comparative advantage case be significant. There is an even greater emphasis on quantifying the degree of improvement claimed for the affirmative plan than had previously been required in the need-plan case. Thus, the first line of negative argument is to show that *the advantage is not significant*. This argument is made along two dimensions, evaluative and quantitative.

The advantage is not significant if the claimed outcome of the plan is merely a change in the present system with no accepted value attached to the differences achieved. For instance, you may trade cars. Before you traded, you drove a Ford; now you drive a Chevrolet. That is a difference, but to what value? Similarly, when the affirmative points out that its plan will result in X differences from the way things are, unless it can prove that X differences possess some positive value, the advantage is not a significant one. The plan can be said to establish a factual outcome, but not an advantage.

The advantage is also not significant if the magnitude of change brought about in the present system is trivial when compared with the magnitude of the problem area under consideration. Some debate theorists even argue that an advantage is not proved to be significant until the affirmative specifically quantifies the amount of advantage which will be achieved by the plan—how many lives saved, for instance, or how much time saved toward achieving the goal of the present policy.

Next, just as an inherent need must be present in the need-plan case, so must a comparative advantage be unique to the affirmative plan. There is a subtle difference between the two approaches. In the need-plan case, the need must be of such quality that only the enactment of the affirmative plan can solve it. The absence of the plan is the cause of the problem. This is not quite true of the comparative advantage case.

Here, the negative cannot overcome the affirmative advantage merely by showing that other mechanisms (repairs, counterplan) can achieve the advantage. The advantage resides in the manner of solving the problem so that the affirmative plan is capable of meeting the goal faster, more economically, or more efficiently than the present system or any other system of policy. Therefore, the negative approach is to achieve the advantages of speed, cost, and efficiency in solving the problem area through methods of repairing the present system.

These two dimensions of the advantage may be combined by the negative. After showing that the advantage is not unique to the affirmative plan except in the area of speed in reaching the goal, for example, the negative could then undertake to show that extra speed has no value in the problem area of concern.

In addition to the negative lines of argument against the advantage, the negative can make arguments against the affirmative plan. The first line of plan argumentation is the same as the argument raised against the need-plan case: *The plan will not work.* The dimensions of the argument are the same: The plan has internal problems that make it unworkable, and the affirmative has neglected to consider important factors in the present system that will operate against the effectiveness of the plan.

Against the comparative advantage case, there is another type of argument available to the negative that is far more important because it introduces constructive reasons for the judge to decide not to accept the plan. The argument is that *the plan is disadvantageous.* The negative not only compares the affirmative advantage against the present system, but also compares the advantage against the disadvantage. If the disadvantage is more significant than the advantage, that is, if the plan causes worse problems than it solves, then the plan should be rejected. No other arguments surveyed thus far give the judge such a positive disincentive against the affirmative proposal. At best, the other lines of argument cast doubts on the extent of the affirmative claims. With the disadvantage argument, the negative can defeat the affirmative even if advantages are granted to the affirmative plan, as long as the disadvantages outweigh the advantages.

There are two general thoughts the negative draws on to establish a disadvantage. In the first, the plan is compared with the present system to determine what aspects of present policy are altered or replaced by the affirmative plan. The positive benefits of the present policy thus removed constitute advantages lost to the present system. In the second method of establishing a disadvantage, the plan is examined to see what new policy requirements are imposed on the present system. The negative aspects of the new requirements constitute disadvantages created by the enactment of the plan. These are separate types of disadvantages, one constituting what is lost to the present system and the other constituting what is created by the affirmative plan. Both these types of disadvantage may be seen as flowing from adoption of the affirmative plan and thus are reasons for rejecting it.

The Criteria-Goals Case

The distinctive feature of the criteria-goals case is its particular emphasis on the goals of the present system and on an asserted set of criteria for measuring policies designed to achieve the goals. Except for that emphasis, the case proceeds as a typical comparative advantage case, and the comments related to the comparative advantage case also apply to the criteria-goals case.

With regard to the goals and the criteria that constitute the distinctive feature of this case, there are several possible lines of negative argument. First, consider the identification of the goals of the present system. Goals are the abstract statements of the basic objectives of the policy system under consideration. In a pluralistic society, there are multiple goals, not all of which agree with each other. For example, in the energy area, among the national goals are these: (1) to develop new sources of energy, (2) to conserve remaining reserves of fossil fuels, (3) to increase the development of those reserves, (4) to utilize energy more efficiently, (5) to allocate supplies of energy fairly, and (6) to reduce environmental pollution associated with energy usage. In the criteria-goals case, as in the comparative advantage case, the affirmative identifies one or more of these goals as the ones on which the national government should place the highest priority. Consequently, the case rests on value judgments. As such, they are subject to interpretation and debate. The negative approach initially could deny the importance of the priority assigned to a goal or set of goals and argue instead for balancing those goals against equally important competing goals. It could argue for the rejection of the affirmative goals in favor of an entirely different, opposite goal.

Second, in addition to refutation of the affirmative goal, the negative may challenge the criteria by which the affirmative wishes the judge to evaluate its policy. These are the standards against which the policy should be measured, not the goal the policy is designed to achieve.

Negatives should be especially alert to guard against attempts by the affirmative to translate the terms of the resolution into the ideal criteria against which any policy should be measured. For instance, in the resolution "Resolved: That the federal government should establish a comprehensive program to significantly reduce energy consumption in the United States," the affirmative might declare that the goal of U.S. energy policy is to conserve energy (the precise object of the debate resolution). Next, the affirmative might argue that the criteria for measuring a program to achieve this goal include these: The program should be federal and comprehensive (the defining characteristics of the policy called for by the resolution). If the affirmative convinces the judge that these initial value judgments are true, then they hardly need to prove any rationale for change. The affirmative strategy is a trap designed in essence to lead the negative to prove that the resolution should not be adopted, a neat reversal of presumption in the debate.

When the negative is alert, however, it will go to great lengths to turn any one of the criteria around on the affirmative. By the same token that the acceptance of these criteria equals acceptance of the resolution, rejection of any of the criteria (or acceptance of an opposite criterion) equals rejection of the resolution. What the negative should attempt to do in this example is to argue that conservation is not the goal of United States energy policy, or at least not the only goal. Next, the negative should argue that any conservation policy should be private, local, state, or regional, rather than federal. Finally, the negative should argue that the policy should be differentiated and targeted rather than comprehensive. If any of these value judgments of the negative are accepted, then the resolution itself is undermined.

When the affirmative criteria do not duplicate the terms of the resolution, less is at stake in the debate regarding whether the criteria are accepted or rejected. You can be sure that the criteria are tailormade to describe the main features of the affirmative plan, however. Typically, the criteria will be initially argued in general terms, such as that the policy should be efficient, cost-beneficial, or equitable. Such terms are value judgments that could be applied to existing mechanisms in the present system by the negative in order to show that the affirmative cannot claim any unique quality for its plan based on such criteria. The negative could also assert additional criteria for measuring policies related to the problem area that tend to run contrary to the policy requirements called for by the resolution.

The Net Benefits Case

The net benefits case is another innovation in academic debate case construction. It is even newer than the alternative justification case. At the college level, recent surveys have indicated that a majority of judges at the National Debate Tournament preferred the systems analysis approach, in which their role is to choose between competing proposals for change. The authors' opinion is that, at the high school level (and even at the college level on a broader scope than the National Debate Tournament judges), a smaller proportion of judges would indicate such a strong preference for the systems approach. It could happen that the systems approach will continue to gain in acceptance and popularity. It remains to be seen, however, whether this innovative case technique will become widely used and accepted in the future.

The net benefits case is drawn from systems analysis, rather than traditional debate theory. Under traditional analysis, the debate judge applies standards of logic to determine whether the affirmative case is *prima facie* by virtue of carrying the burden of proof and overthrowing the presumption that favors the present system. Under systems analysis, evolutionary policy change is presumed, rather than a static continuation of things as they are. The issue of the debate is over who should determine the shape and direction of change, the affirmative or the negative. Hence, under the traditional approach to defeat the affirmative case, the negative need only defeat one of the stock issues. Under the systems approach, the judge expects the negative to present a policy system it is willing to defend in comparison with the affirmative policy.

For the time being, what should the negative do? Should it pursue the traditional stock issues method of defense and attack, or should it be prepared to advocate an alternative policy?

One answer is suggested by the attitude of many debate judges that theory is less important than the specific issues generated by a given debate. Many judges are willing to judge a debate on the basis of the guidelines accepted for use by both teams. If the teams do not agree on the theoretical rules to govern a judge's decision, then the judge considers the arguments over theory as just another area of clash in the debate. Just as the judge is impartial with regard to the resolution *per se*, he or she may also be impartial with regard to the theory that should inform the decision making.

Within this context, the negative should feel free to refuse to use systems analysis, if that seems to be the most productive strategy in a given debate. In the net benefits case, the affirmative demands that the negative either prove the superiority of the present system or present a counterproposal. What is suggested here is that, for many judges, the negative is not obligated to do either. The negative may appeal to the judge to evaluate the affirmative proposal on the basis of the stock issues and grant the usual initial presumption to the present system. In making this suggestion, we also urge the negative to be prepared to defend the theoretical soundness of this strategy to the judge when the affirmative clashes with its validity. The difference between judging an affirmative on stock issues and judging it on systems analysis comes down to whether each of the major affirmative burdens is assessed independently (the stock issues approach) or all are viewed as interdependent (the systems analysis approach). A stock issues judge will see if the affirmative has not proven one of its obligations and, if such is the case, she or he will vote negative. For example, if the affirmative does not prove that the problem is inherent, then there is no reason to adopt the resolution. The status quo will garner whatever advantage is claimed for the affirmative case. The systems analysis judge sees all questions as interdependent and as a matter of probable judgment. She or he is likely to see the debate this way: What percentage of harm uniquely attributable to status quo structures or attitudes can be eliminated by the affirmative plan? Is that increment of greater significance than the increment of disadvantage uniquely caused by the affirmative plan? Whereas the former perspective emphasizes issues in isolation, the latter looks at all issues in combination.

In taking this stance, the negative should note these potential avenues of argumentation against the net benefits case:

First, when the affirmative claims a certain cost-benefit ratio in favor of its plan, the negative should examine and analyze the basis of both the claimed costs and the claimed benefits. The objective of the negative is to maximize the costs of the proposal and minimize its benefits. These tasks correspond closely with the traditional division of labor between the two speakers on the negative team.

In examining and analyzing the claimed benefits of the affirmative plan, the negative should treat this avenue of argument in the same way as it would be in the comparative advantage case. Is the claimed benefit of the affirmative plan significant? Is it unique to the plan? Likewise, in examining and analyzing the cost-benefit ratio of the present system as presented by the affirmative, the negative should realize that this section of the affirmative case is designed to indict the scope and limitations of the present system. Hence, the negative attack should focus on the inherency and repairs potential of the case. The negative should seek to enlarge the cost-benefit ratio assigned to the present system and reduce the cost-benefit ratio assigned to the affirmative plan.

For attacking the plan, the negative strategy is no different from the comparative advantage case attack. The negative should analyze the workability and practicality of the plan and point out its disadvantages. The net benefits case itself admits that its plan has risks. The risks identified by the affirmative should be labeled as disadvantages. If possible, these risks should be amplified by the negative. Moreover, the negative should initiate additional disadvantage arguments. These added disadvantages serve not only as the warrant for a decision against the plan, but also to reveal incomplete analysis by the affirmative on case side, where the cost-benefit ratio of the plan was calculated without including the disadvantages pointed out by the negative.

All of the above discussion is meant to be suggestive and permissive, not directive. We do not advocate that the negative refuse to defend a policy system in the event that the affirmative presents a net benefit case. Everything said above hinges on the reservation that the negative *prefers* to engage in a debate against the affirmative case on the basis of the traditional stock issues.

The negative may decide to enter into the spirit of systems analysis and offer a policy system for comparison against the affirmative policy proposal.

From this perspective, both sides accept the notion of an everchanging policy system that requires continual attention and oversight by policy decision makers. Moreover, the systems approach views all policy areas as open systems related directly or indirectly to all other policy areas. Hence, it is not possible or desirable to consider a limited policy area as though it existed in a vacuum, in isolation from its position as only one policy area among many policy areas. In a sense, all policy systems may be viewed as interrelated subsystems that make up an even larger, more all-encompassing system. Consequently, changes in any policy system will have inevitable effects on all the others that must be considered.

Viewed in this larger scale, any policy change aimed at a particular policy area may be seen as simply a modification of the larger system. For instance, in the larger policy area of the energy field, the Department of Energy is the umbrella agency that covers smaller units dealing with nuclear energy, oil and gas, and other energy matters. Yet, the Department of Energy is not the sole decision-making agency in matters related to energy. Decisions made by other agencies may have profound effects on energy. The Department of Transportation, for example, makes rate and route decisions daily, which influence the consumption of gasoline by the nation's truck haulers and railroads.

The State Department and the National Security Council make decisions and recommendations to the President regarding foreign policy, which in turn could have great impact on energy matters. In the larger view, therefore, the basic issue in a debate over net benefits comes down to whether the judge wants to have the present system, plus the modification, advocated by the affirmative; or the present system, plus the modification, advocated by the negative.

When the affirmative presents a proposal to implement the resolution, and the negative presents a counterproposal, the traditional standards for judging are well known. What standards are applied to counterplans generally?

1. The counterplan must be a completely developed proposal for policy change. As such, it must consist of all the same essential components as an affirmative plan: a principle, a mechanism to achieve the principle, a designated agency, its powers, and administrative details.

2. The counterplan must be competitive with the affirmative plan. That is, it must be of such a nature that the judge cannot decide to accept both the affirmative and the negative counterplan simultaneously. The counterplan must be a substitute replacement for the affirmative plan, not merely a supplement to it.

3. The counterplan must also be competitive with the resolution. The counterplan must be of such a nature that adopting it could not reasonably be interpreted as an implementation of the intent of the resolution; it must be contrary in some essential area.

4. The counterplan must be demonstrably superior to the affirmative plan.

In traditional theory, whenever the negative proposes a counterplan, it waives any claim to the presumption of the present system. Support for a counterplan is a tacit admission that there is a need for change. Therefore, both sides must fulfill a burden of proof for the merits of their respective proposals for change by comparison with one another. Once the negative waives its claim to presumption, the affirmative does not necessarily lose just because it loses a stock issue like the workability of its plan or the potential disadvantages of its plan. The negative must prove the superiority of its own proposal, which is not presumed to be desirable or workable until the negative proves it. With no initial presumption awarded to the present system, the judge must accept some sort of change, even a defective plan, because both sides have agreed that a change is needed. The issue becomes, which proposal—the affirmative plan or the negative counterplan—has been shown to be the preferred change to adopt?

How are the alternative proposals for change compared? How does the debate judge determine which one is superior? Traditional theory also has a set of guidelines for this purpose. To be judged superior to the affirmative plan, the counterplan must meet the following requirements: It must (1) achieve the affirmative objective, (2) possess added advantages that the affirmative plan cannot achieve, and (3) avoid the disadvantages that the affirmative plan would accrue.

Because there is no presumption for one side, the judge has no guidance for situations in which the proposals seem approximately equal. In such a situation, there is no clear reason to vote for either side's proposal. Systems analysis has furnished some further guidelines for use in making decisions between competing alternatives:

1. Simpler systems are preferable to more complicated systems. In scientific terminology, the more *elegant* system is preferable.

2. Direct connections between the variables are preferable to indirect connections. For example, a proposal that claims advantages in the energy area should act directly on causative or highly correlated factors, rather than on peripheral components of the system. Indirect effects are both weaker and less predictable than direct effects. For example, it would be preferable to affect the decision-making process of the Department of Energy, rather than the Department of State, if energy conservation were the object of the plan.

3. Less risk is preferable to more risk. Greater change produces greater risks of unpredictable adverse effects.

4. A proposal that requires fewer changes or changes of smaller degree in magnitude is preferable to a proposal that requires more or greater changes in the policy system.

You are now ready to use the preceding foundation for understanding the negative approach to the net benefits case. Again, the negative is not required to support a counterplan, but may instead wish to defend the present system in the problem area of concern.

Defending the Present System as a System

Recall that, in the net benefits case, the affirmative first describes the net benefits of its proposal (considering both its benefits and its costs) and then does the same for the net benefits of the present system (also considering both benefits and costs). If, as the negative, you wish to defend the present system, your basic strategy should be to reverse the comparative values of the affirmative plan and the present system as described by the affirmative case. In other words, your task is to show that the cost-benefit ratio of the present system is superior to the cost-benefit ratio of the affirmative plan. In order to do this, you must (1) show that the costs of the affirmative plan are higher than claimed, (2) show that the benefits of the affirmative plan are lower than claimed, (3) show that the benefits of the present system are higher than claimed, and (4) show that the costs of the present system are lower than claimed.

A counterplan is constructed like an affirmative plan. The negative should state what action the counterplan intends to accomplish and list the mechanisms that the counterplan will use. For instance, if an affirmative case argues that nuclear reactors ought to be banned because of their potentially harmful effects, the negative might offer a counterplan to increase the safety of reactors. The negative would have to list the specific safety measures and specify the amount and sources of funding. The result of such a counterplan is that the negative could concede problems with the present system but argue that the benefits of nuclear power can be retained without safety problems if the counterplan is adopted. Note that the presentation of the counterplan does not require the negative to refute the affirmative case arguments. It does require the negative to defend its proposal, though. So, the first negative should show that the benefits of the counterplan will accrue and that the counterplan will work.

The bottom line of the negative strategy, whether in defense of the present policy system or in defense of a counterplan, is to establish a favorable comparison of the relative cost-benefit ratios for the negative's alternative system and against the affirmative plan.

Offering the Counterplan as a System

When the basis for decision making is the ratio between costs and benefits, what is important is to achieve the widest possible gap between benefits and costs. It would be a poor decision to adopt a policy that accrues a great advantage but at a cost the nation cannot afford. Conversely, it would be a preferable decision to adopt a policy that increased benefits to a moderate degree but at a cost representing an even lower percentage of investment of the nation's resources to obtain them. The cost-benefit ratio, not the absolute size of the advantage, controls the decision. This factor, combined with the axiom that less change is preferable to greater change, should ultimately work to favor the chances for the negative when it defends the present system (with little change), repairs of the present system (minor changes), or counterplans (especially those involving only moderate changes in the present policy system).

There are some potential strategic advantages to the negative for choosing to support a counterplan against a net benefits case. It may be difficult for you to make any inroads into a well-constructed and soundly evidenced net benefits case when you are bound to defend the present system in the problem area selected by the affirmative. However, when you present a counterplan, you can shift the momentum of the debate to the negative side. Just as the negative cannot predict exactly how the affirmative will decide to limit its interpretation of the resolution, neither can the affirmative predict all the potential policy changes the negative may wish to advocate in policy systems apart from (but related to) the energy area.

Just as the negative assumes the burden of proof with regard to a counterplan, so, too, must the affirmative take on a burden to refute the negative proposal. Of course, the affirmative is not obligated to prove that its proposed systematic change has a favorable net benefit when compared with all conceivable alternatives, but the affirmative is obligated to demonstrate the superiority of its affirmative plan over any particular alternative policy system advocated by the negative. Hence, the negative counterplan may become the central focus of the debate and rechannel the judge's attention away from the affirmative case. Your counterplan may force the affirmative to depart from the prepared comparison of its plan with the present system and engage instead in a time-consuming examination, analysis, and refutation of your counterproposal. Such a strategy favors the negative when the counterplan is thoroughly planned and well supported.

The strategic value of the counterplan is further enhanced when you consider that all policy systems are interrelated. The negative counterplan to change the policy guiding government actions in some other problem area may achieve the affirmative objective indirectly, while creating a powerful cost-benefit ratio in its directly related problem area—an advantage the affirmative plan cannot claim. This strategy is vulnerable to the lack of competitiveness, however. When the negative chooses such a counterplan, it must carefully analyze the reasons why the judge cannot accept both this type of counterplan and the affirmative plan.

Consider the following example: The affirmative plan is to ration domestic supplies of gasoline for nonessential driving for the advantage of energy conservation. The negative could choose to defend the present system of conserving gasoline voluntarily; however, the affirmative plan guarantees that a certain quantifiable amount of fuel will be conserved through mandatory rationing. The negative cannot accurately quantify the amount of gasoline the present system can conserve through voluntary measures, nor can it determine the optimal level of increased education/promotional costs to achieve added public cooperation in conserving significant increments of fuel. Therefore, the negative may choose instead to present a counterplan. A nontopical policy change might be to withdraw United States troops from NATO countries. This proposal, in conjunction with increasing conventional military weapons assistance and a stronger nuclear umbrella over Europe, would conserve the amount of fuel required to maintain troops in Europe and possibly also accrue advantages to international relations. This counterplan indirectly meets the affirmative objective of conserving fuel, because it directly affects U.S. defense and foreign policy.

This example illustrates the strategic advantages available to the negative by offering a counterplan. In defending the present system, the negative attempts to launch a frontal attack on the affirmative's strongest ground. However, in the counterplan, the affirmative is enticed to leave its strong indictments of voluntary conservation under the present system and instead attempt to compare the cost-benefit ratios of its plan and the negative counterplan. Also, as mentioned, this negative counterplan is vulnerable on the point of competitiveness. The negative must be able to show why the judge could not adopt the affirmative plan to ration gasoline, and, simultaneously, withdraw United States forces from European bases.

To recapitulate the negative counterplan approach to the net benefits case, the following outline represents the arguments the negative should be prepared to make.

1. State the affirmative policy objective.

2. Present the negative counterplan.
   A. Describe the principle and the mechanism of the counterplan, including the proposed agency, its powers, and administrative details.
   B. Demonstrate how the counterplan achieves the affirmative policy objective.

3. Demonstrate the cost-benefit ratio of the counterplan.
   A. Prove the benefits (advantages) of the counterplan
      (1) in achieving the affirmative objectives and
      (2) in achieving added advantages in other areas.
   B. Compare with the costs (disadvantages) of the counterplan.

4. Compare with the cost-benefit ratio of the affirmative plan.
   A. Minimize the benefits of the affirmative plan and
   B. Amplify the costs of the affirmative plan through
      (1) amplifying the admitted costs and
      (2) developing unadmitted costs (new advantages).

Summary

In this chapter, negative approaches to each of the affirmative case construction methods previously covered were discussed: traditional need-plan, comparative advantage, criteria-goals, and net benefits.

In summarizing the affirmative case analysis methods, a simple analogy was used: Suppose, instead of explaining debate case constructs, we were discussing how to sell real estate. Let us continue that real estate analogy. What would be the negative alternatives?

If the need-plan case is like trying to convince the judge to build a trading post on the frontier, the negative strategy would be to argue that there is no need to build it. Other means exist for delivering and distributing necessary supplies to the settlers. Settlers can probably get what they need by hunting, farming, or bartering with the Indians. Even if the judge decided a trading post is needed, the affirmative plan to build one would not meet the need.

If the comparative advantage case is like trying to convince the judge to buy a store on Main Street because it generates a high gross income, the negative approach would be to argue that buying that particular store would not be comparatively advantageous because the amount of income generated by the store is not significant and because the judge's other properties could be improved by better management or other internal repairs to generate more income without buying a new store. There are also disadvantages to buying the new store, so that any possible advantages would be outweighed—it has too high an overhead cost, for instance.

If the criteria-goals case is like the comparative advantage case, but with the added line of argument that the store in question meets some ideal set of criteria for doing business, then the negative approach would be the same regarding the comparative advantages portion of the case. Regarding the criteria-goals, the negative would argue that the possible purchase of a new store on Main Street should be considered in light of additional goals not included in the affirmative case, or even contrary goals, and that the affirmative criterion for judging the store as an ideal way of business is either incomplete or incorrect. "Generating a high gross income" may be the affirmative criterion for judging the potential attractiveness of their store, but the negative might want to add the criterion that "overall profits after overhead is deducted" should outweigh gross revenue as the criterion for deciding whether to buy the store.

If the net benefits case, based on systems analysis, is like an offer to sell the judge a store on Main Street based on its overall profit picture, then the negative must come up with a better offer or else lose the sale to the judge. The negative could try to convince the judge to defer a decision to buy anything at all and to consider only whether to buy or reject the affirmative offer. By contrast, the negative could play the game and make comparisons between alternative policy options, which include a conscious choice to refuse to buy a new investment on the grounds that the judge's present portfolio of holdings is better off without adding any new purchases. Finally, the negative could offer a counterplan to the judge. It could offer the judge a different piece of real estate. Also, since the decision to invest involves the judge's limited resources, and since the judge cannot buy every desirable piece of real estate, the negative could point out that other investment options exist. Since policy systems are interrelated, perhaps it would be wise to look at the other possibilities than the one in the area of the affirmative resolution. Then, the negative counterplan might be to offer the judge stocks, bonds, life insurance, or any other form of investment that would compete with real estate for the judge's investment decision. Finally, the negative would show how the counterplan is a superior option.

Overall, there is a variety of negative approaches available for any affirmative case construction. Study them carefully and be sure you exercise your best option.

Questions for Discussion

1. Define *presumption.*

2. Explain what role presumption plays in debate.

3. Does presumption always reside with the negative position?

4. Why are topicality arguments important?

5. What difference could it make to a judge if an affirmative plan plank is proven to be extratopical?

6. What difference could it make to a judge if an affirmative advantage is proven to be extratopical?

7. Of five options available for developing a negative position, which is the most useful and which is the most difficult?

8. Give some examples of quantitative and qualitative measures of significance and distinguish between them.

9. Differentiate between structural and attitudinal inherency. Give examples.

10. Discuss the differences between a negative position grounded in straight refutation and a negative position that is designed to conduct a defense of the status quo.

11. Identify two different ways a plan could be found to be unworkable.

12. A disadvantage can be argued in combination with straight refutation or with a defense of the status quo. What must the negative do differently in each instance?

13. When is it appropriate for a negative to present a counterplan?

14. What is the relationship of the affirmative advantages to the negative disadvantages in terms of the judge's assessment of the debate?

15. What are the requirements of a counterplan?

16. What arguments must be won by the negative to defeat the affirmative in a round of debate that features a counterplan?

17. What are the strategic values of the counterplan strategy?

Activities

1. Write a short paragraph that introduces a negative position for a debate. Use either affirmative cases developed for previous chapters or reconstruct an actual round of debate and develop a position other than the one that was employed in the debate.

2. Develop a list of the most common challenges you have observed in straight refutation. Which challenges are most useful? Which are least useful?

3. Write a disadvantage to any affirmative plan that spends a significant amount of federal tax dollars.

4. Deliver a speech that compares a disadvantage to an advantage. This short speech should be given once comparing disadvantages that are in the same area as the affirmative advantage.

5. Discuss the strengths and weaknesses of disadvantages you have heard pertaining to different cases on the current national topic.

6. Write a counterplan and practice delivering it. What cases would the counterplan be used for refuting?

7. Conduct a practice round of debate in which a counterplan is used as a negative strategy.

Chapter 9

Principles of Cross-Examination Debate

Objectives and Key Terms

After studying Chapter 9, you should be able to

1. Explain the obligations of each speaker in a round of cross-examination,

2. Explain and demonstrate the objectives of the cross-examination period in debate, both as the examiner and the witness, and

3. Participate effectively in a round of cross-examination debate on both the affirmative and negative sides.

After reading this chapter, you should understand the following terms:

clarification of points

exposing errors

obtaining admissions

role of questioner

role of witness

preparing for cross-examination

T he cross-examination format was introduced into academic debate during the third decade of this century. Because of its place of origin, it was frequently referred to as Oregon-style debating. For many years, it was regarded as innovative or experimental. However, in the past few decades, it has become the most common form of debating in high school and has recently been adopted as the official format for the American Forensic Association's National Debate Tournament on the college level.

Nature of Cross-Examination Debate

The format of cross-examination debate is similar to that of standard debate, except for the insertion of question periods. Consider the following:

First Affirmative Constructive	8 minutes
Negative Cross-Examination of First Affirmative	3 minutes
First Negative Constructive	8 minutes
Affirmative Cross-Examination of First Negative	3 minutes
Second Affirmative Constructive	8 minutes
Negative Cross-Examination of Second Affirmative	3 minutes
Second Negative Constructive	8 minutes
Affirmative Cross-Examination of Second Negative	3 minutes
First Negative Rebuttal	4 minutes
First Affirmative Rebuttal	4 minutes
Second Negative Rebuttal	4 minutes
Second Affirmative Rebuttal	4 minutes

On the college level, the format for cross-examination varies.

Conventions of Cross-Examination

The cross-examination period of a debate is a time during which there is direct confrontation between opposing members of the two teams. Certain conventions are observed. First, during the cross-examination period, one speaker asks questions and an opponent answers them. Neither the questioner nor the person being questioned should attempt to abuse that time by extended speechmaking. If, however, the questioner does not control the period, that is likely to happen.

Second, this period is a time to establish an attitude toward yourself on the part of the opposition and the judge. Sarcasm, evasiveness, browbeating, or generally obstructive behavior does not advance your status in the round. Although there will be many occasions when the opposition will give you ample reason to retaliate with behavior of this sort, remember that doing so makes you seem immature. No one finds it easy to pass up the opportunity to be clever with words or to make the other person look inadequate. However, blatant bad manners are no more in order in the cross-examination period of a debate than in any other formal setting.

The cross-examination period is one in which a public question-and-answer exchange takes place for the purpose of influencing a judge. As a consequence, the two debaters should not face one another, but rather stand side by side and face the judge. There should be no conference by either of the debaters with either of their partners during the exchange. If a question is asked that has to do with an argument or piece of evidence advanced by your partner, it is improper to get help from your partner in answering. There is nothing wrong with the response, "I don't know" or "My partner can deal with that better than I." Of course, if such responses are used too frequently, they will weaken your impact as a team member, but they may sometimes be the best answer.

The cross-examination period is not meant to give an opportunity for direct argument between the two debaters involved. To argue with one another is not only juvenile, it is counterproductive. Both the person questioning and the one responding should always remember that cross-examination is the time when you can look really good. It is the time in which you can establish your control of the situation and demonstrate poise and a sense of being in command. But it is also a time when you can erase all those positive impressions by losing your temper and getting upset. Try to avoid such negative behavior.

Objectives of Cross-Examination

There are essentially four objectives in a cross-examination: (1) to clarify points of the opposition's position, (2) to expose factual error or unsupported assertions made by the opposition, (3) to obtain damaging admissions from the opposition, and (4) to set up arguments for use in subsequent speeches by you or your partner. All of these objectives must be pursued in a civil manner.

To Clarify Points

Clarification is an important objective. Probes that begin with such phrases as "Would you explain the use...," "State briefly the ultimate goal of...," "Did you mean that...," or "Restate the...," are valuable in the course of the debate. They allow the opposition to clarify, and they keep you from wasting time and looking foolish by arguing a point that you have misinterpreted. Probes such as these serve to clarify the thinking process by which the opposition arrived at a given position. You cannot attack arguments you do not understand; they must first be clarified and then attacked.

One of the objectives of cross-examination—in the courtroom as in team debate —is clarification.

To Expose Errors

A second kind of clarification that cross-examination can provide is a clarification of evidence. This clarification process, however, should be utilized to expose factual error or lack of substantiation by the opposition. Evidence can be attacked in many different ways. In standard debate, you can criticize evidence, call for clarification and repetition of certain pieces of key evidence, and challenge interpretation of evidence, but you have no guarantee that the opposition will respond. In cross-examination there is no way for the other team to avoid response without impeaching the team's evidence through silence. Remember in the cross-examination period that since evidence is the cornerstone of support for any argument, undermining evidence is a key way to attack an issue. There are four basic attacks against evidence that you can set up through skillful cross-examination questions:

1. The source of the evidence itself may need to be questioned. For example, you might question your opponent in the following manner: "You read evidence from Dr. John Smith in support of the point that solar energy is a viable source of energy for home and industry. What was the date on that piece of evidence?" "Are you aware that six months after that date, Dr. Smith testified before the House Energy Committee that it would be ten years before solar energy would be cost-beneficial on a mass production basis?" Such a line of questioning creates doubt about source credibility. Similarly, if you are aware that the source of the evidence is biased or has traditionally taken the opposite view from the one in evidence, then your questions should move in that direction. The date of the source, the reputation, or direct qualification may also be questioned.

2. You can aim your questions at the content of the evidence. If the evidence is an empirical study, a series of questions on method, the existence of counterstudies, and the size of the sample should be employed. When the evidence is conclusionary, beware of qualifiers in the body of the quotation. The affirmative, for example, could advance an argument on regulation of health care that the present system forms an industrywide cartel precluding the development of prepaid group practices. Listen to the evidence, and question as follows: "In the evidence on an industrywide cartel, please reread the first sentence. Does that sentence use the words 'cartel *may* exist'?" Be aware on this line of questioning of any kind of language in the body of the evidence itself that qualifies its impact: words such as "some," "few," "indications are," and "seem to be."

It is stronger, of course, if you can point out the words by calling for a re-reading of the specific point in the evidence where the qualifier occurs, rather than going on a fishing expedition by asking for a general rereading.

3. Another form of questioning is to pinpoint issues in the case that were not evidenced during the initial presentation. Your approach here is to repeat the opposition's contention and then ask for the repetition of the specific piece of evidence used on that point. You might also ask during cross-examination for additional evidence. For example, "You claim that the United States will be severely energy-deficient by 1995. You give us a projection by Senator B. Since that one contention constitutes the basis for the entire affirmative plan, do you intend to read statistical evidence to support it?"

4. A final line of questioning is to ask about the link between data and claim. Too frequently people have a tendency to assume that the evidence read by the opposition says what they indicate it says. You must listen to the evidence and pursue questions in cross-examination. For example, in a debate on a policy for energy self-sufficiency, the affirmative argues that current federal programs should develop alternate energy sources but are inherently incapable of solving the problem. They then read evidence from a congressional hearing stating that the administrators of the existing programs are inefficient. Your obvious line of questioning in cross-examination would be to establish that the piece of evidence does *not* establish the point advanced by the affirmative. With this line of questioning, you are not attacking the point the evidence *does* make; you are establishing the failure of that piece of evidence to prove what the affirmative has asserted.

To Obtain Admissions

A third goal is to find answers that will damage the opponent's case or plan. This particular objective is difficult to achieve. No opponent is going to confess to the truth of an attack. One should not expect the other team to give up. One should not be frustrated when an opposing speaker does not respond directly to a line of questioning that is damaging. Do not belabor a line of questioning. Simply make your point, and then move on.

Consider a sample cross-examination on the topic of medical care. The affirmative advocates a national system of health maintenance organizations. It establishes the justification for preventive or group care:

Shorter hospital stays reduce iatrogenic or hospital-born diseases. A line of questioning to employ might be similar to this:

> Q: Iatrogenic diseases are the result of exposure to germs that thrive in the hospital environment, right?
>
> A: That is right.
>
> Q: You tell us that a significant number of people are the victims of iatrogenic diseases each year, right?
>
> A: Yes.
>
> Q: Is it your contention that these diseases are contracted because the person is in the hospital?
>
> A: Yes.
>
> Q: And you claim a significant reduction in this type of disease because you reduce the number of days a person will be in the hospital? I believe you said three days will be average under your plan.
>
> A: Yes.
>
> Q: Will you please read the piece of evidence in which it is specified that iatrogenic diseases are only contracted after the third day of hospitalization?
>
> A: Uh . . . I didn't read such a piece of evidence.
>
> Q: Oh, I see. Well, read the piece of evidence which showed an empirical study demonstrating that people who stay in hospitals for more than three days are more likely to contact iatrogenic diseases than those who stay only three days or less.
>
> A: I didn't read that, either.

At this point, you have the admission you want. No causal link is established by the initial presentation. You may invite the affirmative to bring up such evidence later, or you may simply go on to other things. You have established a strong beginning point for an attack on the causality of the affirmative advantage.

Similar lines of questioning can be designed to show appeals to emotions, begging the question, shifting ground, exaggeration of claims, and internal dilemmas or contradictions. A particularly strong line of questions might be developed for the second negative speaker on plan attacks. An affirmative cross-examination that skillfully takes the negative speaker through reestablishing the inherency argument and then quickly pushes back to disadvantages will expose a contradiction or at least a dilemma that the negative will then have to deal with.

To Set Up Arguments

Underlying each of the first three objectives of cross-examination is the fourth and most vital one. Regardless of what you establish in the questioning period, it must set up a line of argumentation that can and will be used in subsequent speeches. Surprisingly enough, many debaters fail to use the results of what they establish in cross-examination. If you gain an admission, it may certainly speak for itself at the time, but you must review it and tie it in with a specific argument. Its significance must be demonstrated—you must help the judge see that the admission is as damaging as a piece of expert testimony would have been. In other words, the results of cross-examination must be used as material evidence in the debate itself. Use statements such as "The negative speaker herself admitted under direct cross-examination that she had no counterstudy to submit"; or "The affirmative speaker admitted to you in cross-examination that he could not tell us how many people are harmed by the conditions he described"; or "Remember that first cross-examination period in which the affirmative admitted that there were no structural barriers to adopting such a system right now. I believe you will agree with me that this is the most important thing the affirmative has said, for in this statement the affirmative forfeits the burden of proof that is their obligation in today's debate." These statements give the judge a direct relationship between what was said in the cross-examination and what was established in the debate. They get the cross-examination period into the mainstream of the debate.

In order to employ cross-examination responses in later speeches, debaters should form the habit of writing down important answers. Not only should the person questioning take notes, but so should the colleague of the person being questioned. It may become crucial later in the debate to have an accurate record of what was said.

Cross-Examination Techniques

Preparation

Preparation is important for good cross-examination debating. There are few debaters who would approach debate without researching their own case carefully and attempting to anticipate what kind of cases they might meet. Rarely does a debater go to a tournament without practice rounds, yet it is not infrequent for debaters to enter into a cross-examination debate without specific preparation for the cross-examination period.

Once you establish an affirmative case, you and your partner should think about possible opposing negative positions. This practice should suggest possible cross-examination questions that the negative might ask after hearing your case. Once you identify some questions that might be encountered, then design appropriate answers. By the same process, you should think of possible questions that might be used in the second examination period and design answers for them. It is not enough to prepare a series of questions; you should anticipate the questions that might be asked and practice answers.

At one NFL National Tournament, a first negative speaker developed a very strong topicality argument without thinking it through to cross-examination. The first question from the affirmative was for the negative to identify an affirmative case that would meet the definitions provided by the negative in the topicality argument. Because the negative had not thought this through, the first negative could not provide an example that could withstand challenges by the affirmative questioner. The second affirmative speaker used this exchange to argue that the definition offered by the negative was unreasonable and that the topicality argument should not be accepted. All the negative needed was one example to win the argument.

Role of Questioner

Consider the role of the questioner. There are a number of guidelines that should be remembered for the role of questioner.

1. Begin the cross-examination period with a question that will capture the judge's attention.

2. Conclude the cross-examination period on a high note. Do not keep questioning about trivia just because you have time left. If you have established a psychological advantage and still have time left, stop.

3. Employ a line of questioning leading to your point. That is, ask for a series of small bits of information that will, when accumulated, lead

to your conclusion about an argument. The concluding question of each line of questions may serve as a summary of what you have accomplished, such as "In view of these facts, is it still your position that. . . ?" Do not expect your opponent to admit that your conclusion is correct, but lead her or him to the point that your judge will accept it.

4. Remember that you are in control of the questioning period. Do not allow your opponent to take control by asking questions, conferring with a colleague, or practicing evasion. When such ploys are used, interrupt the speaker with firm courtesy. Remember, do not lose your poise, but do not lose control, either.

5. Confine yourself to asking questions. Phrase your questions simply and concisely. Do not ask open-ended questions that impart an opportunity to filibuster. Phrase your questions in such a way as to call for short and specific answers, preferably *yes* and *no*.

6. Ask only one question at a time, and get an answer to each question before asking the next one.

7. Use a quiet, moderate style in order to encourage the witness to relax and enter into a fair exchange about arguments in the debate. If you come on too strong, you will set up an adversary atmosphere that might lead to hostility.

8. Avoid questions to which you do not know the answer, with the exception of questions to clarify points in the actual plan or case of the opposition. One questioner gave an opponent an excellent opportunity by asking, "You claim that P.S.R.O.'s unfairly limit the expansion of health maintenance organizations. Can you give even one example of an HMO that was limited by a P.S.R.O.?" The witness advanced the affirmative case by replying, "Yes, I can. I have the records of the HMO in a midwestern city that was kept from. . . ." The point here is that if your own knowledge is inadequate, you may open an opportunity for the opposition with a question to which you do not know the answer.

9. Do not attempt to establish your reputation as the budding Perry Mason. Strutting about, pointing accusing fingers, ridiculing the witness, and putting on a performance may make a good scene in a movie, but it has no place in an academic debate.

Role of Witness

Another aspect of cross-examination debate is the role of the person being questioned. The witness in the cross-examination period has a viable part to play and should be prepared to perform in such a fashion as to win the period. This can be better insured if you prepare in advance by anticipating questions.

1. The witness should stand tall, look directly at the judge and audience, and speak loudly enough to be heard clearly. Every nonverbal message sent should indicate a relaxed, yet alert, individual. A hanging head, evasive eye contact, and soft voice all indicate a person who is unsure or untruthful. Either position does nothing to advance your position.

2. The role of witness is one of answering questions. You are not free to ask questions during this time. There is an exception, however, that should be remembered. If the question was phrased in a confusing manner, if it asked for several items of information, or if in any other way it was difficult to respond to, then you not only may, but you should ask for clarification.

3. Any fair and reasonable question should be answered. When you are the witness, to employ deliberately vague or evasive tactics will only weaken your position eventually. Do not hedge. If you know the answer, give it. If you don't know the answer, say so.

4. It is permissible to qualify an answer, but this should be done briefly. Don't give these qualifications unless they are necessary for clarification. A good technique to use is to state the qualification ahead of the answer. For example, the question "Do you believe that the federal government should control private enterprise?" might best be answered, "To the extent that the federal government is responsible for the safety and well-being of the nation's citizens who are being endangered by a lack of energy, I think the federal government should have a role in the regulation of that private industry."

5. The witness should never underestimate the result of an answer nor lose sight of the fact that every question is designed to weaken her or his own case or help the case of the opposition. Be on guard.

6. When you are the witness, you may decline to answer questions that are ambiguous or loaded. The old technique of posing questions of

the "Have you stopped beating your wife yet?" variety is a trap, and you do not have to respond to them. However, you should decline to answer by explaining that the question is not clear or is leading and ask for it to be rephrased.

7. Do not volunteer information. Answer only the questions that are asked and do so as briefly and concisely as possible. Do not anticipate the next question by answering it ahead of time. You may put arguments into the hands of the opposition that way. Remember, even if the question gets close to a weakness you know your case has, there is no guarantee the opposition will see it. Just wait; don't point the way for them.

The cross-examination period in a debate can be a time of enjoyment and excitement. It is also a time designed to accomplish a valid set of objectives. When the examiner and the witness both understand these objectives, the result is a better debate.

Summary

Cross-examination debate is an excellent format for learning the skills of argument. It enables debaters to question one another and thereby learn the skills of public defense and attack. Like any other debate activity, if it is not handled well it can result in unfortunate exchanges that mar the intellectual excitement of argument. With experience and maturity, however, you should be able to handle even the most tense situation with style and class.

Questions for Discussion

1. What is the value of cross-examination in debate?

2. Outline the four objectives of a cross-examination period.

3. When trying to clarify evidence in a cross-examination period, what are four attacks that can be set up? Provide an example of each.

4. Because the negative gains a tremendous advantage during the negative block, how can the cross-examination of the second negative speaker be used to help the first affirmative rebuttalist? Provide an example.

5. When you question an opponent, why is it important not to ask open-ended questions?

6. It is said that the questioner should not ask questions for which the answer is not already known. What would be the harm of asking a question just to gain more information or to explore an argument?

7. As the witness, you are advised not to volunteer information unless it is asked for specifically. Why?

Activities

1. Using the articles you collected for Activity 4 in Chapter 6, prepare a list of questions you would ask in a cross-examination period.

2. Using your affirmative speech from Activity 4 in Chapter 7 and your negative speech from Activity 4 in Chapter 8, outline questions you feel an opponent might ask. Now outline your answers.

3. Using your flow (notes) from previous affirmative speeches, outline cross-examination questions. Write down what you anticipate the answers to be. How would you use these in your next rebuttal speech?

4. After having participated in a cross-examination debate, go back and review the debate. What questions or answers served you well in the cross-examination periods? Where you had problems, rework your questions or answers.

Chapter 10

Lincoln-Douglas Debate

Objectives and Key Terms

After studying Chapter 10, you should be able to

1. Explain the duties of each speaker position in Lincoln-Douglas,

2. Explain and demonstrate the negative case strategies,

3. Explain the different styles and their appropriateness for particular rounds, and

4. Explain and delineate between the different types of value propositions.

After reading this chapter, you should understand the following terms:

values

negative clash

negative case

constructive speech

rebuttal speech

use of evidence

tournament

judging

policy topics

value comparison topics

single value topics

L incoln-Douglas debate utilizes a two-person format centered around a value proposition. It is far different from team or policy debate not only in its format, but in its style as well. To gain a clearer understanding of Lincoln-Douglas debate, it is important to examine its origins.

History of Lincoln-Douglas Debate

Lincoln-Douglas debate can be traced directly to the famous debates between Stephen Douglas and Abraham Lincoln for the Illinois State Senate race in 1852. In these debates, which would often last over three hours, the affirmative spoke for an hour, followed by an hour and a half negative stance and then a half-hour closing time for the affirmative.

Since then, the Lincoln-Douglas format has been largely limited to political candidates. You may have seen presidential debates on television or witnessed local candidates debating for the office of mayor. But whatever the purpose, this format has long served the needs for the exchange of ideas on important issues of the day. However, it was not until the 1980 National Forensic League Tournament that high school students were able to use the Lincoln-Douglas format.

Since that time, over 100,000 students have competed at local, state, and national levels. At first, comparisons to team debate were the most understandable and appropriate methods for studying Lincoln-Douglas. But now, theory unique to value debate in general and Lincoln-Douglas in particular has been developed and will be further discussed in this and in subsequent chapters.

One of the reasons for the creation of Lincoln-Douglas was to offer an alternative to team debate. Because of this, Lincoln-Douglas debaters only discuss propositions of value. This important difference deserves further attention. To begin, what is a value?

Value Explanation

The *Oxford English Dictionary* defines *value* as "something of worth, to be highly regarded or held in great esteem." In terms of debate, a value is a belief. You may believe in the value of helping a neighbor or donating money to charity. On the other hand, you may believe that laziness and selfishness are bad or undesirable values. These values can be discussed, debated, and argued but they can never be proven true or false. This is one of the most important aspects of any value discussion. You may, for example, believe in the value of a strong military. You can explain your belief by discussing its importance, effectiveness, necessity, even social acceptability, but you can never prove its truthfulness or falsity.

It is also important to understand that values are debated in terms of a specific situation. Consider the topic "Resolved: That gun control is unjustifiable." The debaters will clash over the value of gun control. The affirmative may offer arguments designed to show that owning guns is a good or positive value:

1. "Gun control is unconstitutional."

    Such a statement is designed to show that because gun control is unconstitutional or illegal it should therefore be considered unjustifiable.

2. "Guns are sometimes necessary for personal protection."

    This statement is designed to demonstrate that people have a right to protect themselves in this case by owning a gun. It correlates with the constitutional argument and therefore appeals to the same illegal/unjustifiable argument but with more pathos or emotion.

3. "Many people use guns for sport and recreation."

    This statement is designed to eliminate any possible negative attitudes the judge may have towards guns by showing that they can be fun and safe. It should seem unjustifiable to want to limit or control something that can provide enjoyment in a safe manner.

The negative speaker will argue against the topic by showing the value of gun control to be justified. He or she may make the following arguments:

1. "We currently allow for some gun control to insure that felons cannot purchase guns."

    This statement contradicts the affirmative's first point by stating that properly used gun control does not violate the intent of the constitution and therefore should not be considered unjustifiable.

2. "Many senseless deaths occur from the improper use of guns."

This statement holds two values in contrast: the value of the constitutional right to bear arms as opposed to the value of human life. In developing this argument, the negative would need to state clearly that these two values do not have to be in opposition and that people can maintain their constitutional rights as well as insure that people know how to handle guns safely.

In order for any of these arguments to be truly persuasive, you would need to provide information and further analysis. But you can begin to see that values are debated in practical terms, such as illegality, enjoyment, and expediency—never in terms of truth or falsity. Second, values are debated in reference to something. The values inherent in such actions as gun control, censorship, privacy, and segregation can be debated. The easiest way to insure that the value of something will be debated is to define clearly all of the key terms of the resolution. This is the first responsibility of the affirmative and is further discussed in the next section.

Speaker Duties

The following timetable will provide you with a more thorough understanding of each speaker's position:

Affirmative Constructive	6 minutes
Cross-Examination (Negative vs. Affirmative)	3 minutes
Negative Constructive	7 minutes
Cross-Examination (Affirmative vs. Negative)	3 minutes
First Affirmative Rebuttal	4 minutes
Negative Rebuttal	6 minutes
Second Affirmative Rebuttal	3 minutes

Constructive Speeches

As in standard or cross-examination debate, all definitions and arguments must be presented in the affirmative constructive. Definitions provide a framework for analysis by placing strategic limitations on the interpretation of the topic.

In debating the topic "Governmental invasion of individual privacy is justifiable," it would be necessary to define the terms *governmental, invasion, individual privacy,* and *justifiable.* The first three terms are limitation phrases that enable the debaters to focus on the most important aspects of the topic. The affirmative could not possibly discuss all aspects in just six minutes. Therefore, limitations are imposed. However, definitions must be fair enough to allow the negative an equal chance to present its side. Defining the phrase *individual privacy* as "relating to personal possessions such as a purse or wallet" would be too limiting because a person's home and car could not be debated under this definition.

The next term is *justifiable.* This type of word can be found in most value resolutions. It has been called the "value" or "evaluative term" by college debate directors Robert Norton and Jack Perella. Its function is to enable your opponent and judge to evaluate your interpretation of the topic. If you were to define *justifiable* as that which is legal you would have a very difficult time upholding the resolution because in many instances governmental invasion of privacy is not legal. If, however, you defined *justifiable* as "that which is necessary," then you would have a much easier time offering examples that support this interpretation.

When writing a case, consider that you are building a house. The first thing to construct is your foundation. The foundation is the definitions of the limiting terms. Your foundation supports the walls or arguments. Your arguments support the roof or topic. Obviously, a weak definition will poorly support the topic, while a strong definition will outlast any negative assaults. The value term is then applied to see if your interpretation is strong. Naturally, you will not ask the judge to view your interpretation in light of its weakest points; that is for the negative to mention. You will want to present your case in the most positive terms possible. A solid value term will greatly enhance the judge's impression of your case.

The next aspect of any constructive—affirmative or negative—is the arguments. Much like team debate, arguments are constructed by use of evidence and analysis, but often with a much different emphasis. You will not be expected to have a highly detailed and substructured case as you would in standard or cross-examination debate but, as in these, you are expected to present a well-organized case. For example, using the gun control topic, if you were going to argue that gun control is unconstitutional, you might structure your argument like this:

1. Read the amendment allowing citizens the right to bear arms.

2. Read a short quote stating that gun control is a violation of a citizen's rights.

3. Analyze that because one has the right to bear arms, gun control is unjustified.

Evidence is important in Lincoln-Douglas, but so is analysis and persuasion. You don't need to read everything about the topic, just the most appropriate information.

During cross-examination in Lincoln-Douglas debate, you can question the values underlying the opposition's arguments.

Cross-Examination

The first cross-examination is conducted by the negative. There are many similarities between cross-examination in Lincoln-Douglas and cross-examination in cross-examination team debate. The person who is questioning should make sure only to ask questions, never to make statements, such as "I have read that gun control doesn't work; therefore, you're wrong." Even though you may be tempted to make statements during cross-examination, save them until your next speech.

Other similarities include clarifying information and prodding for weaknesses. You may not have heard everything that was said, so you will want to be sure to ask about whatever points you missed. After filling in the missing information, you will want to begin exposing weaknesses in your opponent's thoughts. Weaknesses can range from poor use of evidence to illogical analysis. Though there are many similarities, there is one area of cross-examination that is unique to Lincoln-Douglas: the questioning of values.

You may be debating the topic "Resolved: The American media do not reflect American values." Suppose the affirmative presented a case in which he or she stated that one of the most important of American values is truth. Next, the affirmative stated that the news programs mostly present stories of death, destruction, and bad fortune. He or she then stated that because the American people are tired of seeing this bad news, the American media do not reflect American ideals. Because the affirmative has also read a great deal of evidence to back up each claim, there is little sense in spending a lot of time questioning it. However, you can question the underlying or most important value. Remember, truth was defined as an important American value. You might want to ask, "Why don't the American people want to view this bad news? Is it because they are disgusted with it and no longer want to face it? Are the media presenting lies to the American public?" At this point, you may have a difficult time in getting the affirmative to answer your questions because you are now exposing a fundamental weakness in the affirmative's value system. American values were defined as being predominantly truth-oriented, but the examples were taste- or preference-oriented. Such a conflict with the value term will make it very difficult for the affirmative to win. As blatant as this example is, it is not uncommon to find such mistakes, especially at the first tournaments of the year.

Negative

As in standard and cross-examination debate, the negative has the basic responsibility of clash, whether that be directly with the affirmative's interpretation of the topic or with the topic itself. You may directly refute the affirmative's case. The best way is by attacking all the arguments one at a time, as they were presented. Make sure to tell the judge where in the affirmative case you are by signposting. For example, stating, "On the affirmative's first contention of unconstitutionality," will help the judge immediately identify what you will be arguing.

The second option has become known as the negative case. The negative case is a direct attack on the topic itself, not necessarily the affirmative's interpretation. In order to create a negative case, you must refute the assumptions inherent within the topic. Such an assumption in the media topic is the idea that reflecting American values is good. Therefore, you must assume that not reflecting American values is good or, conversely, that reflecting American values must be bad.

Using this criterion, you would then design a case, just as an affirmative does, with definitions and contentions. One argument may be that the media should help to challenge beliefs. If the media only reflected our values, then we as a society would become stagnant. Second, because we are such a diverse society it would be impossible to reflect all of our values accurately. Therefore, such a proposal is unobtainable. Generally, negative cases last between three to four minutes, allowing time for straight refutation.

Experience has shown that the best approach for the negative is a combination of straight refutation and your own case. In your presentation, you should first offer straight refutation and finish with your case. This way, you leave the judge with your interpretation of the topic rather than with the affirmative's.

Rebuttal Speeches

Contrary to the pattern in standard and cross-examination debate, the affirmative in Lincoln-Douglas debate is the first rebuttalist. The affirmative also has two rebuttals to the negative's one. For the first rebuttal, the objective is to cover as many negative arguments as possible as well as covering your own. Pay careful attention to your value term, making sure to defend against any negative attacks, as this is the judging criterion you wish to be used. To extend the analogy of the house, the affirmative rebuttalist could consider himself a repairman, fixing any damage to his case inflicted by the negative.

Repairs may be simply answering a question, reading more evidence, restating, or reaffirming. If the negative only questioned your evidence, a simple response may be enough to satisfy the inquiry. It is a good idea to have new evidence ready for rebuttals in case the negative has attacked your evidence as biased or incomplete. You do not want to disregard your original evidence, but by offering further quantification you help to remove any doubt about the integrity of your arguments. If your contentions have not been attacked, then you will need to restate and reaffirm them: For example, "The negative said nothing about contention No. 2—that gun control is harmful to sportsmen." This restatement helps the judge to know exactly which point you are discussing and reaffirming. Another example: "This is significant because we see that many thousands of people will be denied their rights." The reaffirmation helps the judge to better understand the merit of that particular argument. The restatement/reaffirmation phase of the rebuttal becomes even more crucial when you are in the last rebuttal for each speaker. At this point, the restatement/reaffirmation can be broken down into four equal parts:

1. Where you are

2. Opponent's response

3. Your response

4. Impact of argument

Negative Rebuttal

This is your last speech, so you will want to be sure to respond to the affirmative attacks but also to stress what you believe to be the key issues of the debate. Start off with the affirmative case. Use the four-step method for each argument. If there are a lot of arguments remaining because neither you nor your opponent have dropped any, then you have a couple of strategies to choose from. If the affirmative case has many contentions and each one has three to four pieces of evidence, you may not have the time to respond to each piece of evidence. You should try to focus on the basic analysis behind each contention and beat that. Besides, much of the evidence may be redundant. Therefore, you can respond to the entire contention without worrying about each piece of evidence separately. And because Lincoln-Douglas debate stresses the communicative factor, your first concern should be to debate your opponent clearly and intelligibly.

If the affirmative case is very shallow or has very little detail, you may have time to respond to each separate point and piece of evidence. Remember, you must also rebuild your own case, so you should not spend more than three or four minutes of your time on the affirmative case. End with your case. At this point, you will want to focus clearly on the key issues of your case. If you have time, you might try to slow down and persuasively examine why your case beats the topic. You want to leave the judge with a favorable impression of your case and of you. You should use the approach that best fits the situation and your judge. A further analysis of judge criteria can be found in the judge section.

Second Affirmative Rebuttal

You only have three minutes and probably cannot adequately cover all the arguments, assuming the negative has responded to everything you have said. This is when the four-step pattern will help you by allowing you to focus on the case issues you are winning while pointing out the issues in which you believe you have beaten the negative. Such attention to organization is very important because it is a means of making sure you have adequately responded to all attacks and have reasonably extended your case throughout the debate. It is also important because it greatly improves your personal speaking style. In your last speech, you do not want to leave the judge with the impression that you were poorly organized. Style can be a key factor in some debates. Imagine yourself as a judge. Who would you vote for: someone who was so disorganized he or she had to ask you what arguments to discuss or someone who was so confident and organized that he or she actually seemed to guide you through the debate.

Evidence

Well-detailed arguments with abundant substructure are not necessary. Do not mistake this to mean that evidence or organization is unimportant. Lack of evidence or organization only makes for a poor debate. You will find that while a plethora of evidence is not needed, what is given must be precise.

There are several books and encyclopedias important to the Lincoln-Douglas debater. Of course the *Readers' Guide to Periodical Literature* is valuable to any debater. You will find a wide variety of choices of popular reading magazines. Two magazines in particular that you should examine are the *Congressional Digest* and *Vital Speeches of the Day*. The first magazine offers in-depth analysis of a single issue currently being discussed in Congress. An example is "Limiting Political Action Committees: Pro and Con." The second magazine lists important speeches from world leaders on a variety of subjects.

Next is the *Social Index Resource Service* (SIRS). This indexes newspaper articles from across the country. Often, newspaper articles go into more depth than major magazine articles do.

For Lincoln-Douglas debate, research begins the same way it does in standard and cross-examination debate. However, for some topics, magazines and newspapers will not contain the needed information. Consider this topic: "A parliamentary system of government would better meet the underlying values of our Constitution." Much of your information will come from comparative government textbooks and specialized forms of encyclopedias. Three such encyclopedias are the *Encyclopedia of the Social Sciences*, the *International Encyclopedia of the Social Sciences*, and *The Encyclopedia of Philosophy*. These three books offer in-depth analyses of social science and philosophical ideas that can ultimately provide a wealth of information for any value topic.

Some final words on where to find information: Browse, read a major daily newspaper, and ask your librarian for help.

Tournament Procedures

Tournaments vary in length. Some run for two or three days, while others last only for an afternoon. However, certain aspects are the same at every tournament:

1. You will know the topic in advance and will be expected to debate on both the affirmative and negative sides.

2. You will have your own identification code. It may be a number, letter, or just your last name. This prevents judges from identifying your school and possibly being prejudiced.

3. Your code is also used for postings. Postings are the lists of the debates, rooms, and times. Because a Lincoln-Douglas debate usually lasts no more than 45 minutes, two may be scheduled in the same room at the same time. The postings generally look like this:

Affirmative	Negative	Room	Time
10	15	B19	9:30
20	22		
14	12	B20	
18	32		

In this case, there are two affirmatives, 10 and 20, scheduled in the same room. This means that the first line of codes, numbers 10 and 15, debate first at 9:30, and then numbers 20 and 22 debate immediately after. You want to make sure that you are on time for your debate. Even if you are scheduled to debate the second section, you should arrive at 9:30 because someone from the first session may drop out, and you may be asked to debate ahead of time.

Judges

The more you compete, the more adept you will become at understanding particular judges. But, generally, you will encounter three different types: community or parent judges, college judges, and coach judges.

Community or parent judges are very common at smaller, more local tournaments. Though they are genuinely conscientious, they may not be as well versed in debate theory as you are. Because of this, they may not be able to flow as quickly as you can or be as familiar with the intricacies of the specific topic. Be careful to avoid any jargon, either debate- or topic-oriented. L.D.C.'s may mean less developed countries to you but may mean nothing to a community judge.

It is also very important that you be well organized in your presentation. You should always signpost your arguments. The judge may not be taking notes and probably will not remember what Contention 1, Subpoint 3, refers to unless you remind him or her.

College judges are generally quite skilled in public speaking and may be members of college forensic teams. If so, they may flow whatever you tell them. Therefore, you should be prepared for a faster round if you are attending a tournament with college judges. They may even have a background in debate theory and therefore be better able to follow a highly technical debate than a community judge. Do not think, though, that judges will just take notes and figure everything out for themselves. You still have the ultimate responsibility for insuring that the judge understands all the arguments as well as why your arguments are superior.

Debate coach judges are certainly well aware of the topic as well as the arguments and perhaps even the evidence. Often, at large tournaments, coaches are required to judge. But that should not really matter. As long

LINCOLN-DOUGLAS DEBATE BALLOT

ROUND _____ ROOM _____ TIME _____ DATE _____ JUDGE _____

Affirmative (name and code) _____

Negative (name and code) _____

INSTRUCTIONS TO JUDGES

1. Unlike team debate, the resolution to be debated will be a proposition of value, rather than a proposition of policy. Thus debaters are encouraged to develop argumentation on conflicting underlying principles to support their positions. To that end, they are not responsible for practical applications. There is no need for a plan (or for plan attacks).

2. The burdens on the affirmative and negative positions are not prescribed as they may be in debates on propositions of policy; therefore decision rules are fair issues to be argued in the round.

3. In making your decision, you might ask yourself the following questions:
   a. Which of the debaters persuaded you that their position was more valid? (Which debater communicated more effectively?)
   b. Did the debaters support their position appropriately, using logical argumentation throughout, and evidence where necessary?

4. Remember, there should be clash in the debate.

CIRCLE THE APPROPRIATE NUMBER

	SUPERIOR	EXCELLENT	GOOD	AVERAGE
Affirmative	50-49-48-47	46-45-44-43	42-41-40-39	38-37-36-35
Negative	50-49-48-47	46-45-44-43	42-41-40-39	38-37-36-35

AFFIRMATIVE	NEGATIVE
Case & Analysis	**Case & Analysis**
Support of Issues Through Evidence and Reasoning	**Support of Issues Through Evidence and Reasoning**
Delivery	**Delivery**
Reason for Decision	

In my opinion the better debating was done by _____
                                              (affirmative or negative)   code

Critic's Signature _____

FORMAT

Affirmative	6-minute constructive
Negative	3-minute cross examination
Negative	7-minute constructive
Affirmative	3-minute cross examination
Affirmative	4-minute rebuttal
Negative	6-minute rebuttal
Affirmative	3-minute rebuttal

ATTENTION
Judges are <u>not</u> to read evidence at the end of a debate round unless there is a charge of falsification or misrepresentation made by the opposing team during the round.

as you are clear in your analysis and you adapt to whether the coach is flow or nonflow, you should be able to impress even the most particular of judges.

Topic Analysis

The following topics were used throughout different sections and regions of the United States during the 1985–86 school year. They have been divided according to whether they are examinations of a policy, comparisons between two values, or examinations of a single value.

Policy Topics

1. Governmental invasion of individual privacy is justifiable.

2. Protectionism is a positive trade policy for U.S. industry.

3. American foreign policy in the Middle East has lost direction and purpose.

In the first topic, *justifiable* is clearly the value term. The affirmative will be using that word to evaluate the value of invasion of privacy. In any policy evaluation topic, you must be careful not to get muddled in pure policy argumentation. When you debate such topics, it can become easy to debate the policies themselves and not the values implied within the policies—that is, when and where the invasion occurs and what type of invasion it is. These are essential elements to know, but they can best be discussed in the definitions. This debate should focus on whether the government has any reasonable purpose in usurping the constitutional right to privacy. An example could be mandatory drug testing for transportation personnel. It may be considered by some to be an invasion of privacy, but it could also be in the best interests of the public's well-being. The debate would now be about the value of the individual's constitutional right to privacy versus the value of the greater good for the majority. Not all topics are as clear as this one is.

For example, the value terms in topic No. 2 is *positive*. A basic definition of positive is "effective or helpful." Obviously, as applied to U.S. industry, these words refer to saving American jobs. However, such a debate may degenerate from the implied value of protectionism—that is, protecting U.S. employment—to whether or not protectionism will actually accomplish anything. A policy's workability should not be an issue in value debate. What should be debated by the affirmative is that protectionism will insure American jobs and, by the negative, that protectionism does not allow for competition and therefore creates complacency. Unless you are a careful debater, such a topic could easily become a policy debate.

The last topic, No. 3, is the most difficult to debate. The first problem is that the value term is not stated but implied; losing "direction and purpose" is generally considered to have negative implications. As a debater, you can reasonably assume that the framers of this resolution meant that a lack of direction is bad. You may have to make such assumptions when a topic is not worded more explicitly.

The second problem is that this resolution is more of a proposition of fact than of value. In other words, it merely states that something is true. Consequently, many affirmatives would assert that they should win the round once they have shown an example of American foreign policy in the Middle East that seems to lack direction and purpose. However, the affirmative is not excused from discussing values just because the topic is somewhat misleading in its wording. As the affirmative, you have an unstated burden of proof to show that a policy with no direction is in fact bad or evil or disastrous. If you debate only facts or examples and do not debate values, then you are only living up to half of your responsibilities.

The next set of topics can be called value comparison topics. The most important element in debating such topics is that you present a reasonable situation in which the two values are in direct conflict. Without conflict, you can never adequately assess which value is superior.

Value Comparison Topics

1. Shared sacrifice is better than individual sacrifice.

2. Guided justice is superior to blind justice.

For the first topic—"Shared sacrifice is better than individual sacrifice"—a conflicting situation can be found in the Gramm-Rudman Amendment. The issue is whether it is better to single out a few programs for budget cuts (and hurt a smaller number of people) or to spread the cuts across the entire budget. Many would argue that to single out a few programs (often social programs to help the poor or improve education) is unfair because it hurts those people who are least able to protect themselves or to find help through other programs. The case allows debaters to examine the values (and worth) of the few versus the values (or proposed benefits) of the population in general. Remember, in the definition of value terms in this topic, the word *better* is crucial.

One affirmative approach is to be sure to present a situation in which the two values are so clearly in conflict that one must take precedence in order for the situation to be resolved. Obviously, as an affirmative, you would use an example demonstrating that when the value you are defending takes precedence, the conflict is resolved, but that when the other value takes precedence resolution does not occur. It is up to the affirmative to make sure there is no doubt about which value should take precedence.

A very popular negative approach for value comparison resolutions is to show that the two values are equal, that neither one is superior, and that therefore the resolution itself is false. As a negative speaker, you can use this approach to keep yourself out of difficult situations because you never have to take a side. It is much easier to defend two time-honored values than it is to defend one while attacking the other.

The second topic uses a variation of the value comparison by comparing the same value word *justice* with two modifiers, *guided* and *blind*. In essence, these are two forms of the same value, "justice." By offering a pragmatic definition of the value term *superior*, you will be able to set up a scenario in which to view these two forms of justice. Defining *superior* as "better than" does not enable anyone to compare accurately the two types of justice. Defining *superior* as "better able to uphold the value of a fair and speedy trial" helps to establish a pragmatic scenario that is easily understood.

Single Value Topics

The last type of topic is the single value topic. One of the first difficulties is that there is nothing to compare the topic to except itself. In the topic "There is no such thing as a just war," the value being debated is war. A highly specific definition or at least understanding of war is essential. Most people would accept that World Wars I and II were wars. And most people would agree that the U.S. involvement in Vietnam was a war, but (at the beginning of that war) the government referred to it as a "police action." Is war then simply the organized killing of people between two or more countries? Then what about civil wars? There are also "cold wars" in which no one is killed but countries are not on speaking terms. When the Japanese attacked Pearl Harbor, the U.S. was not officially at war with them. Could the attack be considered warfare? Clearly, it is extremely important (and sometimes very difficult) to define value terms in single value topics.

Summary

Lincoln-Douglas debate takes practice, but it is a challenging and exciting activity that will allow you an opportunity to develop your communication and critical thinking skills.

Questions for Discussion

1. What are the different style strategies for different types of judges?

2. What are the three approaches a negative can use in the constructive?

3. What is the easiest pitfall when you are debating a policy proposition?

4. What are some of the reasons for the creation of Lincoln-Douglas debate and how does that make it different from team debate?

Activities

1. Develop an affirmative case outline, using the resolution provided by your teacher.

2. Outline possible negative arguments to the affirmative case outline done for Activity 1.

3. Using the current Lincoln-Douglas topic do the following:
   —find the value term
   —decide the type of value proposition it is
   —prepare an affirmative case with evidence
   —prepare negative arguments with evidence

4. Deliver your affirmative as a speech in class. While other students are delivering their speeches, use the time to practice flowing the arguments.

5. Using one of the affirmative speeches delivered in Activity 4, prepare and deliver a negative speech. Again be sure to practice flowing while other students deliver their speeches.

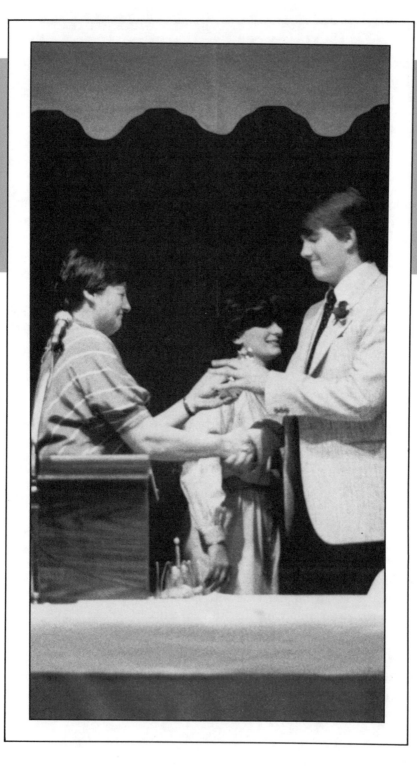

Chapter 11

The Tournament Experience

From Competing to Judging

Objectives and Key Terms

After studying Chapter 11, you should be able to

1. Explain how a tournament works,
2. Explain how to get the most out of attending forensic events,
3. Explain the role of competition in tournament participation,
4. Outline the role of the judge in the debate process,
5. Outline the guidelines of what is expected of a judge, and
6. Outline the questions the judge asks when evaluating a debate for a decision.

After reading this chapter, you should understand the following terms:

preliminary round	ballot
elimination rounds	decision
tournament invitation	oral critiques
judging	written critiques
critical listening	

A cademic debate is centered in the tournament experience. Every year, thousands of high school and college students attend tournaments. The tournament permits students to practice their arguments and sharpen their thinking and speaking skills. This chapter explains how tournaments work and how to get the most out of attending forensic events.

The principle guiding almost all forensic tournaments is competition. Events are divided between preliminary and elimination rounds. A preliminary round at a tournament is comprised of all students who enter an event and a judge who evaluates student performances. Elimination rounds are more exclusive. Only students who have competed successfully advance in the contest. In oratory, for example, those students who have ranked high in their preliminary sections advance to a semifinal and then final round. In debate, those students who have compiled the best win-loss record advance to an octofinal or quarterfinal round.

Before you go to a tournament, it might be a good idea to read the invitation and understand the special makeup of the tournament and its rules and regulations. Not all tournaments offer the same activities; nor are the procedures for participating in each tournament identical. A small tournament may offer only four or six preliminary rounds of debate and begin elimination rounds with the semifinals. A large tournament may offer six or eight rounds of debate and begin elimination rounds with octofinals or even sextodecimofinals. In either case, the tournament proceeds until a final winner is declared.

Tournament Basics

Advance knowledge of tournament customs and procedures is also helpful in determining your preparation. Some tournaments distinguish between novice, advanced, and expert levels of competition. If you are inexperienced, you may wish to enter at a lower level so that you are not under too much pressure. If you have moderate experience, you must decide whether to stay in a lower division or take on greater challenges. Knowing which schools will attend the tournament or which have been there in the past can help you to make this decision. Remember that your coach's suggestions on the number of events and the levels of competition should be heeded.

Tournaments are exciting. It is fun to compete. Winning is always thrilling, of course. And losing usually increases one's desire to learn and do better the next time. But competition is not everything. The trophies that glitter on the center stage are only tokens, symbols of good work. What you get out of tournaments is up to you. The following suggestions may be useful in helping you analyze your own motives for participation.

Tournaments are intense experiences. Debate and other forensic events require a lot of work. It is not unusual for students to work on arguments at a tournament. Especially when unanticipated cases or new disadvantages are unveiled for the first time, a debater may wish to discuss with fellow teammates potential strategies and responses. Likewise, a team may wish to make adjustments in its positions. Sometimes, prepared arguments work well, and sometimes they do not. Small adjustments can mean a lot.

Work at tournaments should be planned in advance. Teammates should agree on a time and place to review arguments. If a school has multiple teams at a tournament, its members should arrange short meetings at which information can be shared. Too much work is not good. Tournaments can be tiring. The days are long, especially when a person is participating in several debates and individual events. When changes are introduced into a speech, they may or may not improve the speech. When changes are extensive, there is simply not sufficient time to practice the new material. Before the tournament, set up a plan of work and revision and stick to the schedule.

A tournament is a social occasion. It is a place where people who share similar interests can make friends. While all the people at a tournament are competitors, in a real sense the same people form a small community. To argue against someone, you have to listen to what they say and take their ideas seriously. Others extend to you the same courtesy. You should always remember that no matter how intense the competition or how great the rivalry, you should treat people with the same respect that you would like them to treat you.

Finally, a tournament is a place where you are able to test your own ideas and values. Some students see the tournament experience as only a game, like Monopoly. For them, the tournament is a shallow experience. After all, games are just a pretended reality for passing time. But other students use the opportunity for argument in better ways. For them, the tournament offers an opportunity to develop ideas about the world and to determine which courses of policy are useful and good for the country. Although you probably should not be personally committed to each and every argument (after all, you could be wrong), it is better to take discussion seriously than to reduce it to the level of a sporting event.

It is likely that at some point in a tournament you will be eliminated from competition. There has never been a debater, an orator, or an extempor who has won all his or her rounds of competition. Even if you are very good, the tournament is set up in such a way as to confront you with increasingly more difficult levels of competition. Somewhere along the line, you will usually meet a person who has done more work, has a better case, or simply meets the preferences of a judge or panel better than you do. Even in cases where contestants are quite equal in preparation, skills, and appeal, the other person may simply have a better day. It is tempting to conclude that the tournament is at an end when you are defeated. However, it is better to think of that time as the beginning.

Observing at tournaments is quite useful. As a debater, you see the arguments from a limited viewpoint. In fact, you may become so engrossed in producing arguments that you do not stop to ask about whether the judge can understand them. Observing permits you to take the position of a judge and to see what strategies and stylistic devices work well and which become barriers to communicating ideas. At any time in your forensic career, it might be a good idea to attend a tournament just to listen. This may give you a perspective on your own performance that is very helpful. When you lose, you should always watch other participants and put yourself in the role of a judge. This will help you understand the process of evaluation and help you to compete more successfully.

The following section explains the general rules for judging debates. If you follow these rules, you will be able to improve your skills at critical listening and argument evaluation. Becoming a wise judge of arguments is every bit as important as being a good advocate.

Judging Debates and Critical Listening

Each contest at a tournament has a judge. Sometimes judges are experts in the subject matter; sometimes they are not. In either case, there are certain guidelines that all judges try to follow to make sure the forensic event is fairly and productively executed.

The primary duty of a judge is to reach a decision. In a round of oratory or extemporaneous speaking, the judge has the duty of ranking contestants, indicating which ones did the best job, the second best job, and so on. The judge also assigns quality points to each performance. In a round of debate, the judge must indicate whether the affirmative or negative did the better job. Additionally, the judge ranks the speakers—first affirmative, first negative, second affirmative, second negative—in terms of who did the best job, the second best job, and so on. Many tournaments ask the judge to assign quality points for each speaker (1–30 on a standard ballot) and quality points for the team (1–30 on a standard ballot).

The following list suggests some general guidelines for judges at tournaments.

1. A judge should be fair.

The integrity of a competitive tournament depends on the honesty of the people who evaluate the participants. While the social atmosphere of tournaments creates friendships, a judge should be strictly neutral when it comes to evaluating a contest. Personal considerations should not influence decisions. Rather, the judge has the duty to develop standards that are applied equally to all students.

After the rounds, debate ballots are collected in the tabulation room to determine ranks and awards.

2. A judge should be attentive.

Judging is an arduous process. Performers only speak for part of a debate and listen to some of the arguments. A judge must take into consideration all speeches in the final evaluation. When the speakers are fresh, exciting, and well prepared, it is easy to listen. When speakers are dull, inarticulate, and confused, attention tends to wander. In either case, the judge must listen to everything in order to make a good decision.

3. A judge should be efficient.

In forensics, arguments can become very complex very quickly. A judge should develop a method that enables him or her to record the event. This record provides a way to jog the memory and to provide a reliable guide for reviewing the development of arguments. Keeping such a record is a skill that is developed only over time. The more the judge can recall and the better his or her notes, the better the decision that can be rendered.

4. A judge should be impartial.

In a forensic contest, the force of the better argument should determine the outcome of the dispute. This means that a judge should suspend preferences or biases in regard to the substance of a position. The question at the end of a debate is not whether the judge feels that the proposition is true or false, but which advocates have done the better job of supporting their case in a particular round.

5. A judge should be polite.

Just as debaters ought to act with civility, a judge should always maintain a calm, friendly demeanor. Sometimes this is hard to do. Debaters, caught up in the heat of the moment, have been known to yell and scream and act rudely. While such behavior may be noted on the ballot, a similar response from the judge does not usually serve a useful purpose. It is especially important to offer restrained comments on the ballot. After all, many of the students who debate are not experts and are just learning. Extremely critical or negative comments may encourage a student either to become so depressed as to quit the activity or to regard the judge as merely a crank.

6. A judge should provide an educationally sound assessment of the event.

All ballots leave room for commentary on the debate. At a minimum, a judge is obligated to write down her or his views that led to the decision.

The ballot helps students learn what worked well and what did not. Ballots that are illegible or incomplete, composed of fragmented impressions, or turned in without commentary are of no value. Ballots that are thorough, well reasoned, and coherent are of great value.

While these suggestions provide general guidelines for the judge, they do not spell out *how* to judge a debate or a forensic event. There are no specific rules as to how debates *must* be evaluated. Indeed, as several recent works have shown, there are several different models that might be applied. Some people find these models of judging useful. They like to pretend that they are applying the rules of policy making or testing scientific hypotheses in a debate round. Their judging models are quite elaborate. If you become interested in judging debates, you might investigate these works and become an expert yourself. By and large, though, these models are esoteric and of limited use.

The best rule of thumb is to examine the substance of the arguments and see which side did the better job of showing the resolution to be a good idea or a bad one. More elaborate decision making machinery does not necessarily make the better decisions. Rather, exotic views of debate theory may impede prudent judgment. Unless theory becomes an unresolved issue in the debate itself, theoretical prejudices should not be imposed on the outcome of the arguments.

When reaching a judgment, ask yourself the following questions:

1. Is the affirmative interpretation of the resolution legitimate?
Make sure that the affirmative has offered a reasonable presentation. If the negative has not challenged the definition of terms offered by the affirmative, you are expected to accept the affirmative as topical. If the negative has challenged the terms, then you must decide whether the affirmative definition is adequate or if the negative has a better definition.

It may be that only part of the affirmative case does not fall within the boundaries of the resolution. When that happens, excise that part of the plan from the debate and judge only on those issues that remain relevant.

It may be that the negative has offered a counterplan that falls under the affirmative definition of the resolution. If that happens, there is no choice but to vote for the affirmative because the negative has no position in the debate to defend.

2. Does the affirmative establish a significant problem?
A significant problem is a flaw in the status quo that someone cares

about. If no one cares or if people care but they see the so-called problem as a positive good, then there is no reason to vote affirmative because the resolution does not act as a remedy.

In evaluating the significance of a problem, you will want to compare affirmative and negative evidence. You must decide what impact negative challenges have on affirmative evidence and how much the significance is reduced.

An affirmative can still win a debate even if it does not demonstrate a significant problem. Remember the comparative advantage case merely obligates the affirmative to improve the status quo, not to erase a significant problem.

3. Does the affirmative establish that the problem is inherent in the status quo?

If a problem has been recently ended or if it can be expected that a problem will soon be resolved because of incentives or forces operating within the status quo, then the rationale for adopting the affirmative is weakened.

In judging inherency, one should compare the likelihood that a problem will be sustained or grow worse under the existing mix of private and public activities against the likelihood that effective action is being or will soon be taken. Thus, the judge should compare affirmative and negative claims on this matter.

4. Does the affirmative claim significant advantages to adopting the resolution?

In arguing advantages to a plan, an affirmative will often identify several consequences that flow from a single course of action.

Evaluation demands that each advantage be considered. If the negative can prove that the advantage is not of substantial value—that either the plan's effects will not be widespread or, even if its effects are widespread, they are of little consequence—then the rationale for adopting the resolution is reduced.

5. Can the plan produce its claimed effects?

If a plan has trouble working or if it gives rise to other factors that prevent it from bringing about advantages or resolving a harm, the rationale for an affirmative decision is weakened.

The judge must compare affirmative and negative evidence to decide whether and how much solvency is gained by the plan.

6. Are there undesirable consequences of the plan?

Most of the time, the negative argues that a plan has disadvantages. These arguments are used to offset the affirmative reason for change. When comparing affirmative and negative evidence, it is important to ask two questions.

First, are the disadvantages of sufficient magnitude to warrant rejecting the affirmative plan? Ultimately, the judge must decide what is better or worse and compare the likelihood of disadvantages against the likelihood of desirable effects from the plan.

Second, are the disadvantages that the plan brings about really harmful? Sometimes, a disadvantage can be resolved by affirmative action. In this case, the argument "turns around" and supports the affirmative. The disadvantage is then added to the affirmative side of the ledger.

7. Is the debate a tie?

If the judge finds a relatively equal number of good effects and bad effects, then he or she must vote on presumption. Presumption is usually thought to reside with the status quo, and a decision on presumption is usually one that favors the negative. However, in some debates the affirmative might be able to show why presumption should favor the resolution. In these instances, the judge must evaluate this argument as well.

The above questions establish an overall framework for evaluating a round of debate. All decisions depend on smaller, microlevel judgments. A judge, like a debater, should be familiar with the tests of evidence. When comparing the strength of positions on an issue, the judge should grant a team an issue if it has the superior evidence. If an opponent has no evidence for a claim, then in almost every class (except where patently false or outlandish claims are made), the team with evidence should be awarded the issue. Where evidence is contested, the quality of the source and its relevance, conclusiveness, date of observation, and agreement with other authorities should be taken into account.

These are the most frequent questions raised by a debate. Of course, things can become much more complex. But by systematically working through the major questions, any judge should be able to work through a complete and accurate understanding of the round.

Debate Ballot

Aff. No. _____ vs. Neg. No. _____ Round _____ Room _____

Instructions to the Judges

In arriving at your decision take into consideration the following aspects of good debating:

Analysis: Getting to the heart of the question
Proof: Supporting contentions with sufficient and convincing evidence
Argument: Sound reasoning; logical conclusions
Adaptation: Clashing with the opposition
Refutation: Destroying opponent's contentions; reinforcing your own
Organization: Clear, logical presentation of material
Speaking: Effective delivery; favorable impact on audience

Please award points to speakers from 18 minimum to 30 maximum.

1 Aff. _____ (   )   1 Neg. _____ (   )
            name   pts.   name   pts.

2 Aff. _____ (   )   2 Neg. _____ (   )
            name   pts.   name   pts.

REASONS FOR MY DECISION

The better debating was done by team No. _____ upholding the _____

ATTENTION
Judges are <u>not</u> to read evidence at the end of the debate
unless there is a charge of falsification or misrepresentation made by the opposing team during the debate.

_____
Signature of Judge

Special Questions

There are several procedures that are not settled matters but are frequently discussed in hosting tournaments. Readers should be alerted to these issues so that they will be prepared to think through to a position.

Should judges reveal decisions? In class, it is possible to engage in an oral critique of the argument. The judge and the debaters engage in a give and take. Oral critiques are quite useful. All participants remember the arguments and can respond quickly. In tournaments, because of time constraints, oral critiques have generally been eliminated.

Some debaters may desire oral critiques, perhaps not as much for their educational benefit as for finding out who won. It is our suggestion that judges not engage in such critique because it makes some contestants privy to information while denying it to others. Moreover, in the heat of a contest situation, critique is usually not well received.

Should judges announce their decision-making preferences? At the National Debate Tournament, all judges are required to submit some kind of philosophy that describes prejudices. Some educators feel that this is a good policy because it permits debaters to adapt their arguments to the judge. Others see it as unwise because it may distort arguments as debaters bend to theoretical prejudices rather than concentrate on substantial issues.

Should judges read evidence? Some people think that a judge should confine observations to arguments that are orally communicated. By reviewing speech texts and cards after a round of debate, it is argued, a judge encourages poor communication practices and biases the decision by reconstructing inferences. Others say that the right to read evidence ought to be reserved, especially in cases where key sources are in contention and the judge wants to reach a more certain decision. Generally, a judge should follow the custom of the tournament.

Should judges hear a team more than once during a tournament? be assigned on the basis of quality? be constrained by regional or institutional factors? be selected by a system of mutual preference or random draw? These are emotional issues. There is little, if any, data that suggests that one method of assignment is better than another. We suggest that those who decide to attend a tournament ought to abide by the procedures stipulated in the invitation. The diversity expressed in local custom may be a strength of the forensic community.

Summary

The tournament experience is the culmination of hours of hard work. But beyond that, it represents an opportunity to try out new ideas, to refine arguments, to polish critical listening and thinking skills, and perhaps to form friendships that will last a lifetime.

Through the tournament experience, you learn to persuade others—sometimes contrary to their initial beliefs. You also learn to respect the decisions and value judgments of others. If you continue in tournament debate, you will have the opportunity to serve as a judge as well as a participant. An activity, which may have seemed at first frightening, will in time take on the thrill of competition, whether you win or lose.

Questions for Discussion

1. After learning the fundamentals of debate, why should you consider participating in a debate tournament? What purpose does competition serve?

2. Why should you observe debate rounds when you are not participating in a tournament?

3. What are the obligations of the judge in a debate round?

4. Outline the general guidelines for judging a debate round.

5. When evaluating an argument as a judge, how important is evidence? Why?

Activities

1. Attend a local debate tournament. Take the judge's ballot and your flow from one of the rounds. After going over the two, explain why you won or lost the round and what arguments could have been developed differently.

2. After you have been eliminated from a debate tournament (or attend as an observer), listen to debate rounds. In the round, take a flow of the debate. Write out a ballot explaining how you would have voted in the round and why.

3. In your debate class, organize a debate tournament. Set up a pairing of the rounds (to be held in class or after class). Use other students in the class as judges. Where possible, also have an observer for each round. Remember each team should have the same number of affirmative and negative rounds and that no team should meet the same team more than once. How often did the participating teams agree with the judge's decision? How often did the observer agree with the judge's decision? Prior to the actual debate each student should distribute a copy of his or her judging philosophy.

Part Three

Student Congress

Deliberative Decision Making

The democratic tradition values the individual. It is built on the importance of collective action by informed individuals. Individuals often collectively solve problems they could not deal with alone. In our society, when we wish to enact policy for the larger group, we have chosen to do so through representatives in legislative groups. Student congress is an event that gives to you, the forensic student, an opportunity to work, speak, and function in that deliberative decision-making environment. This section is designed to introduce you to the principles, structures, and organization of student congress. Further, you will be shown how to prepare for student congress and how to utilize some strategies for success in that activity.

Chapter 12

The Nature and Purpose of Student Congress

Objectives and Key Terms

After studying Chapter 12, you should be able to

1. Discuss the nature of student congress debate, especially as it differs from conventional debate,

2. Understand the purpose of parliamentary procedure and its three main principles,

3. Appreciate the skills needed to become a member of a student congress assembly, and

4. Discuss various student congress events held throughout the country, especially those authorized by the National Forensic League.

After reading this chapter, you should understand the following terms:

legislative debate

student congress

National Forensic League

National Speech Tournament

senate

house

parliamentary procedure

T he application of persuasion in the legislative setting differs from any other situation in one major way. Speaking in legislative debate, or in student congress, is done within a structured environment of specific procedural rules known as parliamentary law. These rules or principles evolved out of the experiences of individuals, action groups, and law-making bodies as rules of order to permit groups to work together efficiently and successfully. In a democratic society, the foundation of parliamentary procedure is rooted in three principles: (1) the will of the majority ultimately decides action and policy; (2) the rights of the nonmajority to speak and otherwise participate must always be protected; and (3) the rules exist to serve the organization and are equally applicable to all of the membership. If you wish to persuade in student congress, you must not only invent the argument and find the data to support it, you must also understand parliamentary rules and the application of those rules in the student congress. You must be sensitive to the shifting weight of opinion within the group and be prepared to offset arguments that are given in opposition to your position. Finally, you must develop the skill of disagreeing with ideas without being disagreeable. This activity allows you to extend your skills of extemporaneous speaking, debate, and interpersonal communication.

The Value of Student Congress

A librarian interviewed by one of the authors contended that of all the students who used the school library for research—forensic students or otherwise—the ones most astute, most politically aware, and most knowledgeable about the techniques of research were the student congress competitors. The attributes necessary to be a competent student congress member are attributes necessary to survive in the "real world" of politics, political science, and persuasion. In addition to practicing a variety of public speaking events, from oratory to extemporaneous to impromptu speaking, student congress calls on skills necessary for successful participation in discussions, debates, and parliamentary situations. An added flavor is provided by the fact that student congress mimics real-life legislative assemblies and presents its participants with an insight into some of the issues and problems that actually confront our lawmakers. What better choice for a learning experience and competitive event than student congress?

The Types of Student Congresses

The National Forensic League, a national honorary society that promotes high school speech competition, recognizes three types of student congresses. *Practice congresses* can be held by any school and may be organized in conjunction with a regular speech tournament or as a separate event. Schools that are not affiliated in any way with NFL may attend and participate in such congresses. However, if NFL points are to be awarded to NFL members, a minimum of four schools must attend. Such practice congresses are very important to the training of student congress members, and if they are available to you, you are fortunate. Every NFL District should try to have at least one practice congress during the year. Coaches who wish to host a competitive activity but who feel that they cannot handle a full forensic tournament should certainly consider hosting a practice student congress.

A second type of student congress is held only once each year for the express purpose of sending students to the NFL National Student Congress. Each NFL District may hold a *District Student Congress* and may send as many as two Senators and two Representatives to the National Student Congress if there are at least twelve schools in attendance at the District Congress.

The third type of student congress promoted by NFL is the *NFL National Student Congress*. The student congress was first held in 1937. Although procedural alterations have been made from time to time, the basic format has remained much the same in the intervening years. The National Student Congress, which meets during the National NFL Tournament, is held in high esteem by students and coaches alike. With over 250 participants each year at the National Congress, the contest is organized into five Senates and five Houses. There are special rules for the National Student Congress, but most of them have to do with the awarding of points and the selection of Superior Congress award winners who advance to a final bicameral session. The legislative deliberation in any of these types of student congress is essentially the same. Specific NFL rules are printed in the form of two booklets entitled *Preparing for*

Student Congress and *Student Congress Manual.* Both are published by the National Forensic League and are available from the NFL National Office in Ripon, Wisconsin.

Besides the National Forensic League, a number of other organizations sponsor congressional events. Many of these are parliamentary procedure events. Others are geared to teach the principles of citizenship and government through direct practice. To participate in most of these activities, a student must apply for acceptance. However, some are available to any student who is a member of the particular organization. Some of the most notable are the Junior Statesmen of America, Youth-in-Government (sponsored by the YMCA), state activity league congresses, and Boys State and Girls State, which are sponsored by the American Legion. Students who are chosen to participate in these latter programs organize their own city, county, and state governments. They choose their own officials and introduce and argue their own bills in the legislature.

The 4-H Clubs of America, the Future Farmers of America, and other clubs that emphasize a knowledge of parliamentary procedure have competitive events that make use of teams trained in parliamentary procedure. In addition, their national conventions are organized to give legislative experience to students in attendance.

The types of student congresses in which you may participate and compete are many and varied. However, they all share the common goal of giving experience to students in the use of legislative debate. Because this book is aimed at students who are interested in building skills in the competitive areas, the discussion and examples used here will be drawn primarily from the materials supplied by the National Forensic League and from the experiences of the authors and their students in NFL Student Congress. However, all student congress events have things in common. If you are involved in other groups besides NFL, you can apply the basic principles discussed here within the framework of rules and regulations specified by other groups.

Student Congress Hints

You are now well on your way to becoming an informed member of a student congress assembly. There are only three goals you need to achieve in order to become a proficient and effective participant: Prepare better on each bill (on one or both sides) than other members do, know how to prepare briefs correctly and how to use them in your debating, and know the Table of Most Frequently Used Parliamentary Motions and how to use it better than even the Presiding Officer does! Are you up to the task? Each of these three key elements of superior congress participation will be covered in-depth in the chapters that follow.

The area that seems to cause the most concern to students at the beginning phase of learning student congress is having to use parliamentary procedure. You need not be clever in using involved motions, but you should know how to put common motions into the proper form and know when to make such motions. You will be provided with a table of frequently used motions and with suggestions on when and how to make correct motions. If you hope to chair an assembly as its Presiding Officer, then you must have special interest in and understanding of parliamentary procedure and know why and how it is used. You should know how to state a question in correct parliamentary language, how to take a vote properly, which types of votes to use, and how to announce the result and effect of the vote. For this reason you should carefully study the role of the Presiding Officer found in an upcoming chapter. If this commentary about parliamentary procedure frightens you a bit at this point, please don't worry; just remember that the purpose of student congress is to *debate*, not to show off knowledge of parliamentary procedure.

Summary

Student congress offers you a chance to practice most of the skills used in political discussion and public speaking. The National Forensic League promotes a variety of congresses at all levels of competition. As a participant, you will need to be familiar with the mechanics of student congress, including bill preparation and parliamentary procedure.

Questions for Discussion

1. What is parliamentary procedure? What are its three main principles?

2. What are the three types of student congresses sanctioned by the National Forensic League?

3. How would you answer a novice student congress member who asked you what it takes to become an effective congress participant?

4. In general, what is the purpose of congressional debate as part of our legislative system?

Activities

1. Read, as a minimum, the Preface and the section on Definitions in *Robert's Rules of Order.* As an added challenge, read *Robert's* Introduction on Parliamentary Law and Article I, "How Business Is Conducted."

2. Identify the two U.S. Senators from your home state. Compose a biographical sketch of each, including political party, length of Senate service, prior political experience, and noteworthy congressional accomplishments.

3. Pinpoint your own congressional district by number and name your congressional representative. Compose a biographical sketch similar to the sketches you wrote for your senators.

Chapter 13

Student Congress Procedures

Objectives and Key Terms

After studying Chapter 13, you should be able to

1. Understand the purpose of various motions and how to use them in the course of a legislative debate,

2. Understand the purpose of bills and resolutions and be able to compose an example of each that will meet the standards outlined in the text,

3. Use the rules of parliamentary procedure to participate in a smooth-running discussion group or assembly, and

4. List the basic procedural rules that govern a session of student congress.

After reading this chapter, you should understand the following terms:

motion

Second

floor

precedence

bill

resolution

amendment

Certain procedural rules have been worked out by the NFL to insure equity in floor debate. Observing these rules will ultimately benefit all members of the student congress. To participate in student congress, you should be familiar with the rules. You should obey them in order to avoid embarrassment during the debate.

Debate

Procedural Rules

All speeches are strictly timed. No speech, including an authorship speech, may be longer than the specified time. The timekeeper will be instructed to inform the speaker and the Presiding Officer when that limit is reached. No additional time will be given. During a speech, members may ask for recognition and ask the speaker if he or she will yield to a question. Because the time for both the question and the answer are taken from a speaker's allotted time, the speaker may begin the speech by stating that he or she will not yield for questions until the conclusion of the speech. If a speaker specifies this, then the speech is given without interruption. Then questions are answered as time allows at the conclusion of the speaker's remarks. A special rule can be created by an assembly using the motion to suspend the rules. This rule establishes an automatic cross-examination period following every speech. However, it is not an NFL rule. Some assemblies create such a period for authorship speeches only.

The author of a bill or resolution is privileged to speak first. But once the debate has opened, the legislation belongs to the group and not to the author. Thus, it is not necessary to get permission from the author to offer an amendment. Nor is it correct to ask the author what the bill means. A bill means what it says to the assembly. It is not open for interpretation from the author. Nor is the group obligated to interpret the bill in the same way the author intended.

Following the authorship speech, each member who wishes to speak may ask for recognition only if he or she assumes a position that opposes that of the preceding speaker. Observation of this rule accomplishes several things. First, it insures that the debate is truly a debate and not a long series of "me, too" speeches that do not advance the cause of anything but point gathering by members. Second, it insures that both sides will have an equal opportunity to present their position openly and fairly. It also safeguards the Presiding Officer against charges of loading the debate for one side or the other. It further makes sure that a maximum number of issues on each side will be aired.

Because a member's success hinges on getting recognition and being able to speak to the student congress, another set of procedures is enforced. First, Presiding Officers call on speakers in the inverse order of the number of speeches they have delivered—that is, they recognize those who have not spoken or have spoken less often before those who have spoken more frequently. In addition, a member may speak only five times a day. When a member has reached this limit, the Official Scorer will mark his or her name off the seating chart, and he or she may be recognized only if no other member of the assembly wishes to speak. Finally, toward the end of the session, the Presiding Officer may announce that until further notice recognition will go only to those who have not spoken more than once. If, however, debate begins to lag, indicating that those who have not spoken more than once do not desire to do so, the Presiding Officer can return to general recognition.

Etiquette

In addition to the restrictions and limitations placed on the length and substance of floor speeches, you need to be familiar with the etiquette of student congress. There is a right and a wrong way to speak in a legislative session. When referring to another participant, use the terminology "Representative Green" or "the Representative from West Texas." Such terminology helps to keep the entire group aware that their positions, temporarily at least, are ones of dignity and seriousness, and underscores the fact that each competitor is playing the role of a member of a legislative body. The Presiding Officer should always be addressed as "Mr. or Mme. Speaker." If the house has been designated as a Senate, then the term for the Presiding Officer is "Mr. or Mme. President."

The proper way to gain the floor in order to make a motion or to participate in debate is to rise as soon as the preceding speaker has finished and at the same time say, "Mr. President" (or "Mme. Speaker"). If the Presiding Officer recognizes you, he or she will state, "The chair recognizes Representative Green." You may then make your motion or give a speech on the pending legislation. If, however, another member of the assembly is recognized, resume your seat until he or she has finished. To interrupt a speaker for questioning, use the following language: "Mr. Speaker (or Mme. President), will the speaker yield for a question?" The chair will then ask the speaker if he or she wishes to yield. If so, you may then ask one question. If not, you resume your seat and do not interrupt again. The Presiding Officer should discourage frequent interruptions of the same speaker. If the speaker has prefaced his or her remarks by saying he or she will not yield until the speech is finished, then no one will be recognized during the speech.

Under no circumstances are you or any other member of the student congress allowed to argue with the Presiding Officer. He or she has been elected to that position, and his or her decisions are final. The decisions are only discussed if there is a failure to follow parliamentary procedure and a violation of the rights of the assembly. Even then, there are two recourses. First, the Parliamentarian should intervene without any remonstrance from the membership. If this does not occur, however, you may "Rise to a point of order" or "Appeal the decision of the Chair." These should be used only if you have a sound parliamentary reason, not a personal one. (These motions are dealt with in the upcoming Table of Most Frequently Used Parliamentary Motions.)

Parliamentary Procedure

Parliamentary procedure is a useful tool that must be respected and used for the purposes for which it was designed. The basic principles of parliamentary law, once understood and accepted, make its many rules easy to understand. Parliamentary rules, first and foremost, exist to make it easier to transact business. They exist to promote cooperation, not to create disharmony. All groups that operate under parliamentary laws are dedicated to the precept that the majority will decide the action of the group. But they are also equally committed to the concept that all members have rights and privileges that must be safeguarded. Furthermore, particularly in a legislative assembly, parliamentary rules are intended to insure that full and free debate of every proposition will be allowed. Parliamentary law is built on the idea that time and effort should be utilized and that decisions should be reached by the simplest and most direct procedure. Specific rules of parliamentary procedure allow for a definite and logical order or priority for business. They also insure that every member has the right at all times to know what is being done by the assembly. These basic concepts of democratic procedure are accomplished by the judicious and fair application of parliamentary procedure. The most important thing for you to remember is that the ultimate purpose of parliamentary procedure is to insure the rule of the majority and to guard the rights of the minority. Used properly, it will keep debate going and will allow for full discussion. The Parliamentarian, the Presiding Officer, and each individual member should be dedicated to this principle and should strive to guarantee its fulfillment in the student congress.

It is not necessary to be a "parliamentary card shark." In fact, if you attempt to use the floor of student congress to show off long and involved or clever motions, you will be quickly spotted as an obstructionist and will have difficulty getting the floor thereafter. As stated earlier, the purpose of the student congress is to debate, not to show off expertise in parliamentary procedure. A good working knowledge of parliamentary procedure allows freedom of debate and gives you the assurance that the proper language is employed.

A motion is a proposal or a suggestion made by a member of a group that he or she wishes the entire group to consider and ultimately adopt. Most motions require a Second, or a second person who feels that the motion is worth discussing and considering. The proper form for common motions is "I move that . . ." rather than "I make a motion to . . . ." You should have a careful enough knowledge of the chart of precedence that you will not introduce motions that are out of order. Simply stated, if the motion you wish to present in order to accomplish your purpose is higher on the table of motions than the motion currently being considered, then your motion has a "higher" priority. It is in order at that specific time to introduce the motion to the group for its consideration. If you wish to move with poise and assurance through congressional debate, you will carefully study the parliamentary procedure necessary. In a student congress, certain adaptations of the parliamentary procedure as outlined in *Robert's Rules of Order* have been made. A careful look at the chart reproduced below by permission of NFL will indicate where some of those changes have been made. Notice how the motions are grouped by type into four distinct classes. Try to understand the purpose listed for each of the 24 commonly used motions and notice the technical information presented about voting requirements for each. You need not memorize such a chart, but you should have a copy handy for easy reference during a congress session.

Table of Most Frequently Used Parliamentary Motions
Adapted for use in NFL Student Congresses

Type	Motion	Purpose	Second Required?	Debat-able?	Amend-able?	Required Vote	May Interrupt a Speaker
	24. Fix Time for Reassembling	To arrange time of next meeting	Yes	Yes-T	Yes-T	Majority	Yes
	23. Adjourn	To dismiss the meeting	Yes	No	Yes-T	Majority	No
	22. To Recess	To dismiss the meeting for a specific length of time	Yes	Yes	Yes-T	Majority	No
	21. Rise to a Question of Privilege	To make a personal request during debate	No	No	No	Decision of Chair	Yes
	20. Call for the Orders of the Day	To force consideration of a postponed motion	No	No	No	Decision of Chair	Yes
	19. Appeal a Decision of the Chair	To reverse the decision of the chairman	Yes	No	No	Majority	Yes
	18. Rise to a Point of Order or Parliamentary Procedure	To correct a parliamentary error or ask a question	No	No	No	Decision of Chair	Yes
	17. To Call for a Roll Call Vote	To verify a voice vote	Yes	No	No	1/5	No
	16. Object to the Consideration of a Question	To suppress action	No	No	No	2/3	Yes
	15. To Divide a Motion	To consider its parts separately	Yes	No	Yes	Majority	No
	14. Leave to Modify or Withdraw a Motion	To modify or withdraw a motion	No	No	No	Majority	No
	13. To Suspend the Rules	To take action contrary to standing rules	Yes	No	No	2/3	No
	12. To Rescind	To repeal previous action	Yes	Yes	Yes	2/3	No
	11. To Reconsider	To consider a defeated motion again	Yes	Yes	No	Majority	No
	10. To Take from the Table	To consider tabled motion	Yes	No	No	Majority	No
	9. To Lay on the Table	To defer action	Yes	No	No	Majority	No
	8. Previous Question	To force an immediate vote	Yes	No	No	2/3	No
	7. To Limit or Extend Debate	To modify freedom of debate	Yes	Yes	Yes-T	2/3	No
	6. To Postpone to a Certain Time	To defer action	Yes	Yes	Yes	Majority	Yes
	5. To Refer to a Committee*	For further study	Yes	Yes	Yes	Majority	Yes
	4. To Amend an Amendment*	To modify an amendment	1/3	Yes	No	Majority	No
	3. To Amend*	To modify a motion	1/3	Yes	Yes	Majority	No
	2. To Postpone Indefinitely	To suppress action	Yes	Yes	No	Majority	No
	1. Main Motion	To introduce business	Yes	Yes	Yes	Majority	No

*No. 5 Should Include:
1. How Appointed?
2. The Number
3. Report When?
   or
   To What Standing Committee

T-Time

*Nos. 3 and 4 by:
1. Inserting
2. Adding
3. Striking Out
4. Substituting
5. Striking Out and Inserting

Voting

Voting procedures serve best when they are carried out in a particular fashion for student congress. For example, voting on legislation and amendments should always be done by a standing vote unless a roll call is demanded by one-fifth of the members. Preference votes and votes requiring a two-thirds majority should be conducted by either a standing vote or a show of hands. At the discretion of the Presiding Officer, some motions may be disposed of by a voice vote; this can be used to simplify and speed proceedings. A Division of the House may be demanded by any two members on any question on which such a voice vote was taken. This call for a division to verify a voice vote must be made before another motion is placed on the floor. Votes for Presiding Officers and Superior members are by secret ballot.

One form of voting in student congress is a simple show of hands.

Bills, Resolutions, and Amendments

All business conducted in a student congress, aside from elections, centers around either a bill or a resolution. A bill is an enumeration of specific provisions that, if enacted, will have the force of law. Put more simply, a bill is a proposed law that is intended to solve some problem. Once debated and passed by Congress (and signed by the President), a bill becomes a new law. A bill must be definite and must state exactly what is to be done or what is to be discontinued. There must be some enforcement procedure included in it, and it should specify some form of implementation. Specific items, such as phase-in time and financing, may be a part of the bill. A penalty should be stipulated if appropriate, or the law will not have any force.

A resolution, on the other hand, is usually a generalized statement expressing the belief of the group. A resolution is, in other words, a proposition of value or fact. The resolution does not carry the force of law. It may be preceded by "whereas clauses" that state the principal reasons for adopting the resolution, although such clauses are not mandatory. A clear understanding of the differences in the form and substance of bills and resolutions is important. Participation in most student congress events is predicated on your submitting either a bill or a resolution and the thrust of the debate could differ depending on whether a new policy or a value judgment is being debated. A resolution will generally center the debate on the broad principles of the concept; a bill is more likely to focus the debate on the merits of the specific provisions it contains.

As you begin preparing to write your own bill or resolution, you need to start either with a problem area that the congress might attempt to solve by proposing a new law or with a condition that the group sentiment feels needs to be addressed within a resolution. Consider some of the following types of problems that face our country: military, energy, foreign trade, legal and judicial affairs, education, economy, welfare, crime, national security, and technology. As you finalize your choice of topic, remember that your sentiment or proposed solution must be debatable. That is, it must have two sides to it, a pro and a con, or it will not serve the purpose of an item for legislative debate. It must have information available on both sides, and it should be timely and of current interest.

Both the form and substance of these documents are important. NFL has particular rules concerning the form of a bill and of a resolution. Other groups may have different rules, but those from NFL are useful as a model:

1. The bill or resolution must be typed.

2. The typing must be double spaced, and the bill or resolution may not be longer than one page.

3. The first words of a bill are "Be It Enacted . . . ." Following any whereas clauses, the first words of a resolution are "Be It Resolved . . . ."

4. Each line of a bill or resolution must be numbered.

5. A resolution may be preceded by one or more whereas clauses but bills and joint resolutions (bills introduced into both houses of the legislature at about the same time, such as to amend the Constitution) never have them.

6. The language of a bill must always be in the imperative mood. That is, it must state exactly what is to be done by whom.

The following examples highlight the difference in style and format between a bill and a resolution and show how a variety of solutions might be offered when you are dealing with a particular current issue.

Simple Resolution

1.   Whereas, few definitive ethical principles have been
2.   promulgated by either the medical or legal professions
3.   concerning the subject of human organ transplants and/or
4.   artificial organ replacements, and
5.   Whereas, not all patients with organ failures have equal
6.   access to organ transplantation, and
7.   Whereas, the selection criteria to determine which patients
8.   are suitable candidates for organ transplantation surgery are
9.   arbitrary at best and discriminatory at worst, and
10.   Whereas, a disparity exists between the number of patients
11.   in need of transplantation surgery and the number of readily
12.   available organs, and
13.   Whereas, the investment of time, money, personnel, and
14.   facilities for transplant surgery is a grossly inefficient allocation
15.   of medical resources, therefore

16.   Be It Resolved by the House of Representatives in Student
17. Congress assembled that it is the sense of this legislative body
18. that the proliferation of human organ transplants and artificial
19. organ replacements cannot be justified.

A Bill

1.   Be It Enacted by the Senate in Student Congress
2. assembled that
3.   Section 1. A human organ donor organization, titled the
4. National Organ Donor Program, shall be established under the
5. auspices of the Federal Department of Health and Human
6. Services and a universal donor card shall be created to replace
7. the widely varied state donor cards.
8.   Section 2. A national educational program shall be
9. instituted using Public Service announcements on radio and
10. television and within the print media, encouraging people to
11. join the National Organ Donor Program. Said educational
12. program will be funded from the approved budget of the
13. Health and Human Services Department.
14.   Section 3. All state Health Departments and appropriate
15. private agencies shall be invited to join this national donor
16. system and "pool" their available organs, thus establishing a
17. national donor bank. All agencies and states that do join said
18. system shall be linked via a central computer system that will
19. keep records of available organs.
20.   Section 4. The current system of financing and maintaining
21. organ banks shall be transferred to the control of the
22. Department of Health and Human Services and organ
23. recipients shall reimburse the national donor bank through
24. regular hospital charges and insurance payments.
25.   Section 5. Establishment of said National Organ Donor
26. Program shall begin immediately upon passage of this bill, and
27. all necessary operational needs shall be completed on or before
28. the beginning of the next fiscal year following ratification of
29. this legislation.

If you read these examples carefully, you can see what bills and resolutions should include. Note the use of very specific language and the inclusion of monetary conditions. When writing a bill, you should be par-

ticularly sure of what the law is at the present time. Preparing a bill for student congress is much like preparing an affirmative case. The bill is comparable to an affirmative plan. The authorship speech is similar to the affirmative need. It is an appeal for justification for the bill's passage based on conditions that the bill will correct. If you approach that task without adequate research and knowledge, you will probably get the kind of reception you deserve!

A special class is reserved for constitutional amendments. They are classified as resolutions because they must be submitted to the states after they are passed by congress. They are, in reality, only a suggestion to the states. However, they must be specific like a bill. A proposed constitutional amendment should indicate the part of the Constitution being changed and should specify the desired outcome of the amendment.

Bills and resolutions introduced on the floor for legislative debate may generate another kind of consideration, the amendment. In student congress, because the delegates have had the bills and resolutions well ahead of time, there are certain kinds of restrictions put on amendment procedures. First of all, an amendment must be submitted in written form. The written amendment must indicate (by line number) the exact portion of the bill that is being changed. It must indicate what method of change is employed, whether by addition, substitution, or deletion. An example of an amendment, properly worded, for the preceding sample bill would be

> I move that the bill under consideration before this house be amended by altering Section 4 as follows: On lines 22 to 24, delete all words following "Health and Human Services" and substitute with the following: "and all ongoing costs for maintaining these banks and for transporting human organs for use in transplant operations shall be borne by the federal government."

In order to submit an amendment, you must first send the amendment in written form to the clerk. Then you must get recognition from the Presiding Officer. No special consideration will be given because you have an amendment to offer. Once you have the recognition of the chair, you should stand and say, "I move to amend the motion by . . ." and then state the amendment exactly as it is in writing. An alternative method would be to say, "Mr. or Mme. Speaker, I have an amendment to offer and would like permission for the clerk to read it." In either event, it is necessary for one-third of the assembly to second the amendment before discussion is in order. This rule is a departure from the rules as promulgated in *Robert's Rules of Order,* but it is used in student congress to insure that an endless stream of amendments is not presented as a delaying tactic, as is sometimes the case in the U.S. Senate. Once the amendment is on the floor, then all debate must relate to the amendment until it is either passed or defeated. At that point, debate resumes on the bill or resolution in either its original or amended form.

Summary

The procedural rules that govern student congress debate are designed to enable all members to participate. Parliamentary procedure is your key to contributing to student congress. By knowing the rules governing voting, and the introduction of bills, resolutions, and amendments, you can be sure that you are moving the business forward effectively.

Questions for Discussion

1. What is a motion? What are the four classes or types of motions?

2. What is a Second? What is its purpose?

3. How is parliamentary precedence (or priority) determined when you are dealing with motions?

4. Why do debate speeches on a bill alternate from affirmative to negative to affirmative and so on?

5. During your first speech of a session you are interrupted and asked if you will yield to a question of clarification. What can you do on your next stand on the floor if you are concerned that you will again be interrupted at the height of making a point?

6. A member proposes an amendment that you feel is insignificant and would be a waste of debate time. What alternatives are available to you?

Activities

1. Using the four methods employed for conducting votes in a congress session, determine when each could or should be used and list at least one advantage and disadvantage of each method.

2. Make a list of ten current issues or subject matters that you feel could be the basis for a good bill or resolution. The issues could be national, state, or local in scope.

3. Write both a bill and a resolution using two different issues listed in question 2 for turning in to your class student congress hopper.

4. Read Article II in *Robert's Rules of Order*, "General Classifications of Motions."

Chapter 14

The Mechanics of Student Congress

Objectives and Key Terms

After studying Chapter 14, you should be able to

1. Discuss the theory and practice of congressional apportionment,

2. Explain how legislative sessions are scheduled and how an agenda can be developed for a standard congressional meeting, and

3. Understand how a variety of elections are conducted.

After reading this chapter, you should understand the following terms:

apportionment

unicameral

bicameral

legislative session

agenda

Outstanding Member

Superior Member

preferential balloting

F or every student, there is a first-time experience in student congress. Although participation in student congress draws heavily on speech skills acquired in other areas and events, there are many characteristics unique to the student congress event. A complete understanding of the mechanics and structure of student congress will help to insure that the experience is meaningful and successful.

Houses and Apportionment

The student congress is organized to replicate, when possible, the actual legislative bodies of our own nation's government. The number of houses a student congress will have depends on the number of schools and students who participate. Consequently, a student congress may be unicameral, bicameral, or multi-house in its organization. Some local practice congresses have become so popular and so well attended that they are organized with numerous houses, each simulating a group of representatives formed into legislative committees considering a variety of legislation. Some multi-house congresses extend the analogy of the U.S. Congress, being composed of a Senate and a House. Thus, the use of Senator, Representative, or simply Congressmember will be considered as equivalents in this text.

NFL experience has shown that a house with too many members will be unwieldly and will not give enough students the opportunity to participate. By the same token, a house with too few students will not offer sufficient interaction to make the experience worthwhile. Consequently, NFL advises that the optimum membership in a house of a student congress is between 20 and 30.

To govern the number of students participating, the individual NFL District will set a particular apportionment for each chapter in the District Congress. If at least 12 schools are participating, the NFL District may send four members to the National Student Congress and would need a bicameral student congress. The apportionment is usually different for Senate and the House. The NFL District Committee may designate anywhere from one to three senators per chapter. In keeping with the principle exercised in our U.S. Congress, the apportionment of senators would be the same for each NFL chapter, no matter what the size. The House of Representatives, however, is based on population. The population of an NFL chapter is the total number of members and degrees held by that chapter. A typical apportionment might be two senators from each chapter and one member in each house for each thirty members and degrees held by that chapter. Practice congresses and State Activity League Congresses can follow similar guidelines for apportionment. Whatever the formula, the official responsible for it will notify the participating schools prior to the student congress.

When participation in the district or state is large enough, it is a good idea to run a tricameral congress and to designate the house that will not be sending representatives to the National Student Congress as the "Novice House." The Novice House provides students who have not previously participated in student congress with an opportunity to learn and experiment with the event without competition from experienced participants. Some NFL Districts restrict such a house to freshmen and sopho-

Student congress committees have responsibilities similar to those in the U.S. Congress. They help insure cooperation between the houses.

mores, and some even eliminate participation by students with debate experience. The idea is to provide a training ground for students and, in effect, to help quality of future student congress participation.

If the student congress is set up as bicameral, an effort can be made to parallel the actual relationships between the Senate and the House in the U.S. Congress. This can be done by following the suggestions made by NFL. For example, when a bill is passed by one house, it can be sent to the other house with the request that the other house concur. If agreement is not reached, or if amendments are offered and not accepted by the initiating house, then a conference committee can be formed to reach consensus. A report from a conference committee or a report from one house to another shall be privileged, but may not interrupt a speaker. This kind of relationship between the houses helps to insure good debate and keeps student congressmen aware of the larger group.

Sessions

The length of a legislative session depends on the desires and facilities of the general director of the student congress. Most practice and district congresses hold a one-day session; many others, such as state-wide or invitational congresses, hold two-day sessions. NFL rules specify that each legislative day of a District or National Congress must contain a minimum of five hours of floor debate in addition to the time used for committee meetings or elections. For a one-day congress, it is possible to have a morning and an afternoon session, each of about three hours' duration. When an agenda, or order of business, for a congress session calls for committee meetings, these may be accomplished either formally or informally. Committees frequently are asked to review proposed bills and resolutions, to choose appropriate legislation for later congresses, or to choose the order of debate at the current congress. They may rewrite clumsy legislation or recommend amendments for the entire house to consider. A final purpose might be to write commendatory resolutions.

The sample time schedules that follow contrast various organizational structures.

Sample Time Schedule for a One-Day Student Congress

8:00 A.M.— 8:30 A.M.	Registration and verification of entries
8:30 A.M.—11:30 A.M.	Morning session
11:30 A.M.—12:30 P.M.	Lunch break
12:30 P.M.— 2:30 P.M.	Afternoon session
2:30 P.M.— 3:30 P.M.	Elections and Awards

Sample Time Schedule for a Two-Day Session

3:00 P.M.— 3:30 P.M.	Registration and verification of entries
3:30 P.M.— 7:30 P.M.	Session I

Second Day

8:30 A.M.—11:30 A.M.	Session II
11:30 A.M.—12:45 P.M.	Lunch break
12:45 P.M.— 3:00 P.M.	Session III
3:30 P.M.—	Joint meeting, elections, awards

At the National Student Congress, each house is in session for the length of the National NFL Tournament. This will usually be three full legislative days (in addition to committee meetings and election time) for the preliminary sessions and one additional legislative day for the final session.

Organization

The mechanics of student congress are much simpler than those of a debate tournament. However, because of its unique nature, careful attention to details will determine whether the student congress will be exciting and successful or disappointing to all.

Prior to the actual student congress, bills and resolutions should be distributed to all participating schools. NFL specifies that all schools should receive copies of the bills and resolutions that will be on the agenda at least 30 days prior to the student congress. This amount of time allows for adequate preparation by competing students and guarantees better quality of floor debate.

As students report to the congressional session, certain organizational details must be taken care of. Prior to the session, a seating chart should have been prepared that accurately represents the seating arrangement and the exact number of delegates who will be seated. Each seat should be numbered. A corresponding set of numbers should be prepared for delegates to draw as they register. The number drawn will automatically determine where the delegate will sit. Some student congresses arbitrarily assign seats ahead of time. However, in the interest of fairness, seating should be determined by a random drawing. Even if seats must be assigned ahead of time, a random drawing should be used.

A suggested "Order of Business" is printed in the *NFL Congress Manual*. Although certain legislative bodies may follow a different agenda, this one is suitable for any such group. An agenda, or order of business, is vital to insuring that all items are handled in an orderly and timely manner.

Order of Business for Student Congress

1. Invocation
2. Call to order
3. Roll call of members and confirmation of seating charts
4. Special orders
    a. Review of special rules
    b. Review of congress procedures
    c. Special announcements and questions
5. Consideration of the calendar
6. Election of Presiding Officer
7. Committee meetings (optional) may be held at a time prearranged by the District Chairperson
8. Floor debate on bills/resolutions
9. Selection of Outstanding and Most-Outstanding congress participants
10. Award of congress gavel and plaques
11. Fixing time for next meeting
12. Adjournment

Elections

Presiding Officer

The Presiding Officer conducts the assembly as efficiently and fairly as possible so that the purpose of the congress is accomplished and each member has a full chance to demonstrate his or her ability to speak and subsequently to improve. Because of this responsibility, it is important that the person chosen as the Presiding Officer be the best possible one.

It is also important that the student chosen have a real desire to serve in that capacity and take pride in her or his ability to keep the group running smoothly and fairly. To insure this, students at the District Student Congress are asked to submit their names in advance for consideration as Presiding Officer. If a very large number of names is submitted, the district committee or the General Director will have to select three for each house. Each nominee for Presiding Officer will be allowed to preside for 20 to 30 minutes in rotation. Then the members of the house will select by ballot the one who will preside for the duration of the student congress. At practice congresses, the same selection process can be used.

The procedure at the National Student Congress is somewhat different. At the first session, the General Director will appoint a temporary Presiding Officer. This person will open the session, introduce the Parliamentarian and scorer, and will then accept nominations for Presiding Officer. In most cases, there will be a nominating speech in which each candidate may present qualifications and experience that might suggest an ability to lead the group as its Presiding Officer. After all nominees have been heard, there will be an election by ballot. Each member, including the temporary Presiding Officer, writes the name of one nominee on a slip of paper. When one nominee receives a majority of the vote, the voting ceases, and the winner is announced. However, until that time, the following procedure is used. After each ballot, the person receiving the fewest number of votes (or the persons, if two or more are tied) is dropped from the list, and the members vote again. This procedure is used until one receives a majority and is declared the Presiding Officer for the session. Because the first half day at the National Student Congress is used for committee meetings, the term of office for each Presiding Officer will be one afternoon and one morning, making up a full legislative day. There will be a total of three different Presiding Officers for each of the houses of the National Student Congress. This procedure could be used by practice congresses as well.

Although the Presiding Officer cannot be nominated for the Superior Representative during the session at which he or she presides, an official congress gavel is awarded to the student for that session. There are two reasons for excluding the Presiding Officer from consideration for Superior Representative. First, it should be apparent that the Presiding Officer would have higher visibility than any other member of the group. Further, the natural aura of authority that has to surround a Presiding Officer would create a kind of "halo effect" and give that person an advantage over all others who might be nominated for that session.

However, more important, if the Presiding Officer is in contention for Superior Representative during the session in which he or she presides, his or her objectivity might be compromised. If actively competing for honors, he or she might be tempted to give recognition only to those who would not threaten his or her winning. Instead, giving the Presiding Officer an automatic award effectively removes that person from a competitive frame of mind. It is important to remember, however, that a person who has already been selected Superior Representative for one session may be elected Presiding Officer at another session. Conversely, a person who has served as Presiding Officer for one session may be nominated for superior member during another session.

Superior Members

Each house of the student congress selects outstanding students for awards. The nomination and election procedures that NFL outlines for practice and NFL District Congresses differ somewhat from those used at the National Student Congress. There are major differences in duration and complexity. However, the basic principle of selection is the same in all situations. The nomination for outstanding students is done by the official scorer and the Parliamentarian of each house, each of whom nominates a designated number of students as superior participants. The final selection of the most outstanding student from among the nominees is done by balloting all the student members of the house. The standard terminology that has developed for award winners for student congress recognizes the first place competitor as Most Outstanding, the runner-up as Outstanding, and others nominated as superior participants.

In NFL District and practice congresses, after the nominations have been made without consultation between the two officials, there is a vote at the conclusion of the congress. The same method that is used for the Presiding Officer voting is used. However, when two candidates remain, the one receiving more votes is awarded the gold plaque as Most Outstanding; the second student receives the silver plaque as Outstanding. If the student congress is the NFL District Congress, the students receiving the plaques also qualify for the National Student Congress.

At the National Student Congress, the Parliamentarian and the scorer nominate, without consultation, two students for each legislative session. In addition, the three top point earners of the session are added if they were not nominated by either official. At the end of each legislative day, the names of all nominated students are placed on a ballot, and preferential balloting is used to determine for each Senate or House the Superior Representatives. These students qualify to participate in the fourth, or final, session, from which come the final award winners for the National Student Congress. In preferential balloting, each member marks all names on the ballot with numbers—for example, first through sixth place for a ballot with six candidates. Only one ballot is used to determine preferential winners. The ballots are first separated according to the first choice that is shown on each. The person receiving the lowest number of first place votes is temporarily set aside, and his or her votes are then distributed according to the second choice expressed on those ballots. The person then having the lowest number of votes is set aside, and his or her votes are redistributed. This process continues until one candidate has received a majority of the votes and is declared the winner of the balloting. The same ballots may then be used in a similar manner to determine the second most-preferred candidate once the winner's name has been removed as a further contender. The use of this method of voting insures secrecy of the results until the conclusion of the third session or, in the case of the final session, until the National Tournament Awards Session. Understanding how preferential balloting functions should make a student more aware of the importance of marking the places below first.

Summary

The rules of student congress are similar to those of the U.S. Congress, although the student congress may have more or less than two houses. The houses meet in sessions with a specific order of business. As a member, you will be responsible for knowing the bills and resolutions on the agenda prior to the session. You will also vote to elect the Presiding Officer and Superior Members of your house.

Questions for Discussion

1. In the U.S. Congress, what is the difference in apportionment between the Senate and the House? Why is there such a distinction?

2. What is the difference between a unicameral and a bicameral congress?

3. What are the purposes of committee meetings?

4. Why are student congress award winners nominated by official scorers and Parliamentarians but actually elected by the congress members themselves?

Activities

1. Using a local organization, such as a service club or school council, compose what you feel would be a suitable agenda for a typical group meeting.

2. Using your own state's population in relation to our national population, determine how your state's congressional apportionment was computed in the U.S. House of Representatives.

3. Put together an outline for a short self-nomination speech that you could deliver to your class to highlight the qualities that would make you a suitable Presiding Officer candidate for a session of congress.

Chapter 15

Responsibilities of Student Congress Officials

Objectives and Key Terms

After studying Chapter 15, you should be able to

1. Identify the officials utilized for a student congress and their responsibilities,

2. Serve as a Presiding Officer for a practice session of congress, and

3. Understand the criteria used to judge student congress presentations.

After reading this chapter, you should understand the following terms:

General Director	page
official scorer	timekeeper
speaking points	Presiding Officer
Parliamentarian	gavel

E very student congress must have a General Director who will make arrangements and give general supervision to the entire event. Within each house of the student congress, certain officials are necessary for smooth operation. NFL rules specify that each house must have a Parliamentarian, a Chief Clerk, or both. At the National level, these are always two different persons, but at lower level student congresses, the duties may be performed by one person. An official scorer is also appointed for each half day of legislative session. In addition, the host school or district should provide two students to act as pages for each house. A person responsible for timekeeping is also necessary. In addition to the appointed officials, each house of the student congress elects a Presiding Officer for each session.

General Director

The responsibilities of the General Director of a student congress are, for the most part, supervisory in nature. If the student congress is an NFL District or National Congress, then the arrangements that must be made are outlined by the rules of that organization. The General Director of a practice student congress or any student congress modeled after the NFL student congress must be aware of the many responsibilities the position carries with it.

The General Director is responsible for finding a suitable location for the congressional sessions. Experience has shown that this is a very important matter. Great effort should be exercised to find a meeting area that is not a classroom or an auditorium. If possible, the trustee board room, the city council chambers, a library, or a courtroom should be obtained. The proper location of a student congress helps produce the frame of mind in each competitor that will lead to outstanding performance. The environment should seem like a congressional meeting place.

The General Director is also responsible for securing the services of all the other student congress officials (Parliamentarian, Chief Clerk, scorer, pages, and timekeeper). These persons will directly determine the success of the student congress, and the General Director should select them carefully according to the guidelines of their positions. After selecting them, the General Director should arrange to meet with them, give them written instructions, and make sure they fully understand their responsibilities and the overall activity of student congress.

The General Director is also responsible for securing awards. Each Presiding Officer must have a gavel during the session and to be presented to the Presiding Officer at the conclusion of the student congress. In addition, there should be a plaque for both the first- and second-place competitors from each house, with possible awards for all those nominated as superior participants.

Official Scorer

The official scorer judges student congress performances. Each legislative session has a different scorer. The scorer has the major responsibility for determining the relative merit of each speech and awarding points to it. In NFL and practice student congresses, there is a maximum of six points for each speech, with five or six points awarded for a superb presentation, three or four points given for an average speech, and one or two points reserved to indicate that the presentation was deficient in major areas. These point restrictions are different at the National Student Congress. Because of these restrictions, the scorer must have a firm idea of the standards to be used in scoring, along with a clear knowledge of the rules that govern speaking in student congress. Such factors as persuasiveness, communicative delivery, innovative and effective arguments, sound reasoning and logical analysis, and incisive and knowledgeable answers to questions should weigh heavily in an official scorer's criteria for judging speeches. The speaker's ability to follow the flow of the debate and respond to previous speakers is also important, as is the speaker's ability to support and document assertions. In all, an official scorer is asked to evaluate both the content and the delivery of the speech.

The scorer must know, in addition, that no student may speak more than five times in a legislative day unless no other delegate is asking for the floor. In addition, he or she should realize that no points can be awarded for clerical duties. The scorer must also award points to the Presiding Officer at the end of each hour. These points should reflect the quality of the Presiding Officer's performance during that hour. The scorer's job is difficult and demanding. It should not be accepted without careful consideration of what is involved.

At the end of the session, the scorer will nominate an agreed-upon number of members (usually two or three) for student congress honors. These nominations, along with those submitted by the Parliamentarian, shall be voted on by the students. These nominees should be the students who have done the most outstanding job during that session. Although the scorer awards points only for speeches that were given, every facet of the students' congress performance should be considered when making nominations.

Parliamentarian

Although the Parliamentarian's role is also supervisory, the position requires a great deal of responsibility. The person who serves in this capacity must not only know parliamentary procedure, but also be very familiar with the special rules of student congress and be willing to see that errors in procedure are immediately remedied. As a consequence, the Parliamentarian must be someone whose authority will not be questioned, but also someone who will not assert that authority until it is necessary to do so.

The Parliamentarian must have a clear understanding of the nature of student congress and must be dedicated to advancing it in the most efficient possible way. It is the Parliamentarian's primary duty to back up and reinforce the Presiding Officer. Further, the purpose of student congress is to debate legislation, and the Parliamentarian is charged with the responsibility of seeing that time is not wasted on other matters. The Parliamentarian also nominates students for honors at the conclusion of each session. He or she takes into account total contributions made to the student congress by members during that session.

An accurate record should be kept of all proceedings and, consequently, of any parliamentary problems that arise. Often, the Parliamentarian is responsible for such a record, either keeping it or delegating the responsibility to someone else. A preferred system is a dual one in which either a clerk or a page and the Parliamentarian both keep a written record of legislation and motions and their disposal.

Page

The page for a house in student congress facilitates communication among the members of the house, between the Presiding Officer and

members, and among the officials. The page is, in short, a bearer of mes-
sages. He or she should be seated in an area that is easily accessible to the
Presiding Officer, scorer, and Parliamentarian. The location should also
provide a clear view of the assembly for the page to respond to a sum-
mons from a member. Excessive message sending is not to be encouraged, but notes can often allow for better working relationships and offset poor debating conditions. In addition, the page should assist with
clerical duties, such as point recording at the end of each session, passing
and collecting ballots, recording motions and their disposal, and giving
any other assistance to student congress officials.

Timekeeper

Because each speech is restricted to only three minutes and because accurate adherence to time limits insures fairness, a timekeeper is an essential official in the student congress. He or she should be equipped with a
stopwatch and should be instructed to use time cards. The time cards
allow a speaker to see the number of minutes remaining in the speech
and alert the Presiding Officer that the speaker's time is expiring. For
this reason, the timekeeper should be seated in a place that is clearly visi-
ble to the Presiding Officer, Parliamentarian, scorer, and speaker. Strict
enforcement of time limits is necessary.

The timekeeper insures that all
speakers have the same amount
of time to present their
arguments.

Presiding Officer

The Presiding Officer for each session of student congress is elected from the membership of that group. It is absolutely essential to place a person in that position who can exert leadership. The person who is presiding must also know parliamentary procedure, must be willing to use it, and must be able to use it with authority. This does not mean that the ideal Presiding Officer is a martinet who has no interpersonal skills. It does mean that the Presiding Officer is "boss" and should be obeyed within the structure of parliamentary law. A weak Presiding Officer can wreck a student congress and waste everyone's time.

The Presiding Officer must be aware of the restrictions placed on the recognition of speakers and must apply the rules regardless of school and personal loyalties. A Presiding Officer who is not fair in giving recognition will quickly have a group of enemies in the student congress who will begin to be a negative and obstructive force. Although the Presiding Officer is in charge, it is much better to be in charge of cooperative individuals.

In addition to the recognition of speakers, the Presiding Officer is also responsible for insuring the rotation of speakers from affirmative to negative. This is usually achieved by announcing clearly each time, "The chair will now entertain a speech for the affirmative (or negative) side." Furthermore, the Presiding Officer must establish a consistent method of presiding that is clearly understood by all. For example, following each speech the chair can announce, "Procedural motions are now in order." If no one asks for recognition, the Presiding Officer can then call for the next speech. This eliminates misunderstandings of the reason a member seeks recognition. The Presiding Officer must also control time limits for speeches and must have a clear, consistent policy on stopping speakers at the conclusion of their allotted time. One of the functions of the chair's gavel comes into play at this point in the proceedings.

The Presiding Officer must make sure that a member yields only to a question and not in order to allow another member to speak. The main goal of the Presiding Officer should be to insure fairness and equity set out in the rules of student congress, such as the procedural rule specifying that no one shall be recognized to speak a second time if anyone asking for recognition has not spoken for the first time. To allow a person who receives recognition under that rule to yield speaking time to one who has already spoken would obviously circumvent the established equity. If a Presiding Officer fails to enforce such rules, he or she is subject to parliamentary moves from the assembly or to a ruling from the Parliamentarian.

In addition to a leadership role and a procedural role, the Presiding Officer must also fulfill a political role. Unfortunately in our society, the label of "politics" or "politician" has come to carry negative connotations in recent years. However, we use the term in the context of the interpersonal roles that are a necessary part of the student congress environment. The Presiding Officer must work constantly with the members of the assembly to cement and solidify relationships. He or she should be aware, for example, of the pressures under which members of the assembly are working. The Presiding Officer should be sensitive to their desire to be treated fairly but should also help them be conscious of the difficulty of the Presiding Officer's roles. Very minor, yet highly effective, strategies can make such a relationship possible. For example, the Presiding Officer may become aware of a person who has asked for recognition but has not received it and is angry. A quick note explaining that others will have to be recognized first but that the Presiding Officer is aware of the member and will get to him or her in due time may certainly alleviate the anxiety. Such an act by the Presiding Officer can take the edge off the member's frustration and keep that member from turning the frustration into a negative element in the debate ahead.

The Presiding Officer should also be aware of those in the assembly who make the job smoother and easier. The member who makes a helpful procedural motion or the one who handles a problem by suggestion rather than by challenging the Presiding Officer's authority should be acknowledged by the Presiding Officer. The member who gives a particularly outstanding speech or the one who uses valuable speaking time to clarify a rather muddled debate has also made an important contribution to the assembly. The Presiding Officer who is alert to these positive elements in the student congress should send notes or make a point of speaking to these persons during a recess. Each kind of positive move made by members of the assembly makes the performance of the Presiding Officer easier and more impressive to observers.

Interdependency is the key to a successful term as Presiding Officer of student congress. The Presiding Officer should certainly be prepared to deal with intransigent or stalemating members by using parliamentary rules properly and decisively. However, in order to fulfill an obligation to all of the assembly, school, regional, or personal loyalties should be firmly set aside when the Presiding Officer picks up the gavel.

Each official of the student congress, whether appointed or elected, has very specific and important obligations for making the student congress successful. However, these officials function within an environment governed by certain mechanics of procedure that must be clearly understood by all and that were discussed in chapters 13 and 14.

Summary

Although every student congress member plays an important part in the business, officials have special roles. The General Director, scorer, Parliamentarian, page, timekeeper, and Presiding Officer all function to keep debate running smoothly and fairly. Serving in one of these offices can enhance your student congress experience.

Questions for Discussion

1. Why is the job of the General Director so important?

2. What are the roles of the official scorer in a competitive student congress session?

3. What is the purpose of the Parliamentarian in a student congress session?

4. How might the use of time cards assist all participants in a student congress session?

Activities

1. Research the background and historical origins of the gavel.

2. Determine a satisfactory method by which a Presiding Officer could set up a priority system to help recognize both speakers and questioners fairly throughout an entire session of congress.

3. In groups of about five students, take turns serving as Presiding Officer. Recognize a member of the small group to make a motion and then respond to the motion using correct terminology, putting the motion to a vote, if appropriate.

Chapter 16

Preparation for Student Congress

Objectives and Key Terms

After studying Chapter 16, you should be able to

1. Make use of such speech preparation tools as research, library skills, briefing, organization, and outlining,

2. Research and analyze a bill or resolution and set up an "issues file" on the topic,

3. Prepare an authorship speech for a chosen piece of legislation, and

4. Prepare a congress brief for a prospective bill or resolution.

After reading this chapter, you should understand the following terms:

analysis

evidence files

briefs

authorship speech

squad preparation

Once you have a sound understanding of the principles of student congress and have mastered the mechanics of the event, you are ready to begin preparation for participation. Although most students who are part of an NFL chapter will be preparing along with the whole squad, there are a number of things you should do for yourself.

Individual Preparation

Analysis

The first step in student congress preparation is to read carefully and thoughtfully the legislation under consideration. The chapter on analysis earlier in this book contains all the elements you will need to utilize in this process. Remember that in student congress, however, some differences in outlook must be considered. A more global point of view is necessary for student congress analysis than for interscholastic debate analysis. The analysis of bills and resolutions for student congress must fall into the realm of what is good and best for the nation, not just what will win a debate round. A long-range view and a national perspective are important in congress debates. In your analysis, you should strive to get beyond local, partisan, or regional outlooks. This is especially important in preparation for the NFL National Student Congress, but it can be equally important in other levels of student congress.

The student congress representative from the Deep South whose only perception is a southern one may find her or his views rejected outright. He or she may suffer from a credibility gap difficult to overcome. The Texan who sees the energy crisis from the perspective of "Let the Yankees freeze to death in the dark," a sentiment expressed on some bumper stickers in that region, may alienate a large number of people quickly. And so would a student congress senator from New York who asserts that the energy situation is a fraud perpetrated by the major oil companies to hike up profits. This is not to say that these viewpoints are invalid. However, they are not the *only* valid viewpoints. You must attempt to discover many points of view prior to entry into floor debate. You may choose not to espouse them, but you must know that they exist. A purely provincial analysis will not serve you well.

Another area in which your analysis for student congress differs somewhat from that for debate is in the historical perspective. In recent years, it has become the fashion for college and high school teams to indicate in the affirmative plan that "Affirmative speeches will constitute the legislative history of this proposal." What this does, in effect, is to erase all the past history of any other attempts to adopt or reject such a proposal. Consequently, the negative's charge that the "U.S. Congress just last year voted not to fund a proposal to develop solar energy" would have no validity in the debate. Such a practice is not in vogue in student congress, however. Since the student congress attempts to function within the framework of reality, the legislative, political, and judicial history of any proposal is not only relevant, but vital to legislative consideration. If the bill to come before the student congress concerns a moratorium on spending for research and development for the Strategic Defense Initiative, a student who attempts to speak about that bill without an understanding of past arms treaties and without an understanding of the military and political relations between the United States and the Soviet Union on the issue of "Star Wars" has done a poor job of analysis of the bill.

Finally, analysis for student congress must also involve an understanding of the vested interests that are represented by the proposal. It must reflect an awareness of the ultimate effect of the adoption or rejection of the bill and of the possible compromises that may be needed to gain adoption. Having gained this understanding and awareness, you will then know what alliances will be necessary to achieve your goal. In short, the analysis of legislation for debate in student congress involves not only the proposition itself but also the interaction between advocates and opponents. It should be apparent that if there weren't these partisan positions and competing arguments, there would be no clash created and the legislation would be adopted without debate.

Research

As you analyze the bills and resolutions for student congress, you are laying the groundwork for the research process. Read everything you can find on the subjects covered. Collect as much information as you would in preparing a research paper. Talk with people whose ideas might be particularly valuable. Begin by researching generalities on the subject matter. Find out the present problem that the bill attempts to solve or that the resolution addresses. Be sure to research both sides of the question. Ultimately you might decide to give a speech either for or against the legislation. Be aware of the subject matter in the news; approach the situation as if you were an actual legislator dealing with actual legislation. Although you will not accumulate the bulk of files and evidence cards that the average debate team collects these days, you must begin with the notion that special research is necessary for thorough preparation. For this purpose, you will need to consult some sources not traditionally used by debaters. To gain a historical perspective on each bill, a good place to begin is an encyclopedia or a government textbook. Books that would probably not be quoted in a debate round hold a great deal of value for the student congress deliberation.

You must be able to speak with authority about the present as well as the past. Current magazines should be utilized (keep the *Readers' Guide to Periodical Literature* handy), with special emphasis on such publications as *Vital Speeches, Congressional Quarterly, Congressional Digest, The Congressional Record, The Congressional Quarterly Weekly Report,* and *Current History.* The value of these particular publications is their regular inclusion of actual legislative debate on issues that would be similar to those considered by the student congress. *Facts on File* for the current year, as well as for the past several years, is an important source of specific examples and statistical data. The current issue of an almanac such as *Information Please Almanac* will give up-to-date materials. If your squad maintains extemporaneous speaking files, they will have a wealth of current information on many of the bills. In addition to these sources, you may want to write to your own United States congressional representatives for materials. Personal letters, telephone conversations, newscasts, and personal interviews are admissible as evidence in student congress as long as they are accurately and carefully cited. Evidence in student congress is necessary just as it is in debate, and a great variety of sources is useful. The same care for accuracy and ethics in evidence usage must be taken in student congress as in debate.

A final note on research. After you have researched the subject matter on each bill and resolution, another area of general research will prove very valuable. Get facts and statistics together concerning the decision-making process as it relates to government spending. How much money is being spent and how much the national debt is growing are important facts and should be readily available to use in floor debate. Beyond these obvious facts, you need to know more about how the specific bills considered by the student congress fit into an overall budget picture in the current economic and fiscal situation in the nation. Be creative. Find out how much money is going into "pork barrel" projects, congressional junkets, strange research subjects, such as the mating habits of the three-toed sloth, and other areas in which government money might be said to be wasted. Investigate government bureaucracy and departmental organization. These facts might seem trivial, but they can frequently serve you well as you are pressed to demonstrate priorities. Such material injected into the floor debate can also alleviate tension through the judicious use of humor.

Organization

Once you have gathered the evidence you need for each bill and resolution, you must put it into a form that will make it easily retrievable and usable. Many students have used various methods of organizing their congress files. Two methods used with a high degree of success by students of the authors are offered here as examples.

A *vertical file* organization is flexible and easy to set up. Secure one legal-sized manila file folder for each bill or resolution. On the outside of the folder, draw a vertical line that divides the front into two equal parts. On one side, list all the arguments in favor of the bill. On the other side, list all the points against the bill. Devise a simple numerical code beside each argument, such as A-1, A-2, and so on. Place the numerical designation beside each argument. Inside the file folder, place all the evidence you have collected to support each of the points listed on the front. Each piece of evidence should be given the numerical code corresponding to the point it supports. You should laminate or glue the actual bill or resolution to the inside front cover of the file. In this way, all the pertinent materials about each bill are easily accessible for quick reference during floor debate.

A second method of organization is the use of a *loose leaf notebook*. A section is set aside for each bill or resolution by means of a divider properly labeled with the name of the item. Plastic "slick sheets" are used to hold the bill at the front of each section. Next, a section of all arguments for the bill is set up. On a sheet of paper, outline all the arguments in favor of the resolution or bill. Immediately behind that page, all evidence is entered to support those points. After the section in favor of the bill, a page of outlined arguments against the bill is placed, followed by evidence to support those points. In this kind of organization, photocopies of articles with pertinent sections underlined or highlighted can be number coded in the margin to match the section on the outlined arguments. You can also put together a series of congress briefs for each bill or resolution. Briefs contain a multitude of arguments in outline form, including interspersed evidence taken from a variety of sources. Such a brief becomes a "living document" that could be used during the floor debate. If a few of your own arguments happen to be used by one or more speakers, you could cross off those points from your brief. As new issues or challenges arise, it is easy enough to add arguments or responses onto your brief. As you seek recognition for your speech, it is easy enough to order the major points remaining on your brief and add an introduction, transitions, and a conclusion to round out the speech. The ability to speak from an outline is indispensable to this style of organization. Regardless of which method you use, remember that in congress just as in debate, citations should be shown for all evidence.

Additional kinds of organization may occur to you. Students frequently group bills by broad categories, such as Foreign Aid, Energy, or Defense. General information is then collected and filed in corresponding categories. Other students prefer to take extemporaneous speaking files into the congress meeting room. Whatever works well for you should be used. The point is that you must impose some organization on your material. The student congress competitor who arrives with a group of loose papers clutched in hand, a randomly selected magazine or two under the arm, and no clear idea of what to say is at a severe disadvantage. The student who comes with organized and well-supported positions will be able to get into the debate quickly and will give a good accounting of herself or himself in the bargain.

Preparing Speeches

After analyzing, gathering, and organizing evidence, you should carefully look at each bill and resolution to determine if you would like to offer any amendments. If so, they should be written out, and evidence should be gathered for each one and filed according to the organizational scheme you are using. Of course, amendments may grow out of the debate, in which case they cannot be prepared in advance. However, careful thinking about each bill may reveal several possible amendments that can be prepared and researched ahead of time.

If you have submitted a bill or resolution to the student congress, you will need to prepare your authorship speech carefully. This speech will be the first one given on the bill and will serve to introduce it to the assembly. Because the speech can be prepared ahead of time, it can and should have the careful construction and audience appeal of an oration. The authorship speech could be used to spike out the major objections that the opposition might try to voice. Anticipating and preempting arguments will make the position of the bill stronger initially and will make it more difficult for the members who wish to oppose it to find a valid argument. As with all congress speeches, the authorship speech should begin with an arresting introduction to challenge the audience, contain a well-organized body, and close with a thoughtful summary and conclusion.

Remember that during this individual preparation you will be collecting far more than you will be able to utilize in actual speaking situations in student congress. The problem is that you will not be able to anticipate just what you will get to say or the circumstances under which you will be able to say it. If you plan only one specific issue to cover only one side of a bill, you may find yourself unable to use it for a variety of reasons. The first person to get recognition may say precisely what you had planned to say, therefore effectively neutralizing your impact if you should get a chance to speak. Or it may be that a great many students wish to speak on the same side you had originally planned for, making it difficult for you to get the floor. However, no one may have been prepared to speak on the opposite side, leaving the floor wide open for you if you are suitably prepared on that side as well. Since participation is the door to success in student congress, it should be obvious that broad and careful preparation is the key to that door.

Squad Preparation

Ideally, a speech and debate squad will have several opportunities during the year to participate in practice student congresses. Sometimes, however, the only student congress of the year is the NFL District Congress. Whether student congress is a continuous event throughout the year or a once-a-year occasion, a squad working together can do a great deal to get all its members ready to participate. Squad participation in the preparation process is important even if only a few are allowed to attend, because experience needs to be built for future participation.

Attitude

The most important part of a squad's preparation for student congress is the setting of attitudes. A coach should talk about and help prepare for student congress to grant it the importance that it is due. The squad should see student congress as a respected and valuable activity. A clear understanding of the principles of student congress and of the place such experience has in the forensic progression can help build those attitudes that will foster success for the individual as well as the group.

A valuable aspect of squad preparation is participation in a practice student congress.

Bills and Resolutions

Each member of the squad should already have written at least one bill or resolution. There are several reasons for this. First, you will gain a great deal of understanding about analysis of a bill from doing the research necessary to produce one yourself. You will then be better able to evaluate the merits of the legislation actually used in the student congress. You will be able to detect a weak bill or one that is not in proper form. There is also the pragmatic need for practice bills for the squad practice sessions. Requiring everyone on the squad to write at least one bill will produce an ample supply for that purpose. Finally, the school will usually be required to submit at least one bill or resolution for use in the debate at student congress. The more bills the squad has to choose from, the better the quality of the bill eventually sent to the General Director of the student congress.

Once the bills have been written, it is useful for the squad to read them carefully, evaluate them as to form and substance, and make suggestions for revision. Then the squad should make some initial analysis of the bills as a group. This squad analysis gives you practice in preparation for the time when you will have to analyze the bills that will be used in the student congress in which you will compete.

Research

Squad research is another important tool. This is not to say that individuals will be excused from their own research. Quite to the contrary, each person must conduct independent analysis and research in any given area. But a certain amount of background for particular bills can be assigned to squad members who can then share the information and save time for the group. The specific arguments that you will bring up for or against a bill must then be researched by you, but the overall background of the topic will be common to all, regardless of your position on the bill.

Parliamentary Procedure

Individual students can read the parliamentary rules and review a precedence chart. But the way to achieve a working knowledge of parliamentary procedure is through practice and use. This requires a group effort, and it is one of the most important things a squad can do to prepare for student congress. After an initial review and discussion of motions, precedence, and rules, the coach should appoint a Presiding Officer, hand out a bill that has been researched, and begin a series of practice sessions in class. The coach can prescribe motions to be made at given points or can simply encourage students to experiment with all the motions. The Presiding Officer should be rotated with each new bill so that all members of the squad can learn the rudiments of presiding. In this fashion, you can find out in the relative safety of the classroom which motions can be used and what their effect on an assembly will be. A word of caution here is appropriate. Expect the first several sessions to be somewhat chaotic and confusing. This is not the fault of parliamentary procedure but rather the result of inexperience. That, in itself, should encourage a lot of practice sessions before competing in student congress. You might consider inviting a current or former member of your forensic squad with some congress experience to serve as Presiding Officer for your first practice session.

During these parliamentary practice sessions, it would be a good idea for the coach or an outside observer to score the speeches given. This will give the squad some idea of how well their speeches were structured and what each one needs to do for improvement. A clerk should also keep records of the parliamentary procedures used during these sessions so that the coach can check at the end of the session for motions that may not have been used. Through practice, the group will get a great deal of experience in the use of parliamentary rules and legislative debate. Make sure there is time and a method for debriefing after each practice session so that the experience constitutes learning, not just the repetition of mistakes. The old adage that "Practice makes perfect" might, without such a process, better be stated, "Practice makes perfectly awful!"

Rules and Regulations

In addition to practicing parliamentary procedure, the practice sessions conducted by the squad should familiarize everyone with the rules and regulations governing the congress that will be attended. Rules restricting speaking, time limits, methods of addressing the chair, and other procedural rules should be strictly enforced during practice sessions. If the squad uses these rules enough, they will learn them thoroughly. They will feel more secure in the student congress. And they will have time during student congress debates to think more about what they are going to say than about the form in which they should be speaking or other procedural considerations.

Summary

You prepare for student congress both by yourself and with your squad. On your own, you analyze and research the bills and resolutions and then organize your information. You also prepare your authorship speech or any amendments you wish to propose. As a member of a squad, you develop bills and resolutions for an upcoming congress and practice parliamentary procedure.

Questions for Discussion

1. What are the differences in style and method of research between conventional debate and student congress debate?

2. How would you respond to the statement, "Student congress is the easiest style of debate because you don't really have to worry about extensive research and a plethora of evidence"?

3. Why is knowledge of the status quo of a bill's subject matter useful in preparing student congress arguments?

4. How is squad preparation an important supplement to individual preparation?

Activities

1. Take a walking tour of the reference section of your school or community library, making a list of the variety of political, legal, historical, and statistical reference books and specialized encyclopedias that could be used for student congress research.

2. Using a piece of legislation written for Chapter 13, prepare a file of notes, articles, reproductions, and other pertinent materials that could later be used in putting together a congress brief for use in an actual legislative debate.

3. Using an additional piece of legislation written for Chapter 13, use the "squad preparation" technique of brainstorming a series of pro and con arguments relating to the bill. Work from the class's knowledge of the background and current situation as it applies to the bill in question.

4. Plan to devote a future week of your class to a five-day congress session. This will require utilizing the principles and procedures presented in Chapters 13, 14, and 16 of this textbook, including writing bills and resolutions and researching the legislation in order to prepare congress briefs. Classmates will serve as Presiding Officers, and your teacher should fill the role of Parliamentarian. Possibly, a school administrator could be invited to serve as official scorer.

Chapter 17

Strategies for Success in Student Congress

Objectives and Key Terms

After studying Chapter 17, you should be able to

1. Understand the various types of congress speeches and the strategic uses of each,

2. List the personal competitive qualities that are necessary to be a successful participant in student congress, and

3. Participate in an actual floor debate as part of a session of student congress.

After reading this chapter, you should understand the following terms:

interpersonal relationships

political "games"

refutation

clash

I f you plan and prepare to participate in a student congress, you will, of course, aspire to succeed in the activity. But, although your advance understanding and thorough preparation are major determinants of success, these elements are only the first steps. Your actual conduct and your attitude during the student congress are the variables that make student congress participation such a challenge. We have interviewed many successful participants about their impressions of the attitudes and actions most likely to contribute to effectiveness in student congress. Based on their experiences, we offer some suggestions that may be useful to future student congress members. This collection of suggestions is not meant to constitute a money-back guarantee for election to Outstanding congressmember. Your own personality as well as the past relationships that you have had in competition with others in the student congress will affect how well a particular strategy will work for you.

Attitude

Legislative debate is a challenging and rewarding experience for a forensic student. The person who approaches student congress as if it were a step down from debate insults not only the activity but the other participants as well. Such an attitude is usually apparent and will result in immediate and far-reaching negative attitudes from others. If you want to be a successful congress member, you must treat student congress as an event important and respected in its own right. You should demonstrate by actions and words that you care about the activity, that you are prepared to work, and that you see value in the event, regardless of outcome.

The most successful student congress member also approaches student congress as an enjoyable event and works to make it that kind of experience. Such attitudes are evidenced in many ways during the sessions of congress. Promptness in reporting to committee sessions and paying close attention to the task of the committee can indicate the importance that you attach to the activity. Listening carefully to other members during house debate shows enthusiasm and support for those who have the floor and allows you to participate in cross-examination to contribute to the progression of the debate. A positive and concerned attitude should be evidenced at all times by all participants.

Interpersonal Skills

Closely related to the attitude you have as a participant is your ability to relate to and work with others. In no other area of forensic competition is the success of the event directly dependent on how well the competitors work together. Consequently, your ability to work with others and to construct good relationships with them is very important. No one would be naive enough to suggest that the members of a student congress gather together just for the purpose of being nice to one another. It is understood that this is a competitive activity. However, you need to understand that the competition is achieved through the ability of speakers to debate bills and resolutions, not through attacks on the personalities of the participants.

Because developing positive interpersonal relationships is important to the success of the student congress, you should begin early to work on these. If you are the only representative from your school, then you will doubly need to form acquaintances with others, beginning as early as registration. Often, particularly at the NFL District Student Congress, you will be among others with whom you have competed during the year in other events. There may be an understandable residue of hostility or at least reserve among the group. Efforts should be made to set aside those attitudes and to begin fresh with the student congress. One thing to avoid in the early period of the student congress is the tendency to stay among participants from your own school or region. It is important for you to circulate, to learn names, and to begin to build relationships.

One student who was named Most Outstanding congressmember at the NFL National Student Congress indicated that he believed that high visibility as soon as possible is important, especially at the national level, where very few students know one another. This visibility is necessary to the building of interpersonal relationships. It can be achieved in a variety of ways. Being direct and gregarious early in the session, learning the names of others by introducing yourself, asking questions, and giving others an opportunity to respond will all give you visibility. Casual conversation during recesses and at meal time can also promote visibility. One student congressmember observed that these times of talking about everything else except student congress probably had more to do with achieving effectiveness than any debate on the floor. And she was probably correct in terms of building good relationships and giving students an opportunity to appraise each other's ability.

Committee work is another time to build visibility early in the session. Volunteer to chair the committee and then be efficient and pleasant in the work of that committee. You will build a nucleus of student congress colleagues who know and respect you. In addition, you will have made a positive contribution to the success of the student congress itself.

Politics

The United State Congress is a political institution, and members of student congress are no less susceptible to playing politics than their counterparts in Washington, D.C. However, you should exercise much caution, for as national events have dramatically illustrated in recent years, the game of politics can be hazardous.

As a member of student congress, you should realize from the outset that in spite of your best efforts there will be a degree of partisanship or polarization even before debate begins. Some of this has already been alluded to. You may be able to mitigate it, but you will probably never be able to erase all preexisting animosities stemming from rivalries developed during the competitive season. Several personality conflicts or personal rivalries will probably exist, certainly at the district and practice level. In addition, there may be regional prejudice even at the national level, or a residue of animosity built on differences at earlier student congresses. Finally, there will be some members who arrive determined to get their pet bill passed, regardless of the consequences or the methods used to accomplish this end.

Almost every successful former student congress delegate whom the authors interviewed had one absolute word of advice about the politics that such conditions as these create. Their advice was simple: "Stay out of it if possible!" It was the feeling of these former competitors that they served their own best interests and those of the student congress simply by listening with an open mind to the efforts of others to pull them into one group or another and then by simply moving on without making a commitment. There may be some plots laid, even some that are somewhat underhanded, in an effort to destroy a bill or to undermine the credibility of some student who supports a particular piece of legislation. Avoiding such plots and working only for the betterment of debate on the floor is a much better strategy for success.

Perhaps the best way to approach the possibility of politics in the student congress setting would be the one most of us would hope to see followed in the legislatures of our own state or nation. Align yourself with people and causes only after careful study has determined that the cause is worthy and the people are sincere. Overall, the successful student congress members we interviewed felt that political power plays and behind-the-scenes plots did little in the long run to advance the cause of the persons involved. Several interviewees cited examples of promising student congress members who were seriously damaged by involvement in such schemes.

An additional caution: If you get frustrated at the political wheelings and dealings of your session, you become your own worst enemy. If you constantly seem to be saying, "It's just not fair" or "The system is against me," then the danger is that you will either pull back or react in anger. Instead, decide on a method of coping that will not be destructive either to yourself or to the group.

Debate

The strategies for success in floor debate are almost all predicated on adequate preparation and persuasiveness in presentation. It is in the actual act of standing to speak as a participant in the floor debate that you are able to get NFL points, to gain greater visibility among your peers, and to put yourself into a position in which you can command their respect. As a consequence, the strategies for successful debating are vital to the success you may achieve.

Perhaps the most important thing to remember is the limitations on participation. For each session, if you are fortunate, you will get to speak a maximum of five times—and for only three minutes per occasion. Frequently, you will have fewer opportunities. As a result, it is important to be aware of the speaking that is done in the context of the total event. It is also important to realize that although every speech given does not have to be a haymaker, the higher the quality of the speech given, the better the possibility that you will find support for yourself and your position in the assembly. Is evidence given to support assertions and generalizations? Is the argument relevant to the point being made? Is the material structured so that it can be easily understood? Be sure to review the standards for judging the quality of speeches that were specified for the official scorer in Chapter 15 to help you gain an insight into successful styles for legislative debate speeches. For example, while a one-minute speech in itself is not unsatisfactory, how do you think it will be judged by the scorer in comparison to other speeches?

Sometimes it is wise to try to deliver one of the first speeches for or against a bill or resolution; sometimes it is good to listen to the debate for a while before seeking recognition to speak. Listening first allows you to evaluate sides of the issue, to determine which may be the prevailing side, and to set up your own strategy of clashing with the opposition in the debate. Not all the former competitors agreed about which strategy is best. In fact, most of them discovered they had used a little of each. Certainly, success breeds success. The highly competitive student congress participant might want to wait until he or she can be sure of the side that will win and then give a speech favoring that side, extending the arguments and adding clincher arguments or evidence.

A good working knowledge of *Robert's Rules of Order* is one tool for successful student congress debating.

On the other hand, it might be best to accept the challenge of attempting to lead the group in the formulation of opinion. This can be achieved by getting early recognition and attempting to build the bandwagon effect in the assembly. Or, after observing the tide of opinion to one side, the challenge might be to attempt to construct a speech for the side that is losing and to make it a speech so persuasive that it would turn the direction of opinion. Either of these strategies is based on the principle inherent in all debate that either side has valid issues that can be supported by evidence.

Another way to add to the strength of a speech given during debate is to utilize speeches already given by referring to them and making your speech an extension and amplification of them. If, for example, the speaker has simply made a reference to an idea that you see as a potentially strong argument, and if you have the data by which to make it into a fully developed point, you can simply say, "Representative Green's point about the historical significance of this bill is well taken, and I would like to . . . ." Referring to other speeches can actually make your own speech sound more substantive than you could otherwise make it in only three minutes. The practical effect is that you use their data, already introduced, as a springboard to your own position. You gain time and impact. Overall, most scorers look for clear evidence of a spontaneous clash as opposed to a series of unrelated, memorized, pre-prepared orations.

Playing out the newly discovered role of a congressional representative and employing the inherent speaking style is a part of the strategy for use in floor debate. Perhaps the most difficult thing for the debater-turned-student-congressmember to do is to regain the skills of persuasive public address after a season of debating with her or his nose in a flow pad, speaking at a rate of 400 words-per-minute. However, if you want success in student congress, then style must be a part of your delivery. The stylistic considerations that you should make involve not only the traditional use of vocal variety, gestures, vocal intonation, and appropriate volume and pauses, but also sensitivity to the times when a little humor would be a welcome relief, especially if the humor can be used to make a valid point. Examples, analogies, similes, metaphors, paradoxes, and other rhetorical devices, when used properly, are always effective in a congress speech. You should be able to sense when there is an opening for emotional as well as intellectual appeal. Further, you should be alert to moments in the debate when a carefully proposed compromise might swing two factions into agreement and bring about the passage of a particularly hard-fought piece of legislation. These are decisions that must be made at the moment and cannot be prescribed by any other person.

Summary

There are several keys to a successful student congress session. When you prepare for the session and then participate with a positive attitude, you are doing your part to make the session go smoothly. Developing your interpersonal skills is another way you can ensure a successful session. Finally, knowing the rules governing debate and following the arguments carefully can enhance everyone's student congress experience.

In these chapters you have examined the widespread and valuable activity of student congress. You should now have a better notion of its nature and purpose and of the principles that govern it. The structure of the congress activity gives specific responsibilities to the officials and also carries obligations to the participants. You have been given here, too, a clear description of the mechanics of the student congress as well as a careful guide to your own preparation for competition.

The student congressmember who approaches the experience with adequate preparation, with a thorough understanding of the event, and with a dedication to the value of the experience will probably find the strategies for success discussed here a natural outgrowth of her or his own attitudes toward student congress. In the authors' experiences, this event is a true blending of the best of all the forensics events. Perhaps the essence of student congress was best expressed in the March 1978 issue of the National Forensic League *Rostrum* by the late Bruno E. Jacob, Executive Secretary Emeritus of NFL. He said:

> In the student congress the students learn to think about state and national problems in terms of solutions which they can urge their colleagues to accept as necessary and practical. They learn how to influence people favorably. They acquire not only knowledge of lawmaking, but respect for the power of the majority and the rights of the minority—the foundations of the democratic process. This makes leaders.

Questions for Discussion

1. What is the purpose of an authorship speech? of a refutation speech? of an amplification or resupporting speech? of a summative speech? What are the proper organizational patterns for each of these speeches?

2. Why might a congress participant be rated highly by the official scorer but do poorly in the peer voting for Outstanding Member?

3. What qualities would you choose if you were compiling the profile of an "ideal" congress competitor?

4. What are the dangers playing political "games" during a student congress session?

Activities

1. Using the general guidelines for judging the quality of student congress speeches, develop specific, written criteria that could be provided to an official scorer to judge a session of congress.

2. Arrange for a small group of students (or your entire class) to attend a state, county, or city legislative session. If necessary, arrange for release time and transportation and contact an appropriate legislator to meet with you before or after your visit.

3. Plan an after-school practice congress, inviting students in speech or government classes from neighboring schools. Be sure to publish bills and resolutions, an apportionment plan, a proposed agenda, and rules and regulations. Invite visiting teachers to serve as official scorers, and be sure to arrange local media coverage of the event.

Glossary of Debate Terms

The language of debate is a special one. It is filled with terms that are meaningful to those who understand the concepts and theory of debate. Those same terms are necessary in the explanation of debate. The following is a list of terms that have been used in this text and in many others that make up the body of literature relating to debate. Each term is concisely defined. Although the definitions provided here were written by the authors, an effort was made to be consistent with the meanings and interpretations that are found in standard argumentation textbooks.

ABSOLUTE PLAN-MEETS-NEED. A plan-meets-need argument so powerful that, if carried by the negative, it demonstrates the plan to be incapable of producing any positive effects in the problem area claimed by the affirmative case. It is sufficient to win a ballot for the negative in and of itself. (See *Solvency*)

ABSOLUTE SIGNIFICANCE. The total number of units affected by the change wrought by the affirmative plan or negative disadvantage.

ADVANTAGE. A significant improvement over the status quo that can best be gained by the affirmative plan.

ADVOCATE. (v.) To support a position. (n.) One who advocates; a debater.

AFFIRMATIVE. The side that favors (affirms) changing the status quo to conform to the debate resolution.

ANALYSIS. The process of breaking down an idea or a proposition into its elements. In debate, analysis traditionally follows a fairly standard process of seeking pro and con positions on the stock issues.

ANALOGY. Use of comparison to draw a general conclusion. The conclusion drawn is strong in relation to the number of likenesses between the things compared. Classical reasoning indicates that analogies are for clarification rather than proof; however, contemporary argumentation accepts generalizations based on strong analogies.

ARGUMENT. Two senses of this term are important to debaters. In the first sense, an argument is a message consisting of a conclusion supported by a reason documented by evidence. The emphasis is on credible proof and logical structure. In the second sense, an argument is a confrontation between two parties in disagreement over a claim. The emphasis is on refutation. Thus, a debater can *make* an argument that is tested against the standards of evidence and logic; two debaters can *have* an argument with each other that one or the other wins on the basis of his or her refutation of an opponent.

ARGUMENTATION. The study or use of argument, consisting of the dual process of *discovering* the probable truth of an issue through analysis and research and *advocating* it to an audience through appropriate logical, ethical, and persuasive techniques.

ARTISTIC VALUES. Also called aesthetic values. Values that reflect the kind and degree of pleasure one derives from the artistic aspect of persons and objects. We attach great importance to beauty, symmetry, good taste—and their opposites.

ASSERTION. An unsupported statement; a conclusion that lacks evidence for support.

ATTITUDINAL INHERENCY. The tendency of agents charged with creating or carrying out the law to avoid their responsibility. The condition exists in such features of the present system as corrupt officials, pressure groups and lobbies, conflicting laws and goals, and general apathy.

AUDIENCE: The person or persons to whom a message is directed. In academic debate the audience consists of the judge who listens to the debaters, weighs the arguments presented by each side, and then makes a decision about which team's posi-

tion is the most acceptable.

AUTHORITY. One whose experience, training, position, or special study makes her or his testimony or opinion acceptable as evidence; an expert.

BALLOTS. The form used to record the outcome of a debate round or forensic event. All ballots leave room for commentary. This extra room is used to provide reasons for the decision and suggestions for improvement.

BENEFIT. In a need-plan case, a benefit is a positive effect of the plan in addition to the solution of the major need areas.

BIAS. A prejudiced attitude on the part of the source of evidence quoted in a debate. If quoted sources are biased, their opinions are therefore questionable as credible proof. Bias exists in sources when it is shown they have some vested interest at stake in the policy being debated. There can be political or economic bias by a lobby group or political party. As a rule academic and scholarly research reports, or nonpartisan analytical "think tanks," are accepted as relatively unbiased sources in debate. Debaters should seek unbiased sources when possible.

BLOCK. (1) A prepared set of arguments relating to a single point. (2) The second negative constructive speech and the first negative rebuttal considered as a single 12- or 15-minute *block* of time.

BRIEF. An outline of all the arguments on both sides of the debate resolution. An affirmative brief or a negative brief consists of all the arguments on the respective sides of the resolution.

BURDEN OF PROOF. The affirmative obligation to present a *prima facie* case supporting the debate resolution.

BURDEN OF PROVING. The obligation of debaters on either side to prove any argument they initiate.

BURDEN OF REBUTTAL. The obligation of the negative in any debate to meet and clash with the affirmative case.

BURDEN OF REFUTING. The obligation of either side to respond to relevant constructive arguments presented by its opponents and to advance its own arguments.

CARD CATALOG. An alphabetized collection of cards that indicate all the books in the library by author, title, and subject.

CARD FILE. An organized collection of evidence recorded on index cards. A card should contain only one idea or bit of information, preferably verbatim from the source, together with complete labeling of the contents of the card and information about the source, such as the authority's name and qualifications and publication data, including the date of the source.

CASE. A debate team's basic position on the resolution, made up of all the arguments that the team presents in support of that position.

CASE SIDE ARGUMENTS. Arguments that relate to three issues: topicality, significance, and inherency.

CAUSATION. A relationship between two phenomena in which one is believed to cause the other.

CAUSE-EFFECT RELATIONSHIP. A relationship based on the assumption that in the process of interacting, there is a connecting link between one phenomenon and another. Further assumes that this connection is so strong that the relationship is predictable.

CLASH. The process of meeting and dealing directly with an argument of the opposition. Dealing with an argument implies denial or minimization, but not agreement with it.

COMPARATIVE ADVANTAGE. A type of affirmative case structure that shows the proposed policy of the affirmative to have significant and unique advantages over the status quo.

COMPARATIVE ADVANTAGE CASE. A kind of case in which the affirmative shows that although existing programs could possibly be modified in the present system to achieve a solution to the problem area, the affirmative proposal could do a better job. The argument focuses on the comparison between the affirmative plan and the present system. The entire case is presented in the first affirmative constructive speech.

COMPUTER INDEXES. One type of computerized system contains items you would find in a card catalog (primarily books). Most are indexed by author, title, and subject. Another type of system carries periodical listings.

CONCLUSION. The statement one arrives at when evidence is considered and interpreted; an inference; a claim.

CONDITIONAL COUNTERPLAN. A negative strategy of arguing the superiority of the present system over the affirmative plan; but, *on the condition* that the judge agrees with the affirmative that the present system should be changed, the negative also suggests a counterplan it is willing to defend in preference to the affirmative plan. This strategy is risky because potentially it places the negative in a self-contradictory position of claiming no need for a change, then advocating a counterplan to change the present system.

CONGRESSIONAL DIGEST. A magazine that offers in-depth analysis of a single issue currently being discussed in Congress.

CONSTRUCTIVE. (adj.) A constructive argument is one offered in support of, or in opposition to, the resolution. A constructive speech is a time period in which it is permissible to present constructive arguments.

CONTENTION. A subdivision of an issue; an argument essential to support a position on an issue. Contentions may consist of either observations or indictments. The statement of a claim. In debate, a number of contentions make up the affirmative case. For example: The problem is significant. The problem is inherent.

CONTRADICTION. Statements or arguments within a given position that are in direct opposition to each other.

CORRELATION. A statement of a logical relationship between two phenomena showing that the two appear together and that they also vary together, either directly or inversely. In other words, correlation would establish a relationship less than causality.

COST-BENEFIT RATIO. An on-balance comparison of the advantages and disadvantages of alternative proposals for change. The emphasis is on quantified measures of both costs and benefits, with the greatest value assigned to the most favorable ratio between costs incurred for benefits received.

COUNTERPLAN. A negative case approach admitting that the present system should be changed, but which advocates the negative team's proposal rather than the affirmative's. Traditionally, the counterplan is given in the first negative constructive speech; and it is demonstrated to be nontopical, competitive with the affirmative plan, superior to it in the area of analysis attacked by the affirmative, and also less disadvantageous than the affirmative plan.

CREDIBILITY. The believability of a statement or its source.

CRITERIA-GOALS CASE. A kind of case that is an elaboration on the comparative advantage case with greater emphasis on the policy goals of the present system. The affirmative incorporates the identification of the goal of the present system as an integral part of its analysis. Affirmative sets up the criteria to judge the fulfillment of those particular goals. The affirmative shows its proposed plan meets the criteria better than the present system does.

CRITERION. A standard of measurement based on an underlying social value.

CRITIC JUDGE. The trained person whose duty it is to hear an academic debate, determine the winner according to the rules, and furnish suggestions for improvement for the student debater.

CROSS-EXAMINATION. A form of debate in which debaters are permitted to ask direct questions of an opponent during specified time periods, usually immediately following the opponent's constructive speeches.

DEBATE. A contest of argumentation. An affirmative team presents arguments in favor of a resolution, and a negative team presents arguments against it. The contest is won by the team which presents the best arguments in the opinion of the judge.

DEDUCTION. A reasoning process that takes general statements or premises and draws a conclusion about particular or specific elements. In formal logic, deduction is contained in a chain called a "syllogism." This form of reasoning is formal, and the validity of such an argument is based on the logical relationship between premises and conclusion, not necessarily on the truth content of any premise.
Example:
Major Premise: All elementary schools are entitled to public tax support.
Minor Premise: Parochial schools are elementary schools.
Conclusion: Therefore, parochial schools are entitled to public tax support.

DEFINITION. A formality of a debate wherein the affirmative team declares the meaning of the terms of the debate resolution. The definition of terms serves the useful function of limiting the areas encompassed by the resolution. While the affirmative team has the privilege of defining the terms, the negative team has the privilege of challenging any definition considered unacceptable. The most frequently used methods of defining terms are references to authorities, examples, or the dictionary.

DEGREE OF SIGNIFICANCE. Relative value of the advantage. Directly affects the required magnitude of the scope of the problem needed for policy action.

DESIRABILITY. A condition or state of favorability; a value judgment attached to a particular outcome of a plan, especially a benefit or an advantage. Desirability is a state lower in degree than necessity.

DILEMMA. A forced choice of one of only two possible alternatives, either of which would be undesirable.

DISADVANTAGE. An undesirable outcome of a plan, apart from considerations of workability or the desirability of the plan's justifications.

DISTORTION. A misrepresentation of a piece of evidence.

DROP. To neglect to carry on an argument, in future speeches, after the opponent's response.

DURATION OF SIGNIFICANCE. The persistence of a problem. In this sense the condition of inherency overlaps the issue of significance.

EIGHT-MINUTE RULE (or ten-minute). A tournament rule allotting to each team a cumulative total of eight minutes between speeches during the course of the debate that can be used for preparing to speak. There is no specification as to how the debaters may allocate their time.

ELIMINATION ROUNDS. The final rounds in a debate tournament. Only students who have competed successfully in the preliminary rounds advance to the elimination rounds. In debate those students with the best win-loss record advance to an octofinal or quarterfinal round.

EMPIRICAL STUDIES. Scientifically controlled experiments, usually expressed in statistical form.

ENFORCEMENT. That plank of the plan that provides for seeing that the performance or prohibition plants of the plan are carried out.

EVIDENCE. Data that form the basis for conclusions.

EXAMPLE. Single objects or events used to illustrate and show the possibility of generalized categories of similar groups of examples; a type of factual evidence. Negative examples are those used to disprove generalities.

EXPERT. An authority; one whose experience, training, or position and study makes his or her testimony acceptable as evidence.

EXTEND. To carry an argument another step forward in rebuttal; to answer the opponent's challenge and advance beyond it.

EXTENDED ANALOGY. A comparison developed at depth to demonstrate a significant similarity.

EXTRATOPICALITY. The state of nonconformity to the intent of the debate resolution. A plan is extratopical if the needs are solved or the comparative advantages are gained as a direct result of some plank of the plan that does not implement the debate resolution.

FABRICATION. The act of making up evidence.

FACT. Actual, observable objects or events in the real world; useful as evidence in debate, facts usually fall into these types: (a) examples, (b) statistics, (c) empirical studies.

FALLACY. A mistaken inference; an erroneous conclusion based on faulty reasoning. Some common fallacies are the following:

Post hoc: The error of mistaking an association relationship for a causal relationship. For instance, because flies and brides are usually both observed in June, it does not mean that one causes the other.

Hasty generalization: In inductive reasoning this fallacy consists of the error of drawing a general conclusion based on too few, or unrepresentative examples.

False analogy: In inductive reasoning this fallacy consists of the error of comparing two objects or events that are dissimilar in the essential areas of comparison.

Biased statistics: Basing statistical inferences on a nonrandom or unrepresentative sample taken from the population. When the sample is not representative of the whole, no conclusions may be drawn about the whole.

Fallacies in authority-based reasoning: Errors occur when accepting conclusions from authoritative testimony when the authority is not quoted in context, when the testimony is outdated, when the authority is quoted in a matter outside his field of expertise, or when his testimony is at variance with other authorities.

FIAT. An assumed power to put a proposal into effect; a legal mandate binding on the parties involved, overriding their personal attitudes. Debaters are allowed to say their proposals are to be implemented "by fiat" for the sake of avoiding quibbles over whether, in the real world, such proposals could be expected to receive approval. Fiat power is limited to matters subject to law; it is not a "magic wand" to avoid substantive argument. For example, an energy bill could be adopted by fiat, but a new oil supply cannot be discovered by fiat.

FLOW SHEET. A diagram of the arguments in a debate and their relationships. Arguments are charted in parallel columns, with the affirmative case written in the left-hand column, the negative arguments in the next column, the affirmative responses in the next column, and so forth. Thus a "flow" of the arguments can be seen at a glance by tracing each argument and its responses across the flow sheet.

GENERALIZATION. Conclusions drawn from evidence or data.

GOAL. A general objective; an aim. Systems of policy are thought to exist in order to achieve goals. Affirmative cases may be developed on the premise that a laudable goal can best be met through the affirmative proposal.

GOING TO CASE SIDE. A debate expression instructing all parties that the speaker is moving to the case arguments in the debate.

GOING TO PLAN SIDE. A debate expression instructing all parties that the debater is moving to the plan arguments in the debate.

HARM. An undesirable impact resulting from the operation of a policy system. The impact may be stated in terms of deprivation or injury to parties affected by the policy. Harm exists where needs are denied or suffering or loss of life is created.

INDEXES (GUIDES). Books that contain alphabetical listings by author, title, and general subject of magazine articles that have appeared in a particular group of periodicals.

INDICTMENT. An accusatory conclusion; a charge, a contention in a debate will usually state an indictment.

INFERENCES. Conclusions based on possible relationships between known facts.

INHERENCY. The state of being an intrinsic, inseparable, necessary part of a system. The term is used to describe a feature of the status quo that exists and will continue to exist in the absence of the affirmative plan. It may also be applied to the affirmative proposal when the negative charges that disadvantages are in-

herent to the affirmative plan.

ISSUE. A question concerning which the affirmative and negative teams take opposite sides; a major point of disagreement.

JUDGE. (v.) To evaluate a debate against certain ideal standards of debating, to decide who wins and who loses. (n.) The person who fulfills the judging function.

JUSTIFICATION. To fulfill the standards of judgement. A justification argument is one in which it is charged that an affirmative case fails to "justify the resolution." As a negative strategy, the argument shows how the advantages of the affirmative case do not stem from the resolution itself but rather from other extratopical features of the plan.

LAY JUDGE. A term applied to persons who judge debates but who are neither coaches nor current debaters. Judgment of debate by such persons will probably center more on the debater's ability to communicate arguments and make them meaningful than on the technicalities of debate theory.

LINCOLN-DOUGLAS DEBATE. A kind of debate that utilizes a two-person format centered around a value proposition.

LOGIC. The system of analysis that shows the nature of relationships between statements, between facts and conclusions, causes and effects, and deductions from premises. Logic is reasoning based on rules concerning the form in which an argument is put, rather than on the nature and quality of evidence.

METHODOLOGY. The procedure by which an empirical study is conducted. An empirical study's methodology may be challenged along such lines as the size of the sample, the amount of time, the presence of a control group, etc. To challenge the methodology is to test the validity of the conclusions drawn from such a study. Debaters who quote from empirical studies should be familiar with the methodology of the studies.

MINOR REPAIR. An alteration of present policy that gains the affirmative advantage but involves substantially less change than that suggested by the resolutions.

MORAL AND ETHICAL VALUES. Values that form the basis for judgments of right and wrong, just and unjust, good and bad.

NATIONAL FORENSIC LEAGUE (NFL). Sponsor of high school speech and debate activities. Located in Ripon, Wisconsin.

NEED. An evil or harmful situation inherent in the status quo that the affirmative plan will remedy. The need is a necessary element of a traditional need-plan case.

NEED-PLAN CASE. A kind of case that develops the argument that a need for change exists. The case develops the plan and shows how the plan meets the need. The case develops the argument that the plan would be beneficial. The heart of the case is that there is a need and that the plan will meet the need.

NEGATIVE. The side that opposes (negates) the affirmative position and therefore the resolution.

NET BENEFITS. An affirmative case construction in which the affirmative, using a systems analysis approach that change is inevitable, presents a proposal to direct that change and expects the negative to propose its own policy system.

NET BENEFITS CASE. A kind of case based on systems analysis. The case

incorporates four steps: (1) Apply systems analysis to the problem area; (2) determine the components that make up the system and the rules that govern how the components are interrelated; (3) analyze and project what differences could be predicted following a change in policy governing the interrelationships; and (4) determine the most favorable ratio between the costs and the benefits of the proposed change in the system.

NITPICK. To quibble over minor points.

NONTOPICALITY. The condition of failure to encompass the scope or intent of the resolution. A case is nontopical if it fails to justify all the terms included in the resolution.

OBJECTION. An argument against the plan.

OBSERVATION. A descriptive conclusion or assumption.

ONE-MINUTE RULE (or two-minute). A tournament rule in which each speaker is allowed one minute from the time the preceding speaker sits down in which to gather materials and approach the podium to speak. If a speaker exceeds this time, the additional time is subtracted from his or her speaking time.

OPERATIONAL DEFINITION. Practice of defining the resolution through the presentation of the affirmative plan early in the first affirmative constructive speech. Individual terms are not defined; rather, the affirmative plan constitutes the essence of the resolution.

OPINION. A statement of an attitude or belief. Opinion testimony is acceptable evidence in a debate if it is the opinion of a qualified expert.

PLAN. The specific program proposed by the affirmative team to implement the debate resolution. The plan is a necessary part of every affirmative case.

PLAN PLANK. Specific provisions within the affirmative plan, a set of particulars about the plan. Individual planks might specify (1) goal or intent, (2) agency of change, (3) duties or powers, (4) enforcement, or (5) financing.

POLICY. A means of achieving a goal; an action. In a narrow sense, a policy is a governmental program, such as the financing of public schools through property tax revenues. In debate a policy proposition is the proposal of some new governmental program that the affirmative team claims should be adopted.

POLITICAL VALUES. Values that reflect judgments as to what is expedient, that is, what should or should not be done for the common good. Include democracy, rights, justice, and many others.

PREDICTION. A statement of how one thinks present facts are related so that one can expect certain results in the future. Accuracy of predictions hinges on the quality of factual data and the quality of reasoning used in drawing relationship between known facts.

PRELIMINARY ROUND. A round of debate in which all students at the tournament participate, and a judge evaluates performances.

PREMISE. A general statement of a goal or value, from which arguments and conclusions may be drawn.

PREPARATION TIME. In a debate the time that elapses prior to each debater's speech. After the first affirmative speech, each team has a strictly regulated amount of cumulative preparation time allocated to it for the entire debate, which the team members may utilize as they wish. The amount of time and the rules governing its use are determined by the tournament director.

PRESUMPTION. Traditionally, the assumption that conditions and policies should remain as they are. The affirmative side has the burden to prove that the status quo should be changed. The present system is presumed to be adequate until the affirmative team meets its burden to prove that a change in the status quo is needed or would be advantageous. Presumption is analogous to the legal principle that the accused person is presumed to be innocent until proven guilty. Newer debate theories have altered the concept of presumption somewhat.

PRIMA FACIE. The Latin phrase may be translated as "at first look." A prima facie case is one that a reasonable and prudent person would accept "at first look." In debate a prima facie case must include a specific plan to implement the resolution and justification for the plan— either an inherent need in the status quo, a comparative advantage of the plan over the status quo, or some other accepted justification.

PROBABILITY. (1) The relative degree of certainty with which an inference may be drawn. (2) In statistical language the level of confidence that may be placed in a conclusion expressed as a percentage.

PROBLEM AREA. The domain of issues that pertain to a topic. A problem area includes issues of long standing social concern.

PROBLEM STATEMENT. A statement narrows a general discussion area. The beginning point for analysis is a definition of the terms by which the problem is stated. Each forensic event places the problem in a different form, but each states a problem for consideration.

PROOF. That which reduces uncertainty and increases the probable truth of a claim. Evidence is transformed into proof through the use of reasoning, which demonstrates how and to what extent the claim is believable. Proof is what is given in response to the demand "Prove it!"

Proof is a relative concept, ranging from possibility through probability to certainty. The amount of proof needed to establish a claim depends on a number of variables, such as the importance of the claim, the strength of opposing claims, and the credibility of the person making the argument.

PROPOSAL. The specific affirmative plan.

PROPOSITION. A debatable statement; a statement open to interpretation; a statement about which reasonable people may accept arguments on either side. Debate theory incorporates three types of propositions: fact, value, and policy.

PROPOSITION OF FACT. A proposition that involves definition and classification in order to establish the truth or falseness of a claim. An objective statement that something exists. May be about an object or event that can be experienced directly by the senses of sight, hearing, touch, smell, and taste.

PROPOSITION OF POLICY. A proposition demanding that after establishing certain facts and values, a consideration of such things as expediency and practicality leads people to propose a certain defensible plan of action. A statement of a course of action to be considered for adoption. Includes all those problem areas

deemed appropriate for government action.

PROPOSITION OF VALUE. A proposition asking that criteria be applied in order to determine the worth or value of a particular thing. Expresses judgments about the qualities of a person, place, thing, idea, or event.

PUBLIC AFFAIRS INFORMATION SERVICE INDEX. Includes magazine articles, but also lists selected government documents by title and subject.

RATIONALE. (1) The philosophical framework within which a case is constructed. (2) The criteria for accepting a premise or conclusion.

REASONING. The process of drawing appropriate conclusions based on the evidence.

REBUTTAL. A short speech devoted to (1) rebuilding arguments that have been attacked, (2) refuting opposing arguments, and (3) summarizing the debate from the perspective of the speaker.

REFUTATION. The process of attacking and destroying opposing arguments.

REPAIR. A minor adjustment in present policies that would accompany part or all of what the affirmative plan is designed to accomplish.

RESEARCH. To search again. To gather information and evidence and to classify it so that it is easily retrievable for use.

RESOLUTION. a proposition stated in the form of a motion before a legislative assembly. In debate used synonymously with proposition.

RISK SIGNIFICANCE. The fractional proportion of the potential population exposed to jeopardy by the present system.

SANDBAGGING. The practice of presenting an argument initially in skeletal form, with little or no evidence so that it appears weak, and saving a bulk of evidence for second line presentation only if the argument is attacked. The strategy is to make your strongest strategy look like the weakest so that the opposition will focus the debate there.

SECOND LINE. Additional evidence for presentation in rebuttal or extensions.

SHIFT. To abandon an original position and take up a different one.

SHOTGUN. (1) A strategy of presenting a profusion of unrelated, scattered attacks against an opponent's case. (2) A loud, bombastic style of delivery.

SHOULD. Usually defined as "ought to, not necessarily will." This term is always found in propositions of policy. Affirmative cases justify a proposal by showing that it will solve a need or produce a comparative advantage and *should be* adopted even if Congress won't pass the needed legislation, the Constitution forbids it, or public opinion opposes it. This is called the power of fiat for the affirmative.

SIGN REASONING. Reasoning by characteristic. Sign reasoning makes the claim that whenever a character is observed a substance must be present, or when a substance is present a characteristic must follow.

SIGNIFICANCE. (1) The degree of importance of a conclusion. Significance may be qualitative or quantitative. Qualitative significance rests on an established value; quantitative significance rests on concrete units of measurement. (2) In statistical language the level of confidence at which a predicted conclusion may not be rejected, usually ".05 level of significance" or "95 percent probability."

SOCIAL INDEX RESOURCE SERVICE (SIRS). A publication that indexes newspaper articles from across the country.

SOLVENCY. The relationship of workability between a policy and its claimed effects. Solvency is a relative concept ranging along a continuum from insolvency through degrees of partial solvency to total solvency. A plan-meet-advantage argument is an attack designed to decrease the perceived solvency of the proposal.

SPECIALIZED DICTIONARIES. Dictionaries that include technical terms. For example, *Black's Law Dictionary* and *The American Dictionary of Psychology.*

STATISTICS. Descriptive or experimental data, often used in drawing mathematical inferences.

STATUS QUO. The present system; the existing order; that which would be changed by adopting the affirmative plan.

STOCK ISSUES. A series of broad questions encompassing the major debatable issues of any proposition of policy. Some stock issues are (1) Is there a need for a change? (2) Will the plan meet the need? (3) Is the plan the most desirable way to meet the need?

STRAIGHT REFUTATION. For every claim that the affirmative asserts is true, the negative offers a counterclaim asserting that what the affirmative says is false.

STRUCTURAL INHERENCY. A law (or lack of a law) or barrier that prevents the present system from solving a problem.

SYNTHESIS. The result of combining separate elements into a complete whole.

SYSTEMS ANALYSIS. A method of analysis that assumes that everything is in a state of constant change. Its underlying principle is that ongoing decisions must be made about the kinds of changes wanted, rather than whether any change is desirable. Calls for each side to uphold a particular system for controlling the changes the present system is going through.

TESTIMONY. An expression of opinion; a value judgment. Testimony is acceptable evidence in debate if it is from a qualified expert.

TOPICALITY. The state of conformity to the intent of the debate resolution. A case is topical if it justifies the full intent of the resolution. A plan is topical if the needs are solved or the comparative advantages are gained as a direct result of those planks in the plan that implement the resolution.

TOURMAMENT. A competitive setting in which students practice their arguments and sharpen their thinking and speaking skills. Consists of preliminary and elimination rounds.

TURNAROUND. An argument that is the meaning of an opponent's contention is the opposite of its apparent intent so that it counts against the opponent. For example, if the negative team makes a disadvantage argument, and the affirmative rebuttalist points out that the result of that disadvantage is more positive than negative, then the argument becomes a turnaround for the affirmative team.

UNIQUENESS. In comparative advantage analysis, the condition of inherency or inseparability of the proposal and the effects that are claimed to result from it, either advantages or disadvantages.

VALUE. An underlying belief or assumption with wide enough acceptance to validate conclusions that are derived from it.

VARIABLE. A condition that may change and alter a cause-effect relationship.

VERTICAL FILES. Collections of periodical and newspaper clippings that relate to topics of current interest.

WORKABILITY. A condition whereby a proposal could actually operate to solve a problem if implemented as legislation. A plan is said to be workable if it includes planks in its mechanism allowing for an agency, its powers, and administrative details.

Selected Works for Additional Reference

Books

Baur, Otto F. *Fundamentals of Debate: Theory and Practice*. Chicago: Scott, Foresman, 1966.

Bettinghaus, Erwin P. *The Nature of Proof*. Indianapolis: Bobbs-Merrill Co., 1972.

Brock, Bernard L., James W. Chesebro, John F. Cragan, and James F. Klumpp. *Public Policy Decision-Making: Systems Analysis and Comparative Advantages Debate*. New York: Harper and Row, 1973.

Brockriede, Wayne, and Doublas Ehninger. *Decisions by Debate*, revised edition. New York: Harper and Row, 1978.

Brown, Wayne, and Penny Swisher. *Directing Successful Speech Tournaments*. Grandview, MO: Dale Publishing Co., 1980.

Brownlee, Don, ed. *Perspective on Non-Policy Argument*. Wingate, NC: Cross-Examination Debate Association, 1980.

Colburn, William. *Strategies for Educational Debate*. Boston, MA: Holbrook Press, 1972.

Dick, Robert C. *Argumentation and Rational Debating*. Dubuque, IA: Wm. C. Brown Co., 1972.

Edgar, William J. *Evidence*. Lanham: University Press of America, 1980.

Ehninger, Douglas, and Wayne Brockriede. *Decision by Debate*. 2d ed. New York: Harper and Row, 1978.

Freeley, Austin J. *Argumentation and Debate: Rational Decision Making*. 5th ed. Belmont, CA: Wadsworth, 1981.

Goodnight, G. Thomas, and David Zarefsky. *Forensics Tournaments: Planning and Administration*. Lincolnwood, IL: National Textbook Company, 1980.

Goodnight, Lynn. *Getting Started in Debate*. Lincolnwood, IL: National Textbook Co., 1987.

Hensley, Dana, and Diana Prentice. *Mastering Competitive Debate*. 2d ed. Caldwell, ID: Clarke Publishing Co., 1982.

Kahane, Howard. *Logic and Contemporary Rhetoric: The Use of Reason in Everyday Life*. 4th ed. Belmont, CA: Wadsworth Publishing Co., 1984.

Kemp, Robert L. *Assignment: Directing the School's Forensic Program*. Clayton, MO: Alan Company, 1985.

———. *Lincoln-Douglas Debating*. Clayton, MO: Alan Company, 1984.

Kleinau, Marvin D., and Richard Hunsaker. *A Guide to Coaching and Judging Contemporary Debate*. St.

Louis, MO: Springboards, Inc., 1981.

McAdoo, Joe, ed. *Judging Debate.* Springfield, MO: Mid-America Research, 1975.

McBath, James H., ed. *Forensics as Communication: The Argumentative Perspective.* Lincolnwood, IL: National Textbook Co., 1975.

Meyers, Chet. *Teaching Students to Think Critically.* San Francisco, CA: Jossey-Bass Publishers, 1986.

Newman, Robert P., and Dale R. Newman. *Evidence.* Boston, MA: Houghton-Mifflin, 1969.

Patterson, J. W., and David Zarefsky. *Contemporary Debate.* Boston, MA: Houghton-Mifflin, 1983.

Rieke, Richard D., and Malcolm D. Sillars. *Argumentation and the Decision-Making Process.* New York: Wiley, 1975.

Robert, General Henry M., et al. *Robert's Rules of Order, Newly Revised.* Glenview, IL: Scott-Foresman, 1970.

Sayer, J. E. *Argumentation and Debate.* Sherman Oaks, CA: Alfred Publishing, 1980.

Terry, Donald R. *Modern Debate Case Techniques.* Lincolnwood, IL: National Textbook Co., 1975.

Thomas, David A., and Jack Hart. *Advanced Debate: Readings in Theory, Practice and Teaching.* 3d ed. Lin-

colnwood, IL: National Textbook Company, 1987.

Ulrich, Walter. *An Introduction to Debate.* Kansas City, MO: National Federation of State High School Associations, 1986.

_____. *Guidelines for the Debate Judge.* Kansas City, MO: National Federation of State High School Associations, 1986.

_____. *Judging Academic Debate.* Lincolnwood, IL: National Textbook Company, 1986.

_____. *Understanding the Counterplan.* Kansas City, MO: National Federation of State High School Associations, 1986.

Utter, E. C. *Parliamentary Law at a Glance.* Chicago: Henry Regnery Co., 1949.

Wood, Roy V., and Lynn Goodnight. *Strategic Debate.* 4th ed. Lincolnwood, IL: National Textbook Co., 1988.

Zarefsky, David, ed. *The Comparative Advantage Case.* Evanston, IL: Championship Debate Enterprises, 1970.

Ziegelmueller, George W., and Charles A. Dause. *Argumentation: Inquiry and Advocacy.* Englewood Cliffs, NJ: Prentice-Hall, Inc., 1976.

Articles

Balthrop, V. William. "The Debate Judge as 'Critic of Argument': Toward A Transcendent Perspective." *Journal of the American Forensic Association* 20 (Summer 1983): 1-15.

Boehm, G. A. W. "Shaping Decision with Systems Analysis." *Harvard Business Review* 54 (September 1976): 91-99.

Brownlee, Don. "Advocacy and Values." *Perspectiveness on Non-Policy*

Argument (CEDA: 1980).

Brydon, Steven R. "Presumption in Non-Policy Debate: In Search of a Paradigm." *JAFA* 23 (Summer 1986): 15-22.

Burgoon, Judee, and Charles Montgomery. "Dimensions of Credibility for the Ideal Debater." *Journal of the American Forensic Association* 12 (Spring 1976): 171-177.

Cherwitz, Richard, and James W. Hiking. "Inherency as a Multidimensional Construct: A Rhetorical Approach to the Proof of a Causation." *Journal of the American Forensic Association* 14 (Fall 1977): 82-90.

Chesebro, James W. "Beyond the Orthodox: The Criteria Case." *Journal of the American Forensic Association* 7 (Winter 1971): 208-215.

Church, Russell T., and David C. Buckley. "Argumentation and Debating Propositions of Value: A Bibliography." *JAFA* 19 (Spring 1983): 239-50.

Corsi, Jerome R. "Zarefsky's Theory of Debate as Hypothesis Testing: A Critical Re-Examination." *Journal of the American Forensic Association* 19 (Winter 1983).

Cox, J. Robert. "A Study of Judging Philosophies of the Participants of the National Debate Tournament." *Journal of the American Forensic Association* 11 (Fall 1974).

———. "Attitudinal Inherency: Implications for Policy Debate." *Southern Speech Communication Journal* 40 (Winter 1974): 158-168.

Cross, John D., and Ronald J. Matlon. "An Analysis of Judging Philosophies in Academic Debate." *Journal of the American Forensic Association* 14 (Fall 1978): 110-112.

Dempsey, Richard H. and Hartman, David T. "Mirror State Counterplans: Illegitimate, Topical, or Magical?" *JAFA* (Winter 1985): 161-166.

DeStephen, Dan. "Some Implications of a Systematic Perspective for the Affirmative." *Debate Issues* 11 (April 1978): 9-12.

Dowling, Ralph E. "Debate as Game, Educational Tool, and Argument: An Evaluation of Theory and Rules." *JAFA* 17 (Spring 1981): 235-236.

Dudczak, Craig. "Direct Refutation in Propositions of Policy: A Viable Alternative." *Journal of the American Forensic Association* 16 (Spring 1980): 232-235.

Eman, Virginia, and Jeffery Lukehart. "Information Use in Academic Debate: An Information Theory Perspective." *Journal of the American Forensic Association* 12 (Spring 1976): 178-183.

Flaningam, Carl D. "Value-Centered Argument and the Development of Decision Rules." *Journal of the American Forensic Association* 19 (Fall 1982): 107-114.

"Forum on Policy Systems Analysis," David A. Thomas, ed. *JAFA* 22 (Winter 1986): pp. 123-166. (Includes Robert C. Rowland, "The Relationship Between Realism and Debatability in Policy Advocacy," William L. Benoit, Steve R. Wilson and Vince Follert, "Decision Rules for the Policy Metaphor," Allan J. Lichtman, "Competing Models of the Debate Process," William Reynolds, "Harms and Benefits: A Reappraisal," and Jerome R. Corsi, "The Continuing Evolution of Policy Systems Debate: An Assessment and a Look Ahead."

Goodnight, Tom, Bill Balthrop, and Donn W. Parson. "The Problem of Inherency: Strategy and Substance." *Journal of the American Forensic Association* 10 (Spring 1974): 229-240.

Gronbeck, Bruce. "From 'Is' to 'Ought': Alternative Strategies." *Central States Speech Journal* 19 (Spring 1968): 31-39.

Hample, Dale. "Testing a Model of Value Argument and Evidence." *Communication Monographs* 44 (June 1977): 106-120.

Henderson, Bill. "A System of Teaching Cross-Examination Techniques." *Communication Education* 27 (March 1978): 112-118.

Herbeck, Dale A. "A Permutation Standard of Competitiveness." *JAFA* 22 (Summer 1985): 12-19.

Herbeck, Dale, and John Katsulas. "The

Affirmative Topicality Burden: Any Reasonable Example of the Resolution." *JAFA* (Winter 1985): 133-45.

Hill, Sidney R., Jr. "Talking Back to Debaters." *Debate Issues* 15 (March 1982): 6-9.

Hollihan, Thomas A. "An Analysis of Value Argumentation in Contemporary Debate." *Debate Issues* 15 (November 1980): 7-10.

———. "Conditional Arguments and the Hypothesis Testing Paradigm: A Negative View." *Journal of the American Forensic Association* 19 (Winter 1983).

Kaplow, Louis. "Rethinking Counterplans: A Reconciliation with Debate Theory." *Journal of the American Forensic Association* 17 (Spring 1981): 215-226.

Karras, Ray W., and James Veitch. "A Proposed Theory of 'Value' Debate." *Debate Issues* 14 (April 1981): 1-7.

Kellermann, Kathy. "The Concept of Evidence: A Critical Review." *Journal of the American Forensic Association* 17 (Winter 1980): 159-172.

Klumpp, James F., Bernard L. Brock, James W. Chesebro, and John F. Cragan. "Implications of a Systems Model of Analysis on Argumentation Theory." *JAFA* 16 (Summer 1974): 1-7.

Lewinski, John D., Bruce R. Metzler, and Peter L. Settle. "The Goal Case Affirmative: An Alternative Approach to Academic Debate." *Journal of the American Forensic Association* 9 (Spring 1973): 458-463.

Lichtman, Allan J. "Policy Dispute and Paradigm Evaluation: A Response to Rowland." *Journal of the American Forensic Association* 18 (Winter 1982).

Lichtman, Allan J., and Daniel Rohrer. "The Logic of Policy Dispute." *Journal of the American Forensic Association* 16 (Spring 1980): 236-247.

Ling, David, and Robert V. Seltzer. "The Role of Attitudinal Inherency in Contemporary Debate." *Journal of the American Forensic Association* 7 (Spring 1971): 278-283.

Martanen, Michael D., and David A. Frank. "The Issue-Agenda Model." *Forensic* 69 (Fall 1983): 1-9.

Matlon, Ronald J. "Analyzing and Debating Propositions of Value in Academic Forensics." *Journal of Communication Association of the Pacific* 6 (July 1977): 52-67.

———. "Debating Propositions of Value." *Journal of the American Forensic Association* 14 (Spring 1978): 194-204.

Mayer, Michael. "The Study Counterplan: Misunderstanding or Misunderstood—A Reply to Shelton." *JAFA* 22 (Winter 1986): 179-183.

Morello, John. "Defending the Present System's Capacity for Incremental Changes." *JAFA* 19 (Fall 1982): 1115-20.

Newman, Robert P. "The Inherent and Compelling Need." *Journal of the American Forensic Association* 2 (May 1965): 66-71.

Norton, Robert K. "Empirical Evidence on the Judging Criteria in Use in the Cross-Examination Debate Association." *Forensic* (Spring 1981): 13.

Parson, Donn W. "On 'Being Reasonable': The Last Refuge of Scoundrels." In *DA* (1981): 532-43.

Pfau, Michael. "The Present System Revisited: Part One: Incremental Change." *Journal of the American Forensic Association* 17 (Fall 1980): 80-84.

———. "The Present System Revisited: Part Two: Policy Interrelationships." *Journal of the American Forensic Association* 17 (Winter 1981): 146-154.

Rowland, Robert C. "The Debate Judge as Debate Judge: A Functional Paradigm." *JAFA* 20 (Summer 1984): 183-93.

———. "The Primacy of Standards for

Paradigm Evaluations: A Rejoinder." *Journal of the American Forensic Association* 18 (Winter 1982).

———. "Standards for Paradigm Evaluation." *Journal of the American Forensic Association* 18 (Winter 1982).

Sayer, James E. "Debaters' Perception of Nonverbal Stimuli." *Western Speech* 38 (Winter 1974): 2-6.

Schunk, John F. "A Farewell to 'Structural Change': The Cure for Pseudo-Inherency." *Journal of the American Forensic Association* 14 (Winter 1978): 144-149.

Shelton, Michael W. "In Defense of the Studies Counterplan." *JAFA* (Winter 1985): 150-55.

Ulrich, Walter. "An *Ad Hominem* Evaluation of Hypothesis Testing as a Paradigm for Evaluating Argument." *Journal of the American Forensic Association* 21 (Summer 1984): 1-8.

———. "Flexibility in Paradigm Evaluation." *Journal of the American Forensic Association* 18 (Winter 1982).

———. "The Strategic Limitations of the Spread." *Debate Issues* (January, 1984): 3-11.

———. "The Use and Misuse of Evidence in Academic Debate." *Debate Issues* 16 (January 1983): 10-16.

Unger, James J. "Investigating the Investigators: A Study of the Study Counterplan." *Debate Issues* 12 (February 1979): 1-8.

———. "Topicality: Why Not the Best?" *Rostrum* 56 (October 1981): 5-9.

Warnick, Barbara. "Arguing Value Propositions." *JAFA* 18 (Fall 1981): 109-119.

Wenzel, Joseph W., and Dale J. Hample. "Categories and Dimensions of Value Propositions: Exploratory Studies." *Journal of the American Forensic Association* 11 (Winter 1975): 121-130.

Zarefsky, David. "The Perils of Assessing Paradigms." *Journal of the American Forensic Association* 18 (Winter 1982).

———. "The Role of Causal Argument in Policy Controversies." *Journal of the American Forensic Association* 13 (Spring 1977): 179-191.

———. "The Substance of Debate Ethics." *Journal of the Illinois Speech and Theatre Association* 32 (1978): 62-66.

———. "The 'Traditional Case'—'Comparative Advantages Case' Dichotomy: Another Look." *Journal of the American Forensic Association* 6 (Winter 1969): 12-20.

Zarefsky, David, and Bill Henderson. "Hypothesis Testing in Theory and Practice." *Journal of the American Forensic Association* 19 (Winter 1983).

Index